FOOD POLICY

FOOD POLICY

Frameworks for Analysis and Action

EDITED BY
CHARLES K. MANN
AND
BARBARA HUDDLESTON

INDIANA UNIVERSITY PRESS • BLOOMINGTON

Library of Congress Cataloging in Publication Data
Main entry under title:

Food policy, frameworks for analysis and action.

Includes index.
1. Food supply—Government policy. 2. Nutrition
policy. 3. Agriculture and state. 4. Food supply—
Government policy—Developing countries—Case studies.
5. Nutrition policy—Developing countries—Case studies.
6. Agriculture and state—Developing countries—Case
studies. I. Mann, Chip. II. Huddleston, Barbara,
1939–   .
HD9000.6.F589   1985   338.1'9   85-42526
ISBN 0-253-34342-9
1 2 3 4 5   89 88 87 86

CONTENTS

Political Aspects of Food Policy

Trade Aspects of Food Policy

Part II: Approaches to Developing National Food
Policy Capabilities

Mobilizing the Will to Use the Framework

Part III: The Future Agenda

PREFACE

Charles K. Mann

Throughout the world there is a broad commitment to reducing hunger and malnutrition. Increased food production is essential to achieve this objective, but increased production alone is not enough. Reducing hunger means attending not only to food production but also to food distribution, food consumption, and human nutrition.

Government policies have a major impact on all of these dimensions of the hunger problem. However, all too often policy makers look only at the effects of their decisions upon production. Moreover, in making macroeconomic decisions about such variables as foreign exchange and interest rates, they may not even consider the impact on food production, not to mention consumption and nutrition.

Along with many other agencies, The Rockefeller Foundation has sought to make a contribution to improving this situation. For many years the Rockefeller Foundation has supported research on food policy. With the International Development Research Centre and the Ford Foundation, the Rockefeller Foundation assisted in the creation of the International Food Policy Research Institute. More recently, it has participated with several governments in assisting to strengthen their national capability to do food policy analysis and to use it effectively.

There is a broad consensus that the weakness in national food policy capability has several dimensions. First, there is a lack of connection between those working at the micro level and those working on macro policy issues. There is need for a framework within which to integrate both micro and macro policy analysis and decisions, a framework which takes into account cultural, political, and managerial as well as economic factors. Moreover, there is a need to encourage constructive dialogue among those working on micro and macro issues.

Second, many individuals involved with food policy are narrowly trained in one discipline or, at the other extreme, have broad political or administrative experience but little technical knowledge. It is often observed that policy makers often do not know agricultural science, agricultural scientists do not know economics, neither know nutrition, and technical people in general have no appreciation for politics. Here too, a framework can help to integrate knowledge of production, distribution, consumption, and nutrition.

In various forms, isolation often is cited as a problem, particularly in the developing countries: isolation of professionals from their disciplinary peers and information sources; of university scholars from the governmental policy process; of the agricultural scientists from the farmers; of various professional disciplines from one another. Institutional innovation is needed to break down this pervasive sense of isolation, to bring together people working on aspects of common problems.

This analysis of the general nature of food policy problems led the Rockefeller Foundation to focus its food policy efforts on two programmatic themes: capacity and communication. These themes structure the projects where the Foundation has assisted countries to strengthen food policy capability. These activities took place in countries where the Rockefeller Foundation already had a substantial background of experience deriving from on-going activities, and were in response to government requests. The food policy projects ranged from relatively limited inputs in Tunisia and Turkey to more extensive activities in Thailand and Kenya. The variation across these projects yields information on the results of a number of different approaches to strengthening capability.

In all cases, these projects represented extensions of other Rockefeller Foundation country activities, allowing it to make some useful contributions without initiating major new field programs. Projects in Tunisia, Turkey, and Thailand have been completed. The activity in Kenya continues.

The idea for the book emerged as part of an effort to encourage interaction and dialogue among food policy analysts and practitioners from both developed and developing countries at a Food Policy workshop held at Bellagio, Italy, November 1–4, 1982. The book seeks to link disciplines within the context of food policy analysis. It recognizes the roles of intellectual frameworks in structuring thought about complex problems. Part I sets forth such frameworks for food production, nutrition, the political context of food policy, and trade. Against this background, Part II focuses on four operationally different approaches which actually have been used to help develop national food policy capability, all drawing upon aspects of the intellectual foundation presented in Part I. The results of these varied action programs give useful insights as to how theory can guide practice. This interplay of theory and experience suggests a number of activities which can help to better the performance of national food policy systems. These are summarized in part III, "The Future Agenda."

ACKNOWLEDGMENTS

This book reflects the deliberations of many individuals as to how outside agencies could help to improve national food policy making. While our debts are legion in the production of this volume, we thank particularly Dr. John Pino, former Director of Agricultural Sciences, The Rockefeller Foundation, for his support and encouragement of this project; Dr. Malcolm McPherson, now at Harvard University, who helped importantly in developing the approach to capacity-building for food policy analysis reflected in the overall design of the work; Ms. Renee Schiff for her invaluable assistance in getting the manuscript ready for publication; colleagues at the Rockefeller Foundation and the International Food Policy Research Institute for substantial intellectual contributions. A conference at the Rockefeller Foundation Bellagio Study and Conference Center in Italy provided the opportunity to confront the theory with the results of field experience in capacity development. That interaction produced new insights which have become a part of the book. Most importantly, we thank the chapter authors whose work comprises the real substance of this enterprise.

All views presented are those of the individual authors and not necessarily their institutions. Remaining errors and editorial oversights are our responsibility.

Charles K. Mann
Barbara Huddleston

INTRODUCTION AND SUMMARY

Charles K. Mann and Barbara Huddleston

Food is an increasingly urgent political-economic issue for developing countries. Food production is the primary economic activity for the majority of the population in many of these countries, and the supply of food at low and stable prices is the central political demand of growing numbers of wage earners and employment seekers in urban areas. Yet it is only recently that food policy in its broadest sense has claimed the attention of policy makers.

Prior to the 1973–75 shock to world petroleum and cereals markets, policy makers in developing countries had been concentrating on production strategies for both industry and agriculture intended to produce rapid rates of economic growth. Cheap food imports, often subsidized with food aid, were used to keep consumer prices stable when domestic production fell short. The 1973 increases in world prices for cereals, petroleum, and petroleum products (including fertilizer), accompanied by sudden changes in the foreign exchange value of their currencies following the U.S. decision to go off the gold standard, meant that government leaders in many developing countries lost control of their domestic price policies for both essential production inputs and basic food staples. As a consequence, they have since begun to focus attention on the links between production policies, consumption policies, and trade and monetary policies with a view toward assuring that they in the future could guarantee their political followers a stable and adequate supply of food. Examination of such linkages is a principal feature of Part I of this book—Frameworks for Food Policy Analysis.

This section begins with an overview by Timmer based on a longer treatment of the issues in a book, *Food Policy Analysis*, by himself, Falcon, and Pearson, published in 1983 by the Johns Hopkins University

1

Press. Essentially, his message is that food policy governs the functioning of national and international food systems and that it rests on an
analytical base which has three components: a micro perspective on
behavior of producers and consumers of food, a macro perspective on
the influence of monetary and fiscal policies on their behavior, and a
trade perspective on the role of markets and prices in linking them at
both national and international level. He also emphasizes the principle
that the ultimate objective of food policy is to provide adequate nutrition
for all, but that this objective often must be achieved indirectly through
policies and programs which generate employment and purchasing
power for the poor, thus increasing their effective demand for food,
rather than programs which transfer food or income directly to the poor
and have significant fiscal implications without promising any long-run
return.

Structural Aspects of Production

A perspective on the micro behavior of producers is provided by the
three chapters by Gomez, Pino, and Mencher. Gomez uses yield data for
rice, maize, and cassava in Thailand and Nigeria to show that the actual
technologies employed by many farmers in the countries he surveyed still
produce crop yields which are well below those achieved in field tests. He
notes that production performance is considerably better when best farm
yields are used for comparison with field test results, and notes that low
yields on marginal farms which do not use new technologies explain why
the average is so much lower. He also introduces the concept of economic
yield, which is meant to reflect the quantity it is economically profitable for
a farmer to produce. While he uses a rather arbitrary method to quantify
economic yield, this could be done empirically for countries where the data
necessary to estimate production functions exist. The approach offers a
fruitful avenue for researchers to explore in analyzing producer responsiveness to government efforts to introduce new technologies.

Pino discusses the role of livestock in farming systems in many parts of
the world where it supplements crop agriculture by providing a source of
cash income, draft power, status, and occasionally of supplementary food.
He notes, however, that while the farmer often treats livestock as if it had
no costs, there are often hidden costs and the economic return may be low.

Mencher looks at the role of women in agricultural production. She
stresses throughout that women play a significant role in food production
systems which is often overlooked when policies are being formulated. In
Africa, for example, there has been a traditional division of labor between
men and women, with the farmer responsible for cash crops and the latter

for subsistence crops. Resources channeled to male family members for increasing production, therefore, will not necessarily flow into the subsistence crop sector.

In South and Southeast Asia, women and children are assigned certain tasks within the family production unit. These tasks may include activities such as manual preparation of fields, transplanting, weeding, harvesting, and processing, depending on the traditions of the locality. Women and children often also care for vegetable gardens and small livestock within the family compound. New production techniques, particularly mechanization, could displace much of this female labor, with the consequences depending on whether or not the women would nevertheless reap part of the benefit from the improvement in productivity. That women and children are frequently discriminated against when it comes to distributing family income is evident from the fact that they are the principal sufferers from malnutrition.

Approaches to Providing Adequate Nutrition

The importance of integrating nutritional considerations into all aspects of food policy analysis is the theme of Berg's introduction to this section. In a chapter discussing the conceptual framework for how to do this, Pinstrup-Andersen emphasizes the importance of going beyond simple measurement of the amount of impact an intervention has and trying to understand how and why food policies and programs have an impact on nutritional status. He identifies three main factors which directly influence nutritional status and which are in turn influenced by food policies and programs through various other intermediate factors. These three main factors are: ability of households to acquire food, household food acquisition behavior, and intra-household allocation of food.

In case studies for Bangladesh and Turkey, both Chen and Gençağa find that income level, that is, the ability of households to purchase food, is a less important determinant of nutritional status than hypothesized. In the case of Turkey, the educational level of parents and their knowledge of nutritionally sound dietary practices was found to be the most important factor. Apparently families, even at very low income levels, make every effort to satisfy basic food needs, even if the food consumed is not a preferred commodity. Thus food transfers often may have the effect of transfers of income which then is used for other purposes. A technique for identifying malnourished families and individuals so that interventions can be targeted specifically to them is proposed by Dapice in the final chapter of this section.

The Political Environment

Food policy is not politically neutral. Selowsky notes that the returns from policy reform are often realized only in the long-run, while short-run losses may hurt the interests of politically influential groups. He explores the possibility of international lending to compensate the losers while waiting for revenues from the winners to start flowing in.

Delehanty approaches the same issue from the standpoint of contract theory, noting that existing policies generate economic rents and that policy reform will mean redistribution of those rents. Policy reform which generates new rents will be easier to accomplish, but all reform will require renegotiation of existing social contracts.

Bates explores the bargaining process in more depth and suggests that public policy should be viewed as the outcome of political competition among organized groups, rather than maximization of social welfare. Factors which affect the outcome include the cost of organization for different interest groups and the effectiveness of different policy instruments in influencing the outcome of the bargaining process.

The Global Environment

Chapters by Donaldson and Schuh treat two themes—Donaldson's the positive changes which have occurred in the functioning of world cereal markets since the 1973–75 crisis, and Schuh's the deterioration in the effectiveness of formal international institutions in managing the global economy, despite the increased importance of doing so. Schuh notes several developments in the international environment which could impact importantly on food policy decisions and their effects at the national level, including, among others, emergence of an integrated capital market, flexible exchange rates, changing trade patterns and emergence of developing and centrally-planned economics as important markets, international labor migration, and changing comparative advantage. He sees reform of international economic institutions as an essential part of the food policy process.

Part II of the book—*Approaches to Developing National Food Policy Capabilities*—explores how the frameworks set forth in Part I can be used to help develop national food policy capability. Four country case studies illustrate different approaches. Common to them all is the proposition that central to increasing national capability is helping key people in the system to increase their individual capacities and improving communication among these individuals.[1]

Individuals draw upon three types of capacity in making policy: strategic, technical, and administrative. Strategic capacity is the ability to define problems clearly and to formulate a coherent set of objectives for themselves or their institutions. Technical capacity refers to knowledge of specific discipline, such as agronomy, plant breeding, or agricultural economics in order to analyze relevant problems. Administrative capacity is the ability to coordinate the activities of diverse groups of people, such as research workers, project directors, and farmers to achieve particular objectives.

Capacity can be improved by adding depth to an individual's skills in his or her discipline. An economist might be provided training in econometrics, or an agronomist might be given advanced training in soil physics. Often, however, the problem is not lack of capacity in an individual's own discipline, but insufficient understanding or other relevant disciplines. Broadening the range of skills of a specialist is another way to improve capacity. For example, an economist might be provided with training in basic agronomic principles, or an agronomist might be given training in the fundamentals of economic analysis.

Communication—the process of information exchange—can be important to the improvement of the food system. No individual has all of the information needed to determine how a given policy decision will affect various objectives or the interest of different groups. Improved communication helps policy makers by expanding the range of information and perspectives available to them. Moreover, because the "policy makers" usually are located in a variety of organizations, improved communication raises the likelihood that their decisions will be mutually consistent. And finally, those who are affected by the policy are more likely to support a policy if they perceive that their views and interests have been given due consideration. Improved communication helps ensure this by facilitating a two-way flow of information between them and the policy makers.

Deepening or broadening the capacity of individuals who work on food policy problems has little value unless they have a context for using their improved capacity. The frameworks set forth in Section I can help establish such a context and can highlight the key elements of the food system. Such frameworks help the relevant individuals organize their knowledge about the food system, and more importantly, they provide them with a means of assimilating new information as it becomes available.

Two types of frameworks are useful. The first, represented by Timmer's piece, reveals the mutual dependence among key policy variables in the national economy. It helps policy makers and analysts to understand how policy decisions affect the food system, how the welfare of various groups is changed by alternative policies, and how the consequences of different objectives complement or contradict one another.

The second type of framework is exemplified by the fundamental principles of disciplines relevant to the food system. Most technical specialists use a few basic principles to structure their analysis of practical problems. For example, cost underlies most economic analyses. The principle of limiting factors is fundamental to the way agronomists think about most crop problems. It structures the way Gomez approaches the question of why farmer yields are low. He looks for the factors that are keeping yields from coming closer to what is achieved on research stations where all factors needed for plant growth are present.

Using the first type of framework to organize knowledge of these key principles (themselves the second type of framework) places them in a context that can help policy makers integrate new information and guide their decisions and the actions derived from these decisions. The key element in learning these principles and developing a framework within which they can be applied is a dialogue among policy makers and between policy makers and scientists familiar with the food system. In this way, improved communication becomes an integral part of the learning—the capacity development—process. An important means of encouraging such communication is the case method of teaching, which has been adapted to the food policy environment by the International Center for the Improvement of Wheat and Maize (CIMMYT). This is described further in the chapter entitled "Using The Case Method To Improve Food Policy." Used to examine realistic policy problems in the context of an appropriate analytical framework, this approach can help develop both capacity and communication.

Fundamental to improving national food capability is building the political will to do so. Developing this political support is one of the main objectives of the World Food Council and characterizes their approach to building national capability. Maurice Williams, Executive Director, notes that often the perception of need for improved capability comes in the wake of a national food crisis, which galvanizes the national will to emphasize food and agriculture. Indeed, the World Food Council itself was created in response to such a situation on a global scale.

The Rockefeller Foundation experience is consistent with Williams' observations about the role of crisis in creating the desire to develop stronger national food policy capability. In Kenya, for example, the request for Rockefeller Foundation assistance came in the wake of Kenya's first post-independence maize shortfall and long queues for food. These conditions triggered popular demand for a national food policy.

In Thailand, the government recognized that the agricultural expansion based on opening new lands had run its course and that future increases would have to come from higher yields. In Tunisia, the request for

Rockefeller Foundation assistance in food policy grew out of concern for a precipitous drop in cereal production.

Williams observed that given sufficient political will, countries become receptive to using free-floating knowledge, research on food policy outcomes developed outside their borders by various research groups. This is consistent with Alberto Valdes' observation on IFPRI's experience that "good research sells itself." He argues that IFPRI should set its own research agenda according to its own assessment of the urgency of problems, whether or not at any given moment there is the political will to deal with them. Should a crisis develop, the political will can arise very quickly, and it is important to have solidly-based knowledge available in advance of the crisis.

Valdes cited as an example the research by IFPRI staff member Jorge Garcia-Garcia on industrial policy in Colombia. The correctness of the analysis was apparent to the leadership which had the political will to apply the results. Similarly, with the International Monetary Fund (IMF) Cereal Import Facility, a crisis helped to create the necessary political will, which in turn drew in the research results which IFPRI by then had ready for distribution.

Both Williams and Valdes stressed that these findings demonstrate the importance of a mechanism to disseminate research results. Knowledge of what research is available must be spread widely throughout political and staff levels, national public and pressure groups. This free-floating information can then be galvanized at the political level. On an international scale, a good example of focusing political will to develop national capacity was the Bellagio meeting hosted by the World Food Council and attended by ministers of agriculture and donor agencies. This meeting led to the decision for the Council to take a lead role in helping countries to formulate national food strategies. More than 50 countries have asked for such help. By December 1984 sixteen strategies had been completed. While expatriate assistance has been important in most cases, the long-range objective is to help countries develop their own capacity to design and to implement these strategies.

Experience with these national strategies highlights the importance of continuing to work at the political level, stressing the importance of national food policy capability. By the same token, international organizations should continue to generate research results on important issues. Particularly in times of crisis, these research results will be drawn into policy forums and acted upon as the political will mobilizes under pressure of crisis. As government and political leaders come to recognize the benefits of more effective policies, they will insist more on having a strong national capability for policy analysis and implementation. The political will to mobilize such capability is an important step in doing so. In almost any country, there exists some talent which, given a high enough priority, can be assembled to strengthen the national food policy capability.

The Integrated Research Project Approach

The Thai project was born of a deep sense of frustration expressed most articulately by Dr. Snoh Unakul, head of the National Economic and Social Development Board. In requesting assistance from The Rockefeller Foundation, he observed that Thailand had reasonable numbers of good economists and analysts, but that they were all working on small-scale discrete research projects. On the one hand, there was no mechanism to link them together so that their efforts could be cumulative and mutually supportive, addressing major national policy problems rather than a host of unrelated small projects. Analytically, he recognized the inter-relatedness of many food and agricultural issues and sought a means of integrating the work of the separate researchers within a common analytical framework. Institutionally, he sought the creation of the non-government research institute patterned after the Brookings Institution or the Korean Development Institute. Seeing this as the appropriate seat for a strengthened national food policy capability, he viewed the integrated food policy project as a prototype research design and the forerunner of such a larger institution.[2]

The project brought together researchers from Kasetsart and Thammasat Universities and the National Economic and Social Development Board, under Dr. Snoh's leadership.

A great deal of time was invested in developing the project framework and elaborating it in successive stages with the research group. The expatriate economists—George Delehanty and Theodore Panayoutou—played an important part in this process. Much of the researchers' professional growth came from their collaboration on the research design as they worked out the interrelationships among the projects. For a protracted period, they met together almost weekly. Communication between the research team and the national policy institutions was facilitated by a series of three major workshops in Bangkok to which outside resource people were also invited.

While there is a physical product of the project in the form of research monographs,[3] other important outputs are: (1) the professional growth and self-confidence of the researchers; they proved to themselves that they could define a problem, determine the data needed, collect that data, and analyze it; (2) the fact that many insights from the research and the workshops are already being incorporated into Thai policy; (3) the lesson learned that practitioners need to be involved with the project as it develops to provide feedback from the real world of policy making. The integrated project approach—scholars and practitioners working together—increased the impact of research findings on policy making because results were incorporated directly into ongoing decision making. Implementation did not depend upon preparation of a formal document for subsequent distribution to the practitioners.

Operational Approach—Kenya

The Rockefeller Foundation has a long history of assistance in institution building with the major universities of East Africa. It focused on assisting with faculty development, supporting visiting professors and providing fellowships to talented Kenyan students. The Rockefeller Foundation contribution to strengthening policy capacity thus was long run in nature, occurring as people trained under the program gradually moved into positions of major importance.

In contrast to this institution-building approach and stimulated by the 1980 maize crisis, the Permanent Secretary of the Treasury requested The Rockefeller Foundation to provide a senior advisor to work in the Office of the President to help the staff members strengthen their ability to deal with food policy questions. This request offered the opportunity to explore a more operationally-oriented approach to strengthening national food policy capabilities. At the same time, the University and the government saw the need to provide training in food policy analysis for both students and civil servants. Ultimately, The Rockefeller Foundation provided an adviser in the Office of the President—Ralph Campbell—but linked him informally with a senior faculty member—George Delehanty—working simultaneously on helping the University to improve food policy training capacity.

As Ralph Campbell's paper indicates, his presence on the firing line provides an excellent insight into the specific kinds of skills that are most relevant to the government's problems. He points out that much of government is preoccupied with how-to-do-it kinds of questions, whereas the central theme of University training is directed toward the question of what to do.

The two Kenya chapters explore ways to close the gap between the operational problems faced by Campbell and colleagues and the University's proper training role as described by Dean David Ngugi. University research, for example, can be made more relevant to government policy questions. Ngugi suggested some specific approaches to tie the University and the Ministry of Agriculture closer together. Specifically, he proposed a series of Masters level fellowships for University graduates after they have had three years of operational experience in the Ministry. These fellowships would help to make the University training more practical and also provide a vehicle for focusing graduate student research on Ministry problems.

Campbell saw little prospect for linking the Office of the President directly with the University. What most needs strengthening is national capability to implement policies, not to analyze them. Specifically, he called for the creation of a cadre of "expediters" who would ride herd on the implementation of various government programs and projects, monitor their progress, identify bottlenecks, and stimulate responsible agencies to take appropriate action. Relative to the skills of implementing programs, he saw the analytical base as being relatively well developed.

This operational approach has yielded a key insight into the nature of the weakness in national food policy capability. A focus on analysis without reference to implementation would be misplaced. Accentuating this imbalance is a tendency to take no action to work out project implementation until the project or policy change has been approved. Upon approval, government then presses for immediate implementation. For these reasons Campbell urges more focus on implementation issues, less on analysis.

Technology-Focused Approach—Tunisia

While no one would advocate a technology-only approach to building national capacity, the experience in Tunisia indicates the power which technology can contribute to this objective. While the Rockefeller Foundation was assisting the Agricultural Planning Office with a cereals sector review, it became apparent that much of the best talent was being swallowed up in doing large numbers of hand calculations. The capacity lacking was not so much knowledge of the basic analytical tools but the time to employ them, due to enormous quantities of routine calculations. By the same token, reporting from the provincial level was handicapped by the lack of circulating power. Long columns of numbers were being added up by hand, slowing down reporting to the Central Office. Over 40 desk calculators and hand programmable calculators were provided to increase the efficiency of statistical manipulation throughout the Central Planning Office and the related provincial offices. This equipment allowed data to be collected and analyzed in a much more timely fashion, not to mention giving an important morale boost to all the workers involved.

Within the Agricultural Planning Office itself, the ability to manage the enlarged flow of information from the field was improved by the provision of two Apple microcomputers. As competence grew in using these machines, they were applied to more complex analytical and managerial tasks.

What is possible affects what one decides to do. If it becomes possible to carry out a more realistic analysis, one capturing more complex relationships, one can begin to think about doing it. However, if the computational power is not available to handle this complexity, no one thinks too seriously about how to do it. Using computer power to expand physical analytical capacity encourages the parallel development of intellectual analytical capacity. Again, appropriate analytical frameworks are critical to making sense of complexity.

There remains substantial unexploited potential in this technology-enriched approach. The Tunisian experiment will provide important insights into how much of the potential can be realized. For example, it is possible physically to connect over telephone lines the two computers, placing one in the agricultural university, one in the Planning Office. Providing the physical possibility of close cooperation—sharing data sets and analytical programs—may lead to real cooperation between these two institutions.

Once management information can be available on a more timely basis, this physical possibility opens the practical prospect of making mid-course corrections when activities are not going according to plan. Without timely information, one does not even learn of departures from the plan until too late to take such corrective action. The technological breakthroughs in computing and communications thus have an important role to play in capacity development.

The Management Approach

The problems highlighted in the operational approach section provide much of the rationale for an increased attention to the management aspects of national capability. Mendoza outlined his experience in the Philippines where building national capability could be considered a management approach. Developing individual analytical capacity represented a subsidiary activity.

The experience with high-yielding rice under the Masagana 99 program focused on realigning government organizations to carry out policy decisions. Issues of organizational structure appear to have dominated policy decisions.

Much of the rationale for policy analysis is its role in clarifying and improving the environment of incentives within which farmers and consumers act. An aspect of the management approach suggested by Mendoza carries that same principle down into organizational analysis. He cited the example of the irrigation engineer who was urged to encourage community involvement in planning the irrigation project but whose professional rewards were based upon the number of projects actually implemented. Thus the incentives affecting individual employees were opposed to the organization's objectives. Good management can align organizational structures and incentives with program and policy objectives.

Another dimension of the management approach to building national capability is outlined by Huddleston as she identifies the types of skills needed by middle-level food sector managers in Africa and inventories the present institutions providing such training. The need for these skills is evident in the specific shortcomings found by Campbell in the operational approach. Like Campbell's, Huddleston's chapter represents a focus on strengthening the how-to-do-it-dimension, whereas the emphasis of most of the book addresses issues of what to do.

Also related to the how-to dimension of the management approach is the case method, a staple of most business administration training programs. Within the food and agricultural policy area, pioneering work has been done by CIMMYT in developing a series of realistic agricultural policy cases. In a total of five workshops in various regions, they brought together policy makers, agricultural scientists, and analysts. Under the guidance of skilled case method leaders, the group examined real agricultural policy cases and weighed the costs and benefits of alternative policy actions. As with the Indonesian Bulog example described by Peter Timmer, the case method "gets 'em all in the same room together." By working through a common series of cases selected for relevance to actual problems at hand, the group is able to formulate a general approach or framework within which to analyze the case. It opens communication channels among all those participating and identifies agencies which would be involved in implementing policy decisions. The CIMMYT experience has been positive in using the case method as a vehicle to help high-level officials both to define more accurately the nature of problems they face and to develop strategies and courses of action for implementation. To date, most of the case development has been on the side of agricultural as contrasted with food policy with few materials being available to highlight the macroeconomic connections or the impact of policy decisions on consumers.

The Future Agenda

The book concludes with a chapter on the future agenda for helping to strengthen national food policy capability. This is informed by the analytical frameworks of the first section, the operational experience of the second, and the various authors' extensive experience in the developing countries. Specific suggestions are presented for national and donor action to improve food policy analysis and implementation.

NOTES

1. We would like to acknowledge the contribution of Malcolm F. McPherson to the development of the ideas on capacity and communication which follow. In turn, these build upon earlier contributions by Professor Alex McCalla about the nature of "the food policy problem."

2. Subsequently the Thai Development Research Institute has been established.

3. Theodore Panayoton, (ed.), *Food Policy Analysis in Thailand* (Bangkok: Allied Printers for the Agricultural Development Council, 1985).

Part I
Frameworks for
Food Policy Analysis

A FRAMEWORK FOR
FOOD POLICY ANALYSIS

C. Peter Timmer

Historically, most food policy has actually been agricultural policy, and most agricultural policy has focused on ways to increase farm output, frequently just for a single commodity such as rice, wheat, or corn. Such partial or narrow approaches have failed to improve significantly the nutritional status of large numbers of people living in less-developed countries because they have failed to forge a strong link between the expansion of agricultural output and the reduction of hunger. The failure of governmental policies to deal more effectively with hunger, even though trends of food availability are generally rising in the world, reflects a lack of understanding of the direct and indirect causes of hunger and its complex relationship to a country's entire food system.

The set of processes by which agricultural commodities are produced on farms, transformed into foods in the marketing sector, and sold to consumers to satisfy nutritional as well as esthetic and social needs makes up the food system. Its functioning frequently leaves many poor people inadequately fed because of a complicated network of connections that determine their employment and income status, the prices they must pay for food and other goods and services, and their mobility to search out better opportunities.

All food systems must accomplish similar tasks. By organizing the production or provision of food, its marketing, and its consumption by the

This chapter provides a brief overview of the major issues treated in *Food Policy Analysis*, by C. Peter Timmer, Walter P. Falcon, and Scott R. Pearson (John Hopkins University Press for the World Bank, 1983). Neither my co-authors nor the World Bank are responsible for the views expressed here. I am indebted to Carol F. Timmer, who served as editor of the volume, for the substantive and editorial skills that distilled a six-hundred page manuscript into this synopsis.

citizens of the society, food systems around the world end up having much in common. The choices a society faces in organizing these tasks are analogous to the larger economic choices faced by any society whether socialist or capitalist: what to produce, how to produce it, and for whom. Different societies make fundamentally different choices in each area and yet have food systems that are understandable within a common methodology of food policy analysis.

Three integrated components distinguish food policy analysis from narrower sectoral analyses: an analytical focus on micro behavior of food consumer and producer households, a policy perspective on the effects of macroeconomic forces on the performance of the food system, and a trade perspective on the role of both domestic and international markets in linking the micro sector and its household issues to the macro sector and its policy issues.

For analysts to integrate these three topics without becoming lost in the complexity of a functioning economy, they need a basic descriptive knowledge of the food system, an analytical framework that connects statistical data with the process of decision making in the food system, and an acquired sense of the economic, technical, and political forces that are providing direction and momentum to the system at any given time. The minimum data required include patterns of food consumption, production, and marketing, as well as domestic price structures relative to international prices. From the macro side, the analyst needs to know nominal and real interest rates, foreign exchange rates, the rate of inflation, and the size and composition of the national budget and its sources of revenue.

In nearly all food systems, the glue that holds together the various pieces is the marketing sector. The food policy framework focuses on the role of markets in providing both technical services and coordinating signals. Both are important. A major role for governmental intervention is to improve the efficiency with which input supply, storage, transportation, and processing are carried out and to provide a price policy environment in which the costs of these technical market functions are appropriately reflected in price signals to producers, marketing agents, and consumers.

This market perspective also helps build the analyst's sense of what drives the food system. By thinking about how market activities, whether in the private or public sector, connect producers and consumers, the analyst can understand the diverse forces leading both groups to make the day-to-day decisions that determine the performance of the food system. This understanding obviously depends on knowing how producers and consumers behave. Food consumption decisions are influenced by a household's income, the prices faced for food and other commodities, and a host of social and individual factors which may or may not be susceptible to government influence. Similarly, farm households allocate their resources to food and cash crop production in the context of their own knowledge, access to productive inputs and prices of output, and attitudes about what factors will best contribute to improved individual or family welfare.

Food consumers and food producers react to food prices in opposite directions. For consumers, higher food prices restrict the range of purchases of both foods and other commodities and services, while lower food prices offer scope for greater food intake, a wider variety of foodstuffs, and a higher quality diet, as well as an occasional new shirt or a radio. Food prices are especially important to the very poor, for they spend much of their incomes on starchy food staples. For these households, survival itself may hinge on low food prices.

Farm households see food prices as a major factor determining their incomes. For a particular harvest, if the input costs are paid and the yields are already determined, the price received for the output is virtually the sole determinant of farm income. In the longer run, the output price provides a signal to the farmer about how much to use purchased inputs, new technology, and household labor and managerial skills. All of these directly affect the level of output. Food prices reflect relative scarcity and abundance. They communicate to both governments and farmers the collective desire and ability of consumers to acquire food and thus provide adequate incentives to maintain food supplies.

The Policy Dilemmas

The dual role of food prices—determining food consumption levels, especially among poor people, and the adequacy of food supplies through incentives to farmers—raises several price-related policy dilemmas. Indeed, the basic dilemma runs deeper than is first apparent. The incomes of both the urban and rural poor depend on their employment opportunities which are significantly a function of the health and dynamism of the rural sector. Incentive food prices for farmers are important for generating such dynamism in the long run and the jobs that flow from it. But poor people do not live in the long run. They must eat in the short run, or the prospect of long-run job creation will be a useless promise. The micro analytical approach of food policy analysis focuses attention directly on the decision-making environment that creates this dilemma and on the potential interventions that can bridge the short-run and long-run effects.

An additional dimension of the food price policy question is how tightly to link the country's domestic food system to the international economy through trade and competitive price relationships. Governments frequently resort to international trade to implement domestic food price goals. But policy debate occurs over a series of questions about domestic price stability, the use of trade policy instruments to achieve income distribution goals, and the issue of food security. Because fundamental social choices are at stake over these issues, analysis alone, particularly of a country's agricultural price policy, cannot provide answers. At best, it can illuminate the costs and benefits from alternative choices that must be made by the political process.

The price policy debate also includes macroeconomic issues, as Figure 1 illustrates. All countries face budget tradeoffs as various partisan interests seek special advantage for their constituents. From a food policy perspective, one important debate revolves around recurring subsidies (often on food for consumers) versus investment in higher productivity, particularly inputs for producers. Related to this debate is the choice between allocations for short-run consumer welfare versus protection or price supports for producers, a debate that tends to focus on rural interests versus urban interests. Given the source of political support for many governments in developing countries, these dilemmas often have been resolved in favor of short-run interests of urban consumers at the expense of long-run rural productivity and farm interests.

The discrimination against the agricultural sector that grows out of urban bias is only partly an overt manifestation of how budget expenditures are allocated. At least as important is another macro policy manifest in the basic rate of exchange between urban and rural goods and services. This rate of exchange, the rural-urban terms of trade, depends critically on the entire structure of macro price policy and particularly on prevailing foreign exchange rates. An overvalued domestic currency almost always acts as a hidden tax on the rural sector, depressing incentives, growth in production, and rural incomes. The prevalence of distorted macro policies in developing countries raises an obvious question: what can a food policy, however well designed and intentioned, accomplish in the context of a hostile macroeconomic and international environment?

The Macroeconomic Context

The food system has broad connections to macroeconomic policy, and the influence works in both directions. The impact of the macro economy on the food system is so powerful that it frequently dooms all efforts of policy makers within the agricultural sector to make any headway in

Figure 1. Major Connections between Macroeconomic Policy and Food Policy

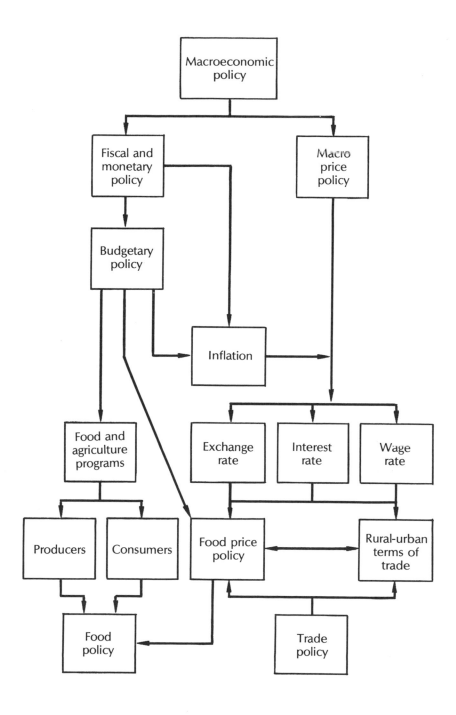

"getting agriculture moving" (to use Arthur Mosher's phrase)[1] when the macro sector is sending contrary signals. A distorted set of macro policies—which typically includes rapid inflation, an overvalued exchange rate, subsidized interest rates for preferred creditors, minimum wages for an urban working class elite, and depressed rural incentives—makes rapid growth in agricultural output extremely difficult while it serves simultaneously to skew the distribution of earned income. Short-run interests of poor people are often protected to some extent by such policies through the availability of cheap food, usually made possible with subsidized imports.

The options available to food policy makers in the context of adverse macro policies are extremely limited: more investment in irrigation, a better agricultural research and extension program, perhaps a subsidy on fertilizer and modern seeds. These will contribute to agricultural growth, but in the constraining environment of a distorted set of macro policies, such programs will not provide the basis for long-run dynamic growth of rural output and incomes, which is the essential base for a food policy that simultaneously increases food production while reducing hunger.

This macro perspective places the food system squarely in the context of economic growth and efforts to alleviate poverty. These efforts involve strategies for the modernization of the agricultural sector, for it is there that much poverty is found. Most poor, heavily-populated countries find that efficient growth in agriculture is required for rapid reduction of poverty in the entire economy. On the other hand, poor performance by the agricultural sector can cause severe macroeconomic havoc in the short run. The policies that create rural dynamism do not all emanate from agricultural planning offices. Most of the decision environment required to stimulate efficient resource allocation, labor productivity, and more jobs is created by macroeconomic policy.

At the same time, the incentives needed to generate much of this rural dynamism can affect adversely the food consumption of poor people. A macro approach to poverty alleviation needs to be complemented by a disaggregated micro perspective on decision making by the poor, both as consumers and producers. Poor consumers have different diets from those of more comfortable individuals in a society, their income sources are usually much less secure, and they are more sensitive to food price changes. Similarly, very small farmers often do not control adequate resources in the form of land, water, or credit to participate fully in the potential of new agricultural technology. Reaching the poor in the short run is always difficult because of their weak links to the food system and the rest of the economy. The task is to find interventions in the micro environment that can protect their welfare while the macro forces strengthen their links to the economy in the long run.

The Analytical Tasks

One role of food policy is to build a bridge between these micro and macro tasks. Understanding the role of trade and markets provides the support for that bridge, but closing the gap between short-run and long-run effects of macro policy relies partly on the effective use of food price policy and partly on carefully targeted food subsidies. Many countries start from a food price policy environment that utilizes food imports and budget subsidies for across-the-board consumer protection, while a host of production-oriented government projects attempt to increase food output. An understanding of the complexity of hunger and its connections to the food system suggests that such a price policy/project orientation may be backwards. The price policy is likely to be more effective as part of the incentive package that induces greater food production from millions of small farmers, while targeted food subsidy projects protect the very poor until they find jobs and higher incomes that result from the new policy environment.

Since much of the environment for rural decision making is dictated by macro policy, rapid rural growth over long periods of time can occur only when this macro environment encourages the efficient allocation of resources. Short bursts of growth are possible from any of the other elements in the decision-making environment—a new seed technology, subsidized fertilizer, or a more effective extension service. But for the long haul, rural growth will falter in the absence of an overall economic environment that encourages, and ultimately forces, the allocation of land, labor, and capital into their most productive uses.

A second important task for food policy analysts is to acquire a sense of food system dynamics—to determine the dynamic consequences of sectoral and macro policies for the achievement of food-related objectives. The dynamic forces are likely to be subtle and operate through feedback mechanisms that are much too complicated to be captured in agricultural sector models or computable general equilibrium models.

If higher food prices induce technical change in food production, for instance, static analysis alone will provide seriously misleading estimates of the actual welfare transfers between producers and consumers and the ultimate impact on the government budget. Price policy can induce changes in land tenure patterns or in choice of production technology. The distribution of income can change not just between producers and consumers but within rural areas as well through indirect effects on hiring patterns and rural wages. Cheap food might have consequences for health and nutrition in the long run not captured by the static analysis. The dynamic effects of food price policy interventions are likely to dominate the static effects in economic terms, but usually the short-run effects dominate political decision making.

Similarly, the dynamic efficiency losses will be compounded if macro policy distorts the allocation of economic factors away from their most productive uses. The distortions usually found—overvalued exchange rates, subsidized interest rates, depressed agricultural incentives, and low food prices—are motivated by short-run concerns over economic growth and the distribution of the output. Using these macro prices (in their broadest sense) to solve short-run distributional problems rather than to allocate resources for long-run growth will eventually lead the entire economy into stagnation and decline. Economic growth, including growth in rural areas, ultimately is inhibited by such a set of macro signals. Nevertheless, it is true that the short-run distributional and welfare problems may be exacerbated if attempts are made to bring the macro prices and macro policy into alignment with the underlying scarcity value of resources.

Determining the impact of a macro reform on important food policy objectives is a crucial analytical task. Such reforms come eventually because serious macro distortions bring enormous pressures for macro policies more consistent with real scarcity values in the economy. Either external creditors—the IMF, World Bank, bilateral donor agencies, or the multinational commercial banks—bring these pressures to bear and force the painful adjustment when a crisis is reached, or else a country's macro policy makers stay ahead of the situation and design new policies that avert a crisis.

Even without specific concern for the food system, such a macro reform is likely to improve the rural-urban terms of trade directly by raising the food price to its international opportunity cost. More broadly, the devaluation that brings foreign exchange rates into equilibrium usually will pump new purchasing power into rural areas, with positive effects on rural employment and improved income distribution. Eventually, scarcity values for labor and capital will induce a new efficiency in resource use.

For the reforms to be effective, many price increases will be needed, and overall budget subsidies must be cut. The real incomes of many workers and civil servants will be sharply reduced, and the urban political base of a government can be seriously threatened in the wake of the painful adjustments needed. From a food policy perspective, those adjustments hinge critically on the likely reductions in food consumption by poor households caused by the higher food prices that almost inevitably accompany a macro reform. Food policy attempts to find a set of food consumption interventions that will prevent the worst manifestations of such a squeeze on the poor, while still stimulating the production response that is the main long-run goal of the reform.

A crucial role for the food policy analyst in the macro debate can now be seen. To enable a macro reform to be politically feasible before an economy has crumbled so far that reform becomes a financial necessity, food policy analysts can design short-run interventions that are both sound in fiscal terms and effective in their impact on the poor. Such designs are possible only within an integrated food policy framework that specifically links the production, marketing, consumption, and macro sectors. By designing short-run targeted food consumption subsidies to help poor people across the bridge to long-run dynamic economic growth, it is easier for macro policy makers to implement the needed reforms in the first place. The political inertia so often observed in the face of macro economies run amok is entirely understandable. An analytically sound food policy can break this inertia by offering macro policy makers a new potential for action.

NOTES

1. Arthur T. Mosher, *Getting Agriculture Moving* (New York: Praeger Publishers for the Agricultural Development Council, 1966).

THE ROLE OF CROPS
IN FOOD SYSTEMS

Arturo A. Gomez

Introduction

The main thrust of this paper is to provide an analytical framework for evaluating the existing and potential capacity of crops to supply the nutritional requirement of an increasing world population. In order to accomplish such a broad objective in such a short paper, I have imposed three simplifying restrictions. First, nutritional requirement will be based primarily on calorie needs, since energy is the most critical component of nutrition for most developing countries and many other components are automatically satisfied when the energy requirement is met. Second, crop productivity assessment will focus on the humid tropics where farm yields are low and population is dense, increasing rapidly and vulnerable to food shortage. Third, crop production estimates will be confined to the three most important food species that supply food calories in the humid tropics: rice, maize, and cassava.

This chapter is divided into four sections, namely:

1. "Promising Production Technologies," which describes a few of the most promising techniques for increasing crop yield;

2. "Levels of Crop Productivity," which estimates the existing and potential capacity of crops as a source of food;

3. "Technology Adoption by Farmers," which describes the important factors that farmers consider in shifting from their existing practice to a new technology; and

4. "From Production to Consumption," which lists the most important requirements for translating adequate food supplies to proper nutrition.

Promising Production Technologies

For densely populated areas where land and not labor is the most limiting resource, a superior production technology is one which brings about a substantial increase in productivity per unit area of land per unit of time. It is on this basis that we identify the following technologies as highly promising:

A. Improved Varieties

Improved varieties are the centerpiece of the so-called Green Revolution that has and continues to increase crop yields in both the developed and developing countries. The yield potential of the best existing varieties relative to the best and most commonly used varieties are shown in Table 1. Also shown are the average farm yields of Nigeria and Thailand. There are three important conclusions that can be derived from the data:

1. Compared to rice or maize, the potential of improved varieties for increasing farm yields is significantly higher for cassava. While the yield of the best test variety for cassava is 103 percent higher than the best farm yield, those for rice and maize are only 29 and nine percent more than the best farm yield, respectively. It seems that the presently-used varieties for rice and maize (where varietal improvement has been initiated earlier) are fairly good and additional improvements are smaller and more difficult to achieve. In addition, emphasis in recent years has shifted more to resistance to pests as a means of stabilizing farm yields. In rice, for example, the number of pests to which the new varieties are tolerant has continuously increased with time.

2. Average farm yields are way below that of the best test variety and even that of the best local yields. Obviously the potential of improved varieties for increasing farm yields is still a long way from being completely realized in actual farms.

3. As a calorie source, root crops have a much higher yield than the cereals. For example, the average yield in calories per hectare per day of the best cassava variety is equivalent to 132,000 compared to 85,000 to 98,000 for rice and maize.

B. Intensive Cropping

In the tropics where temperature is favorable for crop growth all year long, as many as four crops can be harvested from the same piece of land in a 12-month period. In rice, for example, the number of days required from transplanting to harvest can be reduced to 75–80 days so that four

Table 1. **Yields (t/ha/crop) of newly developed varieties in international trials and average farm yields for Thailand and Nigeria**

Yield Levels	Crops		
	Rice[1]	Maize[2]	Cassava[3]
Best Test Variety			
Average	4.9	5.0	37.5
Range	1.7-10.7	2.0-8.6	18.2-64.2
Best Local Check			
Average	3.8	4.6	18.5
Range	0.8-8.0	1.7-7.8	4.5-28.9
Average Farm Yield			
Thailand	1.9	2.1	14.8
Nigeria	1.2	0.9	5.6

[1]Source of Data: IRRI.   1981.   Average of 77 trials.
[2]Source of Data: CIMMYT. 1982.   Average of 67 trials.
[3]Source of Data: CIAT.   1980.   Average of 8 trials.

crops will need only a total of 320 days or 45 days less than one year. Some of the component technologies that enhance the intensity of cropping are:

1. Early maturing varieties that shorten the growing season and, therefore, allow more crops to be grown and harvested per unit time (Table 2);

2. Management practices that allow for early seeding or use of older seedlings, resulting in a further increase in the efficiency of land use; and

3. Intercropping which can structure the crop canopies to make more efficient use of solar energy and therefore increase both total yield and stability of production (Table 3).

Based on the above techniques, it is estimated, for example, that in the Philippines, the number of crops that can be harvested per year can be increased from its present level of 1.6 to as much as 2.5 for maize and to 4.0 for irrigated rice.

Table 2: **Relative yield and maturity of traditional, recommended, and early-maturing varieties for three staple crops**

		Yield	
Species	Maturity (days to harvest)	t/ha/crop	kg/ha/day
Rice[1]			
Traditional	126	–	–
Recommended	110	6.80	62
Early maturing	90	5.40	60
Maize[2]			
Traditional	95	3.77	40
Recommended	98	4.87	50
Early maturing	74	3.53	48
Sorghum[3]			
Traditional	105	4.10	39
Recommended	110	4.46	41
Early maturing	81	3.16	39

[1]Yields are from 1978 replicated trials at IRRI.
[2]Three trials (IRRI 1975, IRRI 1976, Carangal et al, 1977).
[3]Seven trials (Gomez 1970).

C. Others

Although not as dramatic as varietal improvement or intensive cropping, there is a host of other technologies that could increase crop yield or reduce cost of production. Some of these are:

1. Pest and disease management which can stabilize productivity and reduce average cost of production;

2. Use of organic fertilizer such as crop residues, *Azolla*, or animal manures which can reduce cost of production and improve soil properties;

Table 3. **Land equivalents ratios (LER) of various intercrop combinations under different management practices**

Intercrop Combinations	Test Factors	Number of Treatments	LER		Source
			Mean	Range	
Rice + maize	Spacing	53	1.17	0.90-1.52	IRRI, 1975
	Nitrogen				IRRI, 1976
	Varieties				
Maize + legumes	Spacing	127	1.37	0.86-2.12	IRRI, 1975
	Nitrogen				Syarifudin et al, 1974
	Varieties				Pookpakdi, 1975
	Location				Carandang 1979
	Species				Rao et al, 1979
Cassava + others	Species	15	1.62	1.17-2.20	CIAT, 1977
	Date of planting				Moreno and Hart, 1979

Note: Land equivalent ratio represents the land area required under mono-cropping to produce output equivalent to that achieved on one unit of land under the different multiple-cropping patterns indicated.

3. Soil conserving practices for the hilly areas which can greatly increase the land areas that can be grown to crops. Most hilly areas are considered too fragile for crop production and are, therefore, not available for cultivation. Recent findings, however, show availability of several management practices that can arrest soil deterioration even under cultivation. With this technology, substantial land areas that are presently unavailable for cultivation can be added to the cultivated area.

Levels of Crop Productivity

There are four levels of crop productivity that are relevant to the objectives of this paper, namely:

1. Potential yield, the highest yield attainable from the crop based on physiological efficiency;

2. Best farm yield, the yield obtainable in farmers' fields using the best production technology;

3. Economic farm yield, the yield that is profitable for farmers to produce;[1] and

4. Average farm yields.

From these four yield levels the following parameters can be computed:

a. Difference between potential yield and best farm yield, which represents the portion of potential yield which cannot be realized in actual farms. This difference is due to some deficiencies in the farm environment that are beyond the farmers' capability to modify.

b. Difference between best farm yield and economic farm yield, which represents that portion of potential farm yield that is not economical for the farmers to produce. This difference may indicate the lack of proper economic consideration in the development of a production technology.

c. Difference between economic farm yield and average farm yield, which represents the portion of the technology that is immediately ready for farmers' use. This difference represents the non-adoption by farmers of production technologies that are superior to their present practice.[2]

Shown in Table 4 is an estimate of the various yield levels for rice, maize, and cassava. The data show that:

1. Economic farm yield is estimated to be 67 percent of best farm yield, which makes it only 30–37 percent of potential yield. This means that a substantial portion of the biological potential of crops is apparently uneconomical for farmers to adopt. Thus, an attractive research and policy area is one that focuses on ways and means of increasing the portion of potential yield that can be economical for farmers to produce. The two most obvious areas of interest for this type of research are the price of agricultural commodities and the cost of producing these commodities.

Table 4. **Estimated Levels of Yield (t/ha/yr) for Rice, Maize, and Cassava**

Yield Levels	Rice	Maize	Cassava
Potential yield (A)[1]	42.8	34.4	71.0
Best farm yield (B)[2]	24.0	18.0	28.9
Economic farm yield (C)[3]	16.0	12.0	19.2
Average farm yield[4]			
Thailand (D)	2.7	3.2	14.8
Nigeria (E)	1.3	1.2	5.6
A − B	18.8	16.4	42.1
B − C	8.0	6.0	10.7
C − D	13.3	8.8	4.4
C − E	14.7	10.8	13.6

[1] From Table 1.
[2] Authors' estimates.
[3] Computed as two-thirds of B.
[4] FAO production yearbook, 1977.

2. Average farm yield can be as low as eight percent and is usually less than 50 percent of economic farm yield. Note that the realization of economic yield in the farms requires a combination of investment in infrastructure and the education and exposure of farmers to the available technology. For some crops and environments all the biological technique for achieving such a goal is already available and the gap between average and economic farm yield should be one of the easiest and fastest sources of yield improvements. For others, additional biological research is still needed.

Technology Adoption by Farmers

Experiences in many countries demonstrate that farmers are willing to change their existing practice if they can be assured of the availability of:

1. A new and more productive technology;
2. Clear instructions on how to implement the new technology;
3. The required inputs at the right time; and
4. A favorable market.

Absence of any one or more of the above can abort the process of change.

On the basis of a clearly superior production technology, several countries have successfully implemented commodity production programs by providing the required extension, credit and market support. Some outstanding examples are the wheat programs of India and Mexico, the maize program of Nigeria, and the rice programs of Colombia and the Philippines.

It seems clear from these programs that a food-importing country is usually willing and able to provide the necessary support services whenever a clearly superior production technology is available. However, as the initial improvements are incorporated into the farmers' practice, subsequent technologies that are better than the existing practice become more difficult to develop. In fact, it can be expected that the superiority of new technologies over those currently used by farmers should consistently become smaller as time passes. With this smaller and smaller advantage, it becomes necessary to verify and quantify the superiority of these new technologies over the existing farmers' practice. Towards this end, the technology verification procedures being used in a few places in Asia are worth describing.

Technology verification experiments are designed to verify the superiority of a newly-developed technology over that of the existing farmers' practice under actual farm conditions. Thus, technology verification experiments are characterized by:

1. Farmers' fields as the research site;
2. Existing farmer practice as one of the treatments;
3. Farmers' capability and willingness to adopt the new practice as an important parameter to be evaluated;
4. Involvement of extension personnel in the conduct of the experiment; and
5. Use of the experiment as demonstration plots.

Based on the results of these trials, mediocre technologies should immediately be removed from the lists of recommendation while truly superior ones should be widely exposed to farmers to hasten their rate of adoption. The Ministry of Agriculture of the Philippines is presently setting up the institutional framework for a continuous process of technology generation in several provinces of the country, an activity that should be of broad interest.

From Production to Consumption

From the preceding sections, it is clear that the potential of crops for supplying the food requirement of the world population is very bright.

Wortman and Cummings estimate that the carrying capacity on earth, based on calorie requirement, is as high as 76,000 million people or over 15 times the present population.[3]

But an adequate food supply does not necessarily mean a solution to the food problem. Such food supplies must first be accessible to the poorest sector of the economy which is also the most prone to malnutrition and the most vulnerable to food shortages. This, to me, is a more difficult problem than that of production. Let me just enumerate a few of these difficult policy issues.

1. Pricing policy—most of the food prices in developing countries of the humid tropics are greatly influenced and, at times, even controlled by government. What should be the basis for setting these prices? Is it the ability of the poorest sector to purchase enough food? Or the insurance of an adequate margin of profit for the farmer producers?

2. Farm subsidy—should such a subsidy focus on the most responsive farmers who are usually also the most well-off? Or should the poorest farmers be deliberately targeted in spite of the expected slower response?

3. Food security—should each country produce its own food needs even if some items can be imported more cheaply? If so, how is this to be implemented and who should pay for the usually large expenditures required?

While the above issues are clearly beyond the coverage of this paper, they are mentioned in order to stress the interrelationship between the biological and socio-economic components of the food problem. This chapter's focus on the production issue is intended to help in addressing the more difficult problems of food distribution and consumption.

NOTES

1. Editor's note: For illustrative purposes, the author has estimated economic farm yield to be 2/3 of best farm yield, based upon his personal observations of conditions in the Philippines. More precise estimates could be made for any location where data on prices and production response to various combinations of inputs are available. Thus, the analytical framework presented here could be applied to a wide range of situations.

2. Economic yield has been computed from farms where production conditions are quite favorable, including access to irrigation in the case of rice. But average yield includes large numbers of farms where the physical environment is quite poor. This fact helps to explain the difference.

3. Sterling Wortman and Ralph W. Cummings, Jr., *To Feed This World* (Baltimore: Johns Hopkins University Press, 1978).

LIVESTOCK IN
AGRICULTURAL SYSTEMS

John A. Pino

This discussion focuses on the role of livestock in crop production systems, rather than on livestock as a primary production system. It describes the integrated system in which livestock forms a part of the crop production system and comments on its potential contribution to increasing food supply in many developing countries.

In most areas where food crops are the primary agricultural system, farmers keep some types of livestock. They range from alpacas and llamas in the high Andes to pigs and chickens in many of the tropical countries. The range of relationships is quite varied—whether those livestock are used for draft power or whether they are used as a source of food. Livestock also may be used in combination with tree crops as well as field crops. This system offers unrealized potential in many parts of the world. Even in the United States where tree crops are produced, livestock involvement has not been developed as much as it could be.

Of course, there are also livestock systems in which animals are the main enterprise. The most important of these are the rangeland systems found in both humid and arid parts of the world. They will not be treated further in this chapter. However, they are complex systems that have many of the same characteristics as the crop livestock systems and warrant comparable attention because their potential is higher than is currently perceived.

With respect to integrated systems, the crop and livestock mix will vary considerably. A characteristic of most of the livestock activities in crop production systems is that there is a minimum input for the livestock portion of that system. For example, in the case of poultry, there is

This paper draws on a recent Working Paper published by the Rockefeller Foundation.

practically no attention given to them by the family and the poultry (chickens, turkeys, ducks, pigeons) sustain themselves on scraps or foraging. The same is often true in the case of pigs, sheep, goats, and even sometimes with cattle. That does not mean that those systems do not have a potential for increasing their productivity. In many cases the animals in those systems are at the low end of their potential productivity because the farmer does not provide any care or technological input. He does not provide supplementary feed. He does not use improved breeds. He does not very often even provide for health protection measures. Indeed, one of the primary deterrents to improvement in the livestock part of the system is the very fact that losses are extraordinarily high in the animal sector, largely because of diseases and parasites and because the farmer takes little precaution to prevent those losses. Because of the low level of inputs, the system is one in which returns are sometimes considered to be free returns.

In reality, the existing system does involve costs. In the case of pigs and poultry, for example, in many locations farmers will throw out loose grain to the animals. The efficiency of conversion of that grain to meat is very poor, 10 to 15 kilograms of corn for a kilogram of weight gain. So while the production of those animals is perceived very often by the farmer as being something he gets for nothing, in reality very often it is rather costly in economic terms.

Even in the case of poultry, where attempts have been made to encourage farmers to increase the production of poultry by providing them with chicks, one will frequently find that two or three months later, all of those chicks will have died as a result of disease or neglect. The fact is that the animals in the system are secondary, are considered a free good, and there is little capability to properly manage even the few animals the family keeps. Even though there are reasons to explain why these systems have not been very productive, they persist in many areas.

Why do they persist? Very often it is because they provide the only cash income for the farmer and the family who keep the animals. They play a very important part in that context, particularly with respect to the contribution of women to family income. In the case of poultry, it might be eggs or occasionally the chicken, the duck, the goose, or the turkey that is sold. In the case of pigs, it might be the occasional pig that goes to market; or in some instances under some systems, the piglets that are produced might be sold to larger farmers who buy up the large number of small pigs from the mixed systems, place them in pens, and feed them concentrate until they go to slaughter. This system gives a cash income to the farmer. Where the farmer has a cow or two cows, occasionally the surplus milk is collected and sold either to a collector or to other neighbors. Sheep and goats may also be sold individually or for their milk product.

These systems are quite unreliable in that they do not provide the market with a consistent quantity or quality of animal product. The producer is likely to receive a very small return for whatever he sells. Furthermore, as a greater specialization in farming systems occurs, the marginal producers, the ones for whom a few animals are part of the general farming system, are likely to find that they cannot compete in the marketplace, largely because the quality of their traditional produce is unacceptable.

There are economic and cultural reasons for keeping animals. A primary one in some systems, of course, is draft power, which is a very important element in a number of regions of the world. Livestock plays a very important and critical role in many crop systems, particularly in rice systems. Animal draft power enables the farmer to cultivate a larger area. Furthermore, a valuable by-product of the draft animals is manure, often the only fertilizer available to the farm.

Another function that animals serve for the agriculturalist and for those living in rural areas—a function often overlooked—is that of a convertible reserve for cash, goods, or services. Animals represent a "living" banking and insurance system. The farmer or owner will convert the pig, goat, or cow to meet whatever necessity the family confronts. In that sense, for the farmer, the returns outweigh the cost of saving.

A number of these traditional systems are amenable to some degree to the application of new technologies. An example of improving the productivity of animals through application of technology merits special mention. In Mexico in the Puebla project, improvements in the crop system brought about such a change. The Puebla project was primarily designed to increase corn productivity. In that system, before there was an intervention in the form of a crop improvement program, one found a range of crop and animal relationships involving poultry, a few pigs, and some dairy cows. The number of dairy cows in the area was rather small. There might be one or two cows tied behind the house of the farmer or being tended by children along the edge of fields. Yields were low, the cows were scrubby, and so on, but farmers kept them because they felt that whatever they could get was better than nothing. These animals were sustained on a few patches of grass here and there and the surplus forage that was available from the fields.

When the new corn production system was introduced, not only did grain output increase but also the amount of fodder production increased fourfold, that is, the corn stalk, the leaves, and so on. This immediately offered an opportunity for expansion of the ruminant livestock population.

In Puebla, there is a great demand for milk and, since there already were some cattle, the additional feed made it possible for farmers to increase the number of cows they kept. Unfortunately, there was very little technology that had been designed for that level of farmer production of milk. There was technology for highly specialized dairy cattle production, but nobody was paying attention to how a farmer with three or four cows could maximize his returns, based on an increased availability of forage that he now had. Nevertheless, this is a mixed system with considerable potential for increasing the level of income from livestock.

This is only one example of the kinds of relationships that are going to exist in a variety of places where the cropping system changes. And these relationships are going to change the nature of livestock productivity.

One of the things which will be a deterrent in many of those systems is going to be the level of veterinary assistance that is provided to small farms. More and more veterinarians are shifting to practices that emphasize herd health procedures rather than individual animal health. This change has taken place, of course, in the more developed and advanced countries because it simply is too costly for an individual veterinarian to take care of an individual sheep, a cow, and so on. Mortality costs are going to continue to be high for the small farmer. In the case of chickens, it is going to be particularly high. For this reason, chicken production by small farmers is not economically viable. Pig production by small farmers needs a lot of good economic work to show whether it is viable. Yet many countries are trying to promote small-scale livestock production with these farmers. Crop/livestock systems need much more analysis before further resources are expended in perpetuating them.

There are some real problems in crop/livestock systems. The fact that these systems exist is an important point to emphasize. Too often researchers have not recognized the role that livestock plays in farming systems. We really do not know how important that role is or what costs and benefits are really involved. The use of animals for draft power in various crop production systems is quite well understood. There is even some marginal income derived from animals that are kept for draft, in terms of milk usually, or the sale of a calf, for example. But the full range of economic considerations regarding other relationships in the crop/livestock system is not well understood, and there are some costs involved which are generally overlooked. This means there is still a research job to complete before sound policies can be formulated in this area.

WOMEN AND AGRICULTURE

Joan Mencher

The purpose of this chapter is to provide an analytical framework for evaluating the role of women's involvement in agriculture in the formulation of food policy. The question of women in agriculture is not a separate issue but is integral to all discussions relating to food policy. In this presentation, however, I am attempting to focus on some of the crucial issues relating to women and agriculture and to organize them into a conceptual framework for understanding their role in various production systems. The chapter looks at women in agriculture both as producers and as consumers. In this connection, two general concepts will be referred to frequently: (1) efficiency (in production) and (2) equity (which concerns production and income distribution, as well as consumption). While both of these are important issues everywhere, we shall see that in various parts of the world greater stress must be given to one than to the other.

In recent years there has been an increasing awareness of such facts as the following:

1. A very high percentage of the actual labor in food production in Third World countries is provided by women (as much as 90 percent in some sub-regions of Africa);[1]

2. In many areas women traditionally did most of the post-harvest processing of food products;

3. Where food is purchased for home consumption, much of the purchasing is done by women (or by young children under female supervision), and perhaps 99 percent of cooking in the home is done by women;

4. Thus, by implication, in most Third World countries it is primarily the women who are responsible for the nutrition of the next generation, as well as for themselves (and for male members of the household whenever they are at home);

5. In many areas women's productivity (measured per unit of time) is equal to that of men, especially in those tasks for which body mass is not a crucial variable.

This chapter looks first at the ways in which women's involvement in agriculture and women's contribution to agriculture vary among the different world regions, such as sub-Saharan Africa, the Arab world (including North Africa), South and Southeast Asia, and Latin America. The second section discusses some of the ways in which women's participation in agriculture is affected by various institutional arrangements—depending, for example, on whether they participate as landless laborers, as owner-workers, or as owner-supervisors of medium-to-large land-holdings; and from another perspective, in terms of their rights to land vis-a-vis the males in their own families. The third section looks at women in terms of their role in household maintenance and survival, the consequences of this role for their participation in agriculture, and the attendant implications for food policy.

1. Interregional Variation in Women's Participation in Agriculture

Different world regions (and to some extent sub-regions) show significant diversity in the traditional sexual division of labor in food production, a diversity which cannot help but have important implications for food policy.

Sub-Saharan Africa

In sub-Saharan Africa, women traditionally have constituted the bulk of the agricultural labor force, especially in subsistence agriculture, and traditionally have been largely responsible for processing and conservation of food for local use. As cash crops entered the local economies during the colonial era, it was primarily males who took to cash cropping, leaving the females to look after food crops (with very little male input, except for the initial preparation of the land). This was also the case in those areas where males migrated out in search of wage work. This pattern has of course continued in the present post-independence era, and it is striking to note the tendency of most of the African governments to ignore the role of women in production, despite their commitment to meeting their own food needs from domestic production.[2]

In Africa today, one finds a sharp separation between women's crops and men's crops, between women's purses and men's purses, and between women's marketing and men's marketing. Though there is considerable variation in the extent of separation in different sub-regions, it is essential in looking at data on Africa to keep in mind that the household is not as meaningful a unit of analysis as it is in many other areas.[3] This point is brought out very clearly in a paper examining the differential impacts of project intervention on men and women which makes the following points:

1. The amount and seasonality of male and female labor requirements

are affected differently by project interventions because of their different labor roles (both with regard to crops and tasks by crop);

2. Men's and women's income levels and income-earning opportunities will be affected differently by project interventions because of their diverse sources of income and household expenditure responsibilities.

Differences such as these lead to the conclusion that, in order to get a clear picture of the situation in a typical African farm, it will be essential to disaggregate the female and male labor and income components, including month-by-month changes in these throughout the year.[4]

African women work incredibly long hours day after day producing subsistence crops. And since the women and children often eat all they grow on their subsistence plots, they may have no surplus cash to use for fertilizers, pesticides, and other inputs needed to increase their production. Furthermore, because so much female labor is needed for subsistence crops, production of cash crops may also suffer.[5] With governments eager for cash crops that can be exported, the basic grain or root crops — which are raised primarily by women — are consistently given lesser importance. Thus, pressures to grow more profitable cash crops have resulted in women losing their traditional rights to grow their crops on communal lands and have often led to a reduction in basic food production.[6] Furthermore, where labor-saving devices have been introduced, it has been mostly for male farming, rarely for females. Thus, while incomes have gone up, and more people have bicycles and transistor radios than formerly, family nutrition has in many areas gone down as a result of ignoring the female role in agriculture.[7]

In many areas the land on which women grow food crops has become increasingly marginal, as the better land has been given over to cash crops (often export crops). In addition, various studies indicate that households with males present were more likely than female-headed ones to obtain information about agricultural loans or about new improved farming practices.[8]

It seems that developments like those mentioned above result from the habit of planners to focus on only part of the food production system, rather than to look at it holistically.[9] Thus, for example, the intrusion of new, male-dominated large-scale patterns of wholesaling, distribution, and retail trade are likely to erode the traditional patterns of female marketing unless governments are able to provide help to sustain these patterns. Clearly, if women cannot expect to earn cash from their surplus produce, their incentive to increase productivity will be limited.

The Arab World (including North Africa)

This is an area where it has generally been assumed that women have practically no role in production; however, recent studies seem to indicate that this is not always the case. Thus, a UN report for 1978 points out that many Middle Eastern farmers are reluctant to report that their wives and daughters work in the fields, even if they do so. And actually, in some areas there has been a marked increase in women's participation in agriculture: as men migrate to work in Saudi Arabia and other oil-rich countries, women are left at home to look after the family farms. Even in other areas where males migrate for newer types of jobs, there is an increase in female labor on self-managed farms.[10] Clearly, any extension program that hopes to succeed in reaching these women would have to make use of female extension workers in order to respect traditional attitudes.

South and Southeast Asia

Perhaps the most significant way in which South and Southeast Asia differ from Africa in terms of our present discussion is that here, alongside a concern with production, the question of equity looms extremely large. In South Asia, and to a greater or lesser extent in various parts of Southeast Asia, households with an over-abundance of food may co-exist in the same village with a larger number of households at or near the starvation level—in good as well as in bad years.

The whole of Asia has long been more highly stratified than Africa, with South Asia being the part of the world where stratification could be said to have reached an apex. South and Southeast Asia together account for between one-quarter and one-third of the total Third World population. (Indeed, if one includes China, this region accounts for approximately one-half of the total world population.) In this vast region there are substantial differences among the different countries, as well as between sub-regions within countries. The regions that make the most intensive use of female labor in South and Southeast Asia are the rice-growing regions of India, Sri Lanka, Indonesia, Philippines, Thailand, and Burma. Most of the heavy, tedious labor-intensive work in rice cultivation, that is, the manual preparation of the fields, transplanting, weeding, harvesting, and food processing, is done by women in India, Sri Lanka, and most of Southeast Asia. In South Asia, Indonesia and the Philippines, a large part of this work is done by hired laborers of both sexes, who often live close to the survival level. In India, it is striking that the classical family farm where a woman works on her own land is more common in areas where rice is not monocropped, whereas in the primary rice districts it is very uncommon. In Bangladesh all but food processing is done by men, and in Java most of the female harvesters have been displaced by males.[11]

Recent data has shown that when both females and males work as hired laborers in agriculture, a significantly higher percentage of the income of the females is contributed to the household than that of males. So in at least some rural areas, female contributions come to more than those of their husbands or other household males.[12] And it is important to note that this is occurring in regions where women always have been paid less than males, and where, in many instances, even recent modern legislation has codified these wage differentials.[13] Even where male contributions are substantially higher in absolute terms than those of females, it is often the latter which are crucial in keeping a household above the starvation level.

Thus labor displacement, especially the displacement of women, needs to be watched most carefully in this part of the world. Indeed, in such situations improvements in cultivation practices that use more rather than less labor would have a higher equity value and would potentially do more to alleviate hunger.

Nutritional levels among landless women are extremely low, especially in households where there are no male workers, and even more so when there are small children and/or the woman is elderly. Traditionally, elderly women who had no one to feed them (e.g., in India and Java) used to feed themselves by gleaning in the fields after the main harvest was over; but today, with newer and improved techniques that eliminate some of the loss in the fields, such women have lost their main source of food. The long-range implications of this remain to be seen.

Regional differences in female participation in agriculture in this part of the world are often related to the type of crop(s) grown. Thus, for the Philippines, it is reported that 70 percent of women in the labor force are in rice or corn production, where they bear the burden of labor-intensive technology.[14] For India, estimates for female participation in field work are relatively low in the northwestern wheat zones (a third to a half of all agricultural labor). In the rice regions in most of India (including West Bengal), the number of female hours of work per crop season is far higher than the number of male hours, since the operations performed by women are highly labor intensive.[15] However, the vast majority of this female labor is done by untouchable or tribal women, sometimes coming from other areas, especially in areas where rice is the main crop. Female migration for transplanting, weeding, or harvesting is clearly not a new phenomenon in many of the traditional southern or eastern rice zones.

In the areas where coarse grains and millets predominate, there appears to be somewhat less stratification, and there is a greater tendency for women to work as unpaid family farm labor, at least in intermediate-ranking households. It is in these regions that women seem to be much more overworked. Time allocation studies in these areas show women working 14–16 hours a day, whereas in the rice regions (in part as a result of population increase, in part as a result of changes in land/labor relations in the second half of the 20th century) it is the lack of work which is a common complaint, at least at some times in the year.

Throughout South and Southeast Asia, until very recently, women, even women in *purdah*, have been in complete control of food processing. This is now being partly replaced by mechanized rice mills or flour mills. Official statistics about female involvement in agriculture are notoriously poor in reporting the participation of women in field work in this entire region (often for reasons relating to the sex of the census taker, or questions of family prestige among higher-caste Hindus, or higher-ranking Muslims), but when it comes to food processing and conservation, there is virtually no information available. Yet, this is an area where considerable improvement could be brought about in order to decrease food losses.

In Asia women also play a major role in caring for chickens, goats, pigs, and (especially in South Asia) cattle. They have also been traditionally involved in the drying and processing of both fresh and saltwater fish for domestic consumption and at times for the market. In Eastern India, low-caste and semi-tribal women also do line fishing for both home consumption and the market. All of these enterprises, however, remain outside the purview of the extension services, which rarely, if ever, focus on women.

Latin America

Tinker notes that while the proportion of women in the agricultural labor force in Latin America is lower than for Africa or Asia, it still is an impressive force according to the Economic Commission of Latin America.[16] And according to Carmen Diana Deere, this figure is much too low, because only women who had no man in the house were counted as doing agricultural labor, whereas in fact many women with husbands work on their family farms.[17] Women often work on the small *minifundios* that have come into being as large estates are broken up, often being in sole charge while their males go off for wage work. Where plantation crops have come to replace subsistence crops, women have often been forced off their holdings, and then both they and their families are deprived of a regular food supply. Where land reform has occurred, women have seldom been named as owners of land. Blumberg suggests that in Latin America, rural females "seem to suffer from a combination of the negative consequences of both the African pattern (where women work harder, with less help, to grow most of the food crops in the subsistence sector) and the . . . pattern . . . where women work for wages in the cash crop sector, but at the lowest-paid and least stable jobs. . . ."[18]

On the whole, the extent to which Latin American women are involved in agricultural decision making relates directly to the status of women in general. Where western concepts of sex roles predominate, women in agriculture do not generally enjoy status equality. Here, as in Africa and Asia, since agriculture is considered to be a male occupation, very little attention has been given to female roles in production, despite the ideology of woman-the-feeder.

2. Institutional and Cultural Factors

Various institutional and cultural factors can affect the ways in which females are involved in agriculture. Their relationships to land and land tenure arrangements are perhaps the most basic. Thus, a particular policy may have widely differing effects on different groups of women, depending on whether they are landless or marginal agricultural laborers working for payment in cash or kind (as found in many of the rice regions of South and Southeast Asia), or women belonging to cultivating households where the women do all or some of the work on their family farms as unpaid family labor, or women who are involved in supervision and decision making on larger farms. Food policy must take into account what work is done by women and try to estimate how the women will be affected by planned changes, especially the poorest of women who, with their children, are already living close to the margin of subsistence. On the one hand, in areas where women have extraordinarily heavy work burdens, new technologies which involve increased labor can only be accepted if accompanied by some labor-saving devices. On the other hand, to introduce labor-saving devices which benefit landowners in an area with severe under-employment for the poorest group of women could lead to increased starvation and/or severe malnutrition, unless accompanied by plans for alternative employment. Thus technologies which may be equitable in some regions may be inequitable in others, depending on pre-adoption patterns of labor use.

Rights to land use are also relevant. In many developing countries, women's access to land for farming—even when they are the main or sole farmers in the household—is contingent on some male's access to land. In areas where marriage ties are ephemeral (such as much of Africa), a woman working land belonging to her husband is less likely to make permanent investments in the land than when it belongs to her natal kin.[19] (This factor is less important in Asia and Latin America, where marriages are less likely to be dissolved.)

The impact on food policy of proposed land reform measures must also be carefully assessed in terms of women's traditional access and control over land. Otherwise one may end up with land reform measures which appear on paper to be benefiting the poor, but which have the effect of disadvantaging one of the most vulnerable sectors of the poor, i.e., women without male protectors. Likewise, in setting up credit programs, it would make sense to design them so that they will reach women who manage farms but who may not be allowed by social custom (or may be unable because of family responsibilities) to visit government offices or talk in public with male officials.

3. Women's Role in Household Maintenance and Survival

Where both women and men work for wages, it has been found that generally a much higher percentage of women's earnings goes into household maintenance than men's earnings. This has profound implications for government policies, since the normal assumption is that if males' income is increased, the household income will automatically be increased and all members of the household will be better off. But the facts seem to indicate that, even where the male's income is improved, it does not necessarily lead to more income or food for the rest of the household members. Planners who make the mistake of regarding female income as supplementary will fail to realize that innovations which decrease the quantum of work available for females can have disastrous effects on significant segments of the population. Even where actual female income is less than male income, it may still be crucial for family nutrition.

In many parts of the world, women are in charge of subsistence food crops, whereas males tend to work on cash crops. This does not mean, however, that women have no need of cash, nor that labor they perform to earn such cash is unimportant.

Female-headed households, both landless and landed, account for close to 25 percent of all households in the Third World.[20] In these households, the female contribution to the household larder may well be the only one, apart from what is provided by the children. This apart, such households suffer special handicaps in relation to agriculture because of constraints imposed by local custom or other circumstances. Yet these households are largely invisible to policy makers, since they are scattered randomly throughout the countryside and cannot present an organized voice to the government.

Conclusions

In many parts of the world, despite all of the recent work in agriculture, there are problems of stagnant or declining agricultural production in Third World countries. This is not only true in Africa or Latin America, but since 1979, has also been noted for India.[21] It is clear that at least part of the reason for these problems is the failure to look at human factors, specifically the role of women in agriculture. This chapter argues that it is not possible to deal with these problems without understanding how the food production system functions in specific contexts. Thus, in order to formulate projects that will really increase production, it is necessary to examine each different region in detail so that policies can be tailor-made to suit national and sub-regional situations.

In addition, it is necessary to modify the neoclassical model of the farm household and to discard the widespread assumptions of family consensus on the allocation of resources or labor—so that in the African case, male and female labor and income are not taken as substitutable,[22] and in the Asia case, male and female income from wage labor are not considered substitutable in terms of household maintenance. These modifications are necessary in order to make our theoretical assumptions fit with the actual behavior of people.

One general observation that has been made throughout the world, wherever detailed case studies have been carried out, deserves emphasis. The first consideration on the part of females working on farms (whether they own them themselves, are working on their husband's or family's farms, or are working as tenants or wage workers) has to do with obtaining enough food for household consumption. Where women work (along with men) for wages in agriculture, almost all their earnings go immediately to feed themelves and their children, often even the husband, whereas a much lower percentage of male income ever reaches the household in the form of cash or kind.

Any policy that seeks to meet this consumption need, with minimal or no risk, is likely to be strongly supported on the ground by local women. It is only after basic consumption needs are met that women can be free and able to turn to trying to improve their own or their family's well-being in other domains of life. Keeping this in mind, one can clearly see that no policy prescription for achieving an equitable supply of food for Third World people can be brought into being without recognizing female contributions to farming and food systems, by helping to preserve them when they are threatened and by trying to improve them wherever possible.

NOTES

1. According to Monica Fong, a statistician at ILO, Geneva as of 1970, there were 287 million women in agriculture in 1970 and 481 million men, or 37% of

the people involved in agriculture are listed as being female. However, this figure is far smaller than what could be projected as a more realistic figure, since everywhere that intensive data had been collected, what is found is that the quantum of female employment has been grossly underestimated (Ceres 1980). According to UN estimates, women undertake a *major part of cultivation* in over half of Third World societies. Other case studies would seem to indicate that the actual percentage is much higher than this (Ceres 1980:15). These figures, however, leave out all aspects of food processing or supervision of farm operations. They focus solely on actual physical work in the fields.

2. Tinker, quoting a UN report notes that while "Statistics show that one-third of farm managers in Africa south of the Sahara are women, with even higher percentages recorded in some countries . . . women's crops and women's work continue to be largely ignored by extension services." Irene Tinker, "New Technologies for Food Chain Activities: The Imperative of Equity for Women," AID/otr–147–79–14. Distributed by the Office of Women in Development, AID, pp. 11–12.

3. Kathleen Cloud, personal communication.

4. Mary Burfisher and Nadine Horenstein, "Sex Role Differences in the Farming Households: A Framework for Analyzing Differential Project Impacts on Women and Men." U.S. Dept. of Agriculture, International Economics Division Economic Research Service, Africa and Middle East Branch, 1982.

5. Tinker, "The Imperative of Equity for Women."

6. Jeanne K. Henn, "Report on Women Farmers and their Relationship to the ZAPI de l'Est," Washington, D. C. World Bank, Mimeographed (1976).

7. Ingrid Palmer, "Rural Women and the Basic-Needs Approach to Development," International Labor Review, Vol. 11, No. 1 (January–February 1977).

8. K. A. Stawdt, "Agricultural Productivity Gaps: A Case Study of Male Preference in Government Policy Implementation," *Development and Change*, 9:439–457.

9. Rae Lesser Blumberg, "Rural Women in Development," in *Women and World Change: Equity Issues in Development*, ed., Naomi Black and Ann Baker Cottrell (Beverly Hills: Sage Publications, 1981).

10. United Nations, Report of the Secretary General, "Effective Mobilization of Women in Development" (UN/A/33/238) (1978).

11. A. Stoler, "Class Structure and Female Autonomy in Rural Java," *Signs*, Vol. 3, No. 1, pp. 74–89.

12. Joan P. Mencher, "Women's Work and Poverty: Women's Contribution to Household Maintenance in two Regions of South India" (Paper presented at a Conference on Women and Income Control in Third World Countries, Columbia University, November 7–9, 1982).

13. Joan Mencher and K. Saradamoni, "Muddy Feet, Dirty Hands: Rice Production and Agricultural Labour," *Economic and Political Weekly* (December Special Issue, 1982).

14. Gelia T. Castillo, "Is the Family Essential to the Filipino?" (1975), pp. 32–36.

15. In a previous project carried out in Kerala by Mencher and P. G. K. Panikar at CDS, Trivanndrum, in one of the Palghat villages, it was found that landowners on the average used women for 417 hours per acre of wet land per crop season, whereas they used males for only 106 hours per acre though interestingly, males were used for many more diverse tasks than females. For Tamil Nadu, where Mencher collected data earlier (i.e., in 1970–71), she also

found the same pattern, i.e., that while men do a much more varied number of things, there is a greater demand for women because they participate in the most labor-intensive activities. Even here, the ratio is of the order of three female hours of work to two male hours.

16. Tinker, "The Imperative of Equity for Women," p. 23.

17. Carmen Diana Deere, Jane Humphries, and Magdalena Leon de Leal, "Class and Historical Analysis for the Study of Women and Economic Change" (Paper prepared for the Role of Women and Demographic Change Research Program, ILO, Geneva 1979).

18. Blumberg, "Rural Women in Development," p. 49.

19. Chaney, Simmons, and Stawdt carefully point out that when women have use rights but are not the legal owners, it might be helpful to think of them as tenants. This is especially true where divorce is fairly common. They state: "A woman who has no control over the product of her land would have less incentive to increase her labor and enhance her productivity through improved farming methods and inputs if her allocated share of the output would not increase. In other words, to the extent that women are in the position of insecure tenants, their productivity and incentives might be constrained." Chaney, Elsa, Emmy Simmons, and Kathleen Stawdt, "Women in Development," from Background Papers for the United States Delegation, World Conference on Agrarian Reform and Rural Development, FAO, Rome (1979), pp. 9–10.

20. This category includes widowed and divorced women without adult sons, women whose husbands work elsewhere, and those whose husbands are too old or infirm to work—or simply disinclined to do so. The numbers vary from close to 90 percent in some parts of Africa to 10 or 12 percent in other areas.

21. *Economic & Political Weekly* (1982):1629–30.

22. Kathleen Cloud and Catherine Overholt, "Women's Productivity in Agricultural Systems: An Overview" (Paper presented at the International Agricultural Economics Meetings, August 30, 1982).

INTEGRATING NUTRITION IN FOOD POLICY ANALYSIS

Alan Berg

Let me begin with three points on which we can all agree. First, malnutrition is a major problem even by the most conservative of the many estimates that we hear about the size of the problem. Second, nutritional status is greatly influenced and affected by food policies. And third, in food policy analyses, nutritional considerations are largely neglected.

Among many planners there is at least an implicit assumption, sometimes explicit, that given adequate food supply, the nutrition problem will largely take care of itself. Others involved in food planning at least imply that encouraging crop adjustments or intervening in markets in the interests of nutrition may risk ruining a good thing that has evolved sensibly over time.

It *is* a tricky business and clearly one must be cautious in suggesting change. Even though most nutrition effects are not planned, existing food policies do contribute to nutrition in several important direct and indirect ways, and certainly we do not want to derail these. No sensible nutrition advocate wants to kill the goose to save the nutrition egg. But having said this, it still seems reasonable to try harder to understand better and to advance those policies that can at least avoid deterioration of food consumption patterns and at best improve the nutritional intake of vulnerable population groups.

In the fall of 1982, I had an opportunity to look at nutrition problems in Zimbabwe, a country which is considered the bread basket of that part of Africa and which had just had its best crop year ever. I saw more kwashiorkor and marasmus in a month in Zimbabwe than I had in the previous 16 years in all the other countries I visited, including a lengthy period in India during a time of famine. These very severe forms of malnutrition are so rare in most countries that they generally are looked at as medical curiosities. In Zimbabwe, one can stop at almost any health facility at random and see at least several cases of such severe malnutrition. In talking with officials, it is quite clear that those who are making policy decisions from aggregate data are missing the boat. The numbers they have to work with mask the problem. It is quite possible that a closer look—an approach that disaggregates the problem by place, by group, by kind of nutritional risk—could lead to a process of analyzing alternative food policies more responsive to needs. If negative nutritional effects must be accepted because other objectives are more important, and they may well be in some countries, then the trade-offs at least should be explicitly stated. The effects of such policies can be monitored, and ways to moderate nutritionally negative consequences can be considered. Four general needs and three more directly actionable steps offer a framework for approaching this task.

First, we need to be clear about and firmly committed to a nutrition objective that goes beyond keeping people alive. We must aim to keep people healthy enough to be fully functioning and productive, and all that that implies for the development of human capital in both the short and the long run. A clear position on this objective can avoid a great deal of confusion about what we are after and what it takes to get there.

Second, we need to recognize and accept a point that is often repeated in rhetoric and seldom acknowledged in practice: that food policy that does not consider nutrition is not food policy. The identification of improved nutrition as an explicit, quantified objective is quite different than an insertion in national plans about the importance of improving agriculture to meet the needs of malnourished people, while at the same time ignoring nutrition in projects, analyses, and evaluation. Under such circumstances, nutrition is used as an excuse rather than a real objective.

Every government now influences in a variety of ways the quantities of foods being produced, traded, and consumed. Yet, the effects on nutrition of agriculture and food policies seldom are adequately planned or anticipated. There is a need to include nutritional considerations in the design of pricing policies, for instance, and of agricultural research policies. This is not to suggest that nutrition is the main objective or even a major objective of food policy. But, as noted earlier, if negative nutrition effects must be accepted because other objectives are more important, then the trade-offs should be explicitly stated, so that at least there are no surprises.

Third, we need to recognize that although nutrition status is in large part affected by food price policies and incomes, food is only one part of the equation. Adequate food is fundamental to meeting nutritional needs, but of itself it is not going to solve the malnutrition problem.

Fourth, we need to understand better how the process works, with emphasis on the elements that may counteract the good intentions of government. For instance, in targeting supplementary feeding programs to the individual, many unanticipated results occur both because of the substitution of food for non-food consumption and the redistribution of goods within the household. Program planners have not adequately anticipated or understood household behavior. This calls for more behavioral research into the subject and special attention to disaggregation in future data collection. We also need a better understanding of questions of management, implementation, and politics—including the local power structure. Generally we have inadequate understanding of the strength of vested interest groups, of who benefits from specific policies and programs, and of what gets siphoned off. As one colleague put it, "What is leakage to economists is payoff to politicians." In short, we cannot cling to the illusion that a policy or program that makes sense technically, economically, and nutritionally will also fly administratively and politically.

What steps can bring us closer to realizing our goals? We need models of how better to build nutrition into food policy analysis. With all admiration for the World Food Council's initiative and promotional skills in encouraging food sector strategies, the fact is there is little to turn to in the way of solid examples. There is an important psychological dimension to having a couple of successes under the belt, both to show it can be done and to show what to do. To the extent that it is politically possible, it would seem useful to concentrate energies and skills developing and describing two or three success stories, rather than to spread thinly the limited resources at this early stage. In this regard, we probably should not restrict ourselves to thinking in terms of formalized food strategies or food plans. If the work is linked to and even subsumed by another action, e.g., part of a five-year planning exercise, a general price review, or a rural development policy document, our experience is that these channels offer a better prospect of assuring follow-through. There is an already accepted context and perceived important connection for the work; there is an administrative infrastructure, and there is a local vested interest in getting the work done and done well.

In Indonesia, for example, prospects for a food policy analysis study were explored two-and-a-half years ago, amid widespread official indifference. Now, as the country begins preparation of the next Five-Year Plan, the atmosphere is much more receptive. What emerges will not be called a food plan. But most of the concerns addressed in this book will have been covered in the process.

Because we are not talking just about a plan but also about its implementation, we need to look more closely at the assumption that what is being proposed can be sustained. To achieve sustainability, we need to insure to the extent possible that the work is done by or at least involves people in the countries concerned. We must aim for more than permission for a group of expatriates to do a study that satisfies the whims of the donors.

This leads to the need for an improved local analytical capacity and the training—and time and patience—which that implies. It is not enough just to pour money into preparing a plan. There already is often too much money chasing too few people.

There is also a need to develop international capability to do such work when local capability is not there or will be a long time in coming. According to IFPRI, which probably has the most work under way of any institution on the nutrition side of the food policy analysis field, there are few countries in the near future (India being the most prominent exception) with existing and available professionals capable of designing the kind of work we are talking about.

The lack of existing capacity in industrial as well as developing countries reflects the lack of importance given to food consumption issues in universities and, more particularly, in agricultural economics departments. There is an almost total absence of attention to the subject, for instance, in agricultural economics departments in the major land-grant universities in the United States. The situation is crying out for a department or two with entrepreneurial initiative to take advantage of this void and to move into this important new area.

Finally, what are some immediate steps that might be taken by private foundations with limited resources? First, they might play an important role in encouraging universities to develop programs, with staff serving as marriage brokers between available funds (say, USAID land-grant college dollars) and universities. Second, they might support the development of graduate programs in this area, with priority attention to African countries. Third, they could emphasize the nutritional consequences of agricultural work, including that of the CGIAR system and other national and international agricultural research programs. Fourth, they may be able to foster linkages between health programs and agricultural programs to further food policy aims. Private foundations can experiment with such actions in ways governments and international agencies cannot. They have more flexibility; they can better deal with issues that cut across disciplines, sectors, and organization charts; they can afford to take risks.

Although food policy analytical work, particularly on the nutrition side, has come a long way in recent years, the topic is still new. In a sense it is where economics was in the 1930s. Much pioneering work is still required. What we do know now, however, is that malnutrition is not going to be solved in the normal course of development, at least in the near term, and hence it requires an explicit look. We also know there now are evolving methodologies and some hard tools at our disposal to allow us to begin dealing with the issues analytically. In short, we know a lot more now than we did just a few years ago, and there is every reason to expect more tomorrow. Rather than shy away from work in this area because of its relative sketchiness, we should recognize both the reason for this condition and the opportunities that this suggests for work in a virgin territory.

AN ANALYTICAL FRAMEWORK FOR ASSESSING NUTRITION EFFECTS OF POLICIES AND PROGRAMS

Per Pinstrup-Andersen

Introduction

To assure a high degree of success, efforts to alleviate malnutrition should be based on sound information regarding the nature of the nutrition problem, who is affected, and why. Information on potential or actual impact of various efforts is equally important. Such information provides a basis for selecting and designing the most appropriate nutrition intervention programs and influencing the selection and design of other programs and policies not specifically aimed at nutritional improvements but with a significant nutrition impact. This paper discusses how to provide information useful for the formulation of programs and policies either aimed directly at improving nutrition or with significant potential nutrition implications. No empirical analysis is presented and no suggestions are made regarding the appropriateness of particular programs and policies.

Nutrition Program Evaluation

Nutrition intervention programs are widespread and of varying nature, ranging from clinical treatment of malnourished children, through nutrition education to food transfers to households presumed to have malnourished members. The performance of many past and current programs has been evaluated. In some cases, the evaluations have been very

Figure 1. **Mock Evaluation**

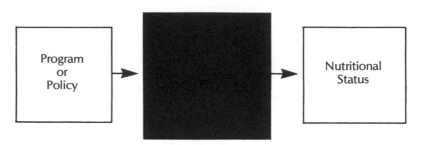

rudimentary, while others have been based on large and complex studies. Many—although by no means all—past evaluation studies have attempted to assess the impact on selected indicators of nutritional status while partly or totally ignoring the intermediate relationships which brought about the impact, as well as other factors which might have exercised impact simultaneous with the program being evaluated.

If the sole purpose of a given study is to evaluate ex post facto the impact of a particular program on the nutritional status of a particular group of people during a particular time period and within certain environmental influences, such an approach may suffice. A caricature of an evaluation of this nature is shown in Figure 1. No attempts are made to analyze the mechanism by which the impact is transmitted, i.e., it is unknown what happened inside the black box. The study merely compares a situation where the program is present to a situation where it is absent, either over time for the same population group or at a given time across population groups.

But if analyses of past and current programs are to be truly useful for the choice and design of new programs and modifications or termination of current ones, it is necessary to know not only by *how much* but also *how* the nutritional status is influenced by the various programs. We must understand *why* some programs are more or less effective than others. There is relatively little work completed on the how and why questions. The job of evaluating a given program then becomes one of tracing the program impact through the process by which impact occurs and estimating the amount of impact on each of the relevant steps in the process.

The key factors and relationships in the black box are relatively few and many of them are common to different kinds of programs. On the other hand, there is an almost unlimited number of possible programs and program combinations which may be designed. If we understand how a given program affects the key factors and in turn how these factors affect the nutritional status within clearly specified or identified environments, we can design effective programs by focusing them on the factors which are most appropriate for a given environment. The number of factors is obviously smaller than the number of possible combinations of such factors which could be affected by different programs. Thus, it is more effective to study the factors than the programs. But to assure an immediate program relevance, a study of the factors should take place within a program framework.

Furthermore, the effects of factors other than those directly affected by a given program, including those falling into what is here called the environment, must be understood and quantified. In the case of a supplementary feeding program, for example, it is important to know not only how nutrient intakes are affected but also how the use of the additional food is affected by sanitary conditions, health factors, and higher educational levels of women, each of which may contribute to a better utilization of the food. While such factors may be assumed constant for the purpose of the evaluation of a single program, such an assumption will not be valid in the case of using the project findings for the design of new programs under different sets of circumstances.

Nutrition Assessment of Other Programs and Policies

Programs and policies not specifically aimed at the achievement of nutrition goals but with significant nutrition implications, e.g., many agricultural and food policies, are only rarely assessed for their nutrition effects. Yet, such assessment—if properly done—would facilitate the incorporation of nutrition goals into the choice and design of such programs and policies with the likely result of improving the nutritional impact.

The processes through which these broader programs and policies influence human nutrition are similar to those related to direct nutrition intervention programs; and while relative emphasis on particular process components may vary, there is, in principle, no reason why the analytical framework to be applied should differ between the two types of programs and policies. Thus, the above discussion applies here as well.

A Proposed Framework: Overview

The processes which determine the nutrition effects of programs and policies are complex. This complexity together with insufficient data and lack of appreciation for the utility of generalizing study findings beyond a particular program, population group, time period, and environment is the most common reason why evaluation studies often avoid an analysis of the process, thus leaving the black box partially or totally untouched. To change this situation, an appropriate analytical framework must simplify the complexity by identifying the most important factors, relationships, and data needs and must demonstrate that these factors and relationships are not program specific and that empirical findings may be generalizable across programs and policies. In the context of previous jargon, the black box must be opened, but rather than emptying everything out—and thus overwhelming even the most ambitious researcher or evaluation officer— we must select the most important parts for study and clearly identify what is left inside.

A set of factors and relationships which might be used to make up such a simplified analytical framework is proposed in Figure 2. Only food-related policies and programs are considered. A similar framework could be developed for health-related policies and programs. The intent of the framework is not that all program and policy assessments should estimate empirically all the causal relationships shown in the figure. The proposed utility of the framework is that it helps in identifying the key factors and relationships for a particular program and policy and the data needs for tracing the program/policy effects through these relationships to the final impact on the specified nutrition indicator.

The framework as shown in Figure 2 contains three main factors through which food and nutrition programs and policies may eventually influence nutrition: (1) the ability of households with malnourished members to acquire food, (2) food acquisition behavior of households, and (3) intra-household distribution of food. These three factors may be influenced by programs and policies through changes in a number of other factors (Figure 2) and may, in turn, influence nutrition through changes in the acquisition of food by households and individuals and the utilization of food by these individuals.

Ideally, analyses would focus on the estimation of the coefficients that explain the magnitude and strength of each of the causal relationships identified in Figure 2, thus linking quantitatively the various factors through which a given policy or program affects the nutritional status.

The most appropriate specification of the analytical model depends on a number of issues including: (1) the type of policy or program and how it is expected to influence the nutritional status, i.e., through which factors, (2) the population groups whose behavior is most important in determining the nutrition effects, and (3) which of many nutrition indicators will be used. Each of these issues is briefly discussed below.

Figure 2. **Relationship of Food Policies and Programs to Nutritional Status**

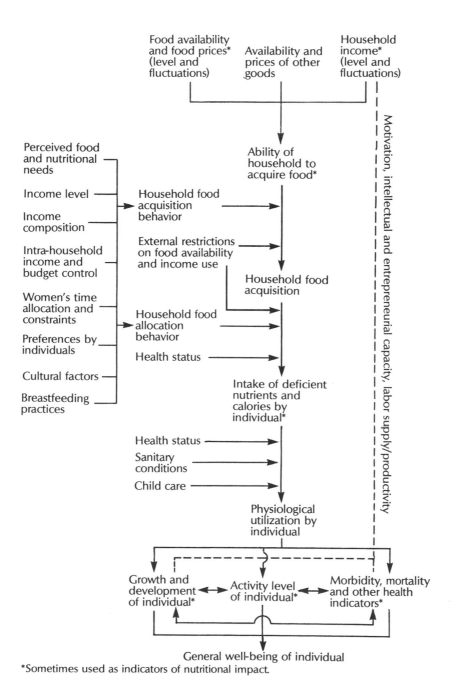

*Sometimes used as indicators of nutritional impact.

Policy and Program Types

Food and nutrition policies and programs may influence the nutritional status through their impact on any of the *factors* shown in the top row and the left column of Figure 2. *Food supply and rural development programs and policies* influence human nutrition primarily through changes in the ability of malnourished households to acquire food. This ability is influenced through changes in food availability on the farm, food prices, and rural incomes, as well as the fluctuations in these factors. The nutrition impact of *consumer-oriented food price policies* (food price subsidies), *food-linked income transfers* (food stamp programs), and *food transfer programs* also occurs primarily through changes in household ability to acquire food. The extent to which the ability to acquire food results in actual acquisition of food by households depends on the pattern of food acquisition behavior of households. It may be hypothesized that policies and programs have a direct impact on this behavior through changes in the relative importance of various income sources, intra-household income and budget control and women's time allocation.

The nutrition impact of a particular program depends on its nature including its limitations to certain commodities, rations and/or target groups. If program rations replace purchases without additional purchase requirements, the effect is expected to be determined by the real income embodied in the transfers. In other cases some substitution between program commodities and other goods is expected to take place. If the intra-household control of incomes from these programs is distributed differently from that of other incomes and if the marginal propensity to spend on the particular foods varies among household members, a direct impact on household behavior may occur. Food transfer programs are frequently targeted to certain household members, e.g., malnourished children or pregnant women. Except for certain program types, such targeting is likely to fail because of offsetting adjustments in food consumption by all members and/or adjustments in food acquisition from other sources. Such failure is usually referred to in the nutrition literature as leakage. Whether in fact leakage of this nature should be considered a serious failure of the program is, of course, open to debate. In spite of large leakages, most food supplementation programs still attempt targeting on particular individuals by imposing various types of restrictions on the use of transferred food.

Nutrition education and awareness programs influence human nutrition through household acquisition and allocation behavior related to food, health, and sanitation. Perceived needs for food, nutrients, and health and sanitary services may change as may child care and breastfeeding practices. Food fortification programs may influence nutrition through the ability of the household to acquire deficient nutrients. Two opposing effects may occur: first, fortification results in a higher content of particular nutrients in a given quantity of food, and second, it may result in a higher price per unit of food. Similar effects would be expected from formulated foods programs.

The Population Groups and Their Behavior

The nutrition impact of a particular program or policy depends not only on the program or policy design but also on the behavior of the various groups or individuals acting within the processes illustrated in Figure 2. These "actors" may enhance or reduce the intended nutrition impact. In some cases they may purposely oppose program objectives. Ignoring at the time of program design the possibilities for conflict between program goals and the goals of the various actors is likely to lead to disappointing program results. Furthermore, as substantiated below, program evaluation which assumes that program goals are shared by all relevant actors is likely to add little to our understanding of why programs perform as they do.

The principal actors are:
1. The consumer household;
2. The individual household member;
3. The food producer/supplier;
4. National government agencies;
5. Local power structures;
6. The program implementation body and individuals within;
7. Marketing agencies and individuals.

The importance of each of these actors varies among program and policy types. The behavior of households, program implementation bodies, and the local power structure are of particular importance for all programs and policies and are further discussed below.

Household Behavior. In-depth understanding of household behavior as it relates to acquisition and intra-household distribution of food is essential to successful program and policy design. Behavior with respect to acquisition of food and its allocation within the household determines the extent to which changes in household ability to acquire food are reflected in food intakes by the malnourished.

Demand parameters such as commodity-specific price and income elasticities go a long way in explaining or predicting the relationships between changes in the ability of households to acquire foods and the resulting change in household food consumption. Since the concern is for households with malnourished members, the parameters must be relevant for these households. In societies with a very skewed income distribution and considerable malnutrition, average estimates are not likely to represent the behavior of households with malnourished members. Thus, the relevant parameters must be estimated by income group. Reliable estimates of such parameters are of recent origin, and their use in food policy design has been very limited indeed. During the last few years, however, there has been a considerable increase in research efforts to estimate demand parameters by income stratum.

Data scarcity is the principal barrier to direct estimation of such disaggregated parameters. Cross sectional data sets may provide an acceptable basis for the estimation of income parameters and, thus, the income effects of price changes. However, they may not serve for reliable estimation of price parameters or the substitution effect of price changes unless they refer to various times or various geographical locations and thus provide for sufficient and relevant price variation. Periodic and directly comparable household surveys over a number of years would alleviate the data constraints.

In addition to reliable estimates of demand parameters related to household incomes and food prices, the ability to predict with a high degree of precision household food acquisition and allocation behavior and the household's reaction to food policies and programs depends on a better understanding of other behavioral factors. Many factors may have a direct impact on household food acquisition and allocation behavior and thus make existing income and price parameters either invalid or incapable of explaining household food acquisition behavior. These include: changes in (1) the demand for women's time, (2) intra-household budget control, (3) income composition, (4) the range of goods and services competing for the household budget, (5) the frequency and fluctuation of household incomes, (6) the degree to which incomes are considered transitory or permanent, and other changes brought about by public policies and programs or structural changes, such as rural to urban migration or transformation of subsistence farming areas into an exchange economy.

Past research on the impact of these factors on food acquisition and allocation is relatively limited. It appears plausible on the basis of available evidence that a number of unexplained behavioral issues reflect the influence of factors such as those mentioned above. However, additional empirical research is needed to provide information in this area which will be useful for policy and program design.

Program Implementation and the Local Power Structure[1]

The process by which national government programs and policies are implemented or translated into action at the local level is a key ingredient in the success or failure of those programs and policies. Yet little is known about the determinants of a successful implementation process. To date, relatively few efforts have been made to analyze how the black box at the local level influences the outcome of specific national programs. Until recently it was erroneously assumed that the black box at the local level was largely passive in nature, i.e., content to carry out policy decisions made at higher levels. However, recent studies have suggested that in many cases what the national government orders or commands is not necessarily what the local level actually does. It may indeed be true that local level forces lack the power and resources to *determine* national policy. Yet since national decisions at the local level must be implemented by or through local forces, these forces possess an important power to constrain or deflect the character of national programs. Local level forces act as a critical filter or prism capable of screening, altering, or even impeding the implementation of national health and nutritional programs.

One of the central problems associated with policy implementation at the local level is that of leakage. One type of leakage occurs when nutritional programs designed for lower income groups fail to reach their targeted groups. Leakage is produced by a variety of factors, such as weaknesses or inadequacies in the delivery mechanism at the local level. Yet the net effect of this type of leakage is always the same, namely a significant difference between the promise of national government programs and the reality of local level delivery.

In many rural areas, the problem of leakage is directly related to the dynamics of local power structure. The skewed distribution of land and economic resources in these areas means that many poor peasants are economically and socially dependent upon the patronage services provided by rich peasants. These patronage services include the provisions of agricultural employment, emergency loans, and intercessionary services with officials. On the other hand, such patronage services are quite important because they ensure the daily survival of large numbers of poor peasants. Yet the importance of these patron-client ties serves to complicate greatly the process of local level project implementation. By virtue of their control over human and material resources at the local level, rich peasants *expect* to dominate all local delivery mechanisms established by the national government. Such expectations are seldom challenged by local level representatives of the national or regional government, whose power is typically not grounded in the economic structure of the local community. In most cases local government administrators simply lack the resources and willpower needed to assure that program benefits reach the target groups. At the same time poor peasants, fearful of alienating the rich peasant on whom they depend, are most reluctant to press for access to national health and nutrition programs. From the standpoint of the typical poor peasant, national programs and policies which come and go are not to be trusted or pursued at the expense of antagonizing the local elite. As a consequence, the benefits associated with national programs and policies are often captured by rich peasants and their favored clients.

Nutrition Indicators

The choice of indicator of nutrition impact varies among studies and is a function of: (1) the particular program or policy being assessed, (2) data availability, (3) cost and time considerations, (4) the disciplinary orientation of the researcher or evaluation officer, (5) implied or assumed relationships among process components, and probably a number of other factors.

The choice of indicator is reflected in the degree of penetration of a particular study into the process as illustrated in Figure 2. In general, data requirements and magnitude of the study increase with increasing penetration. The least penetration is illustrated by the use of program and policy impact on total food availability as an indicator. Although grossly ineffective and often misleading, this indicator is frequently used in food production programs and policies. A slightly greater degree of penetration is provided by the impact on the ability of households with malnourished members to acquire food, e.g., income status. While an improvement over total food availability, this frequently used indicator is still unlikely to be closely associated with the ultimate criteria because it ignores factors and relationships downstream in the framework, e.g., the effect of food acquisition behavior by households, and possible program input on this behavior, food distribution among well and malnourished household members, and health and sanitation issues.

Use of actual household food acquisition as a nutrition indicator is a further improvement because it takes into account household behavior. This indicator is widely used in nutrition assessments of food policies and as an indicator of existing malnutrition and its distribution in a given population. Use of estimates of intakes by malnourished individuals provide an improvement over household food acquisition. However, although sometimes used to evaluate food supplementation programs, particularly those targeted to particular household members, the use of such estimates is not nearly as frequent as the use of estimates of total household food acquisition because of the difficulty of obtaining reliable data.

Anthropometric measures of growth and development are commonly used to indicate the impact of nutrition intervention programs on the nutritional status of children. This is a relatively convenient approach which, if correctly applied, yields reliable estimates of the extent to which the physical development of a particular child deviates from the norm. However, except for severely malnourished children, it may be difficult to separate the effect of nutritional improvements from other effects, such as genetic variation. Also, as opposed to the various food-related indicators mentioned above, anthropometric indicators reflect both food and health-related factors.

The activity level of an individual is another possible indicator of nutritional effect. This indicator is based on the premise that individuals suffering from insufficient energy intakes tend to reduce energy usage by lowering the activity level. Such lower activity levels may affect the development of children and reduce labor supply and productivity. Except for a few studies of the impact of food supplementation on labor productivity, the use of this indicator has been rare. The limited usage is due, at least in part, to the severe difficulties of measuring the activity levels with sufficient accuracy.

The rate of mortality and morbidity have also been used as indicators of nutritional impact. They are probably good indicators of the impact on severe malnutrition provided that: (1) program impact can be separated from the impact of other factors, (2) the sample from which data are drawn is sufficiently large, and/or (3) these rates are relatively high prior to the program. Finally, clinical and biochemical methods are sometimes used as indicators. While the former are used mainly for severely malnourished individuals, the latter are sometimes used in relation to extensive household surveys.

Summary

This chapter addresses the question of appropriate assessment of the nutrition effects of public policies and programs. A large share of past studies has failed to explain how and why certain effects occurred. While useful as ex post facto evaluations of particular programs, such studies offer little assistance for those attempting to design new and improved programs and policies because the results are difficult to apply to programs other than those evaluated. Needed is an approach which not only estimates the nutrition impact of particular programs but also explains how the impact occurred and what would be the impact of certain program modifications. This requires analysis of the processes by which programs and policies influence the nutritional studies. The chapter identifies some of the most important processes and factors and makes suggestions regarding the analytical approach. It discusses household food acquisition behavior, program implementation issues, and the local power structure.

NOTES

1. Richard Adams contributed to the section on Program Implementation and the legal power structure.

local

REFERENCES

Arnold C. Harberger, *Basic Needs Versus Distributional Weights in Social Cost-Benefit Analysis* (Background notes for a seminar, World Bank, Washington, D. C. 1979).

Eileen T. Kennedy and Per Pinstrup-Anderson, *Nutrition-related Policies and Programs: Past Performance and Research Needs*, IFPRI November 1982.

Per Pinstrup-Anderson, "Food Policy and Human Nutrition" (Paper presented at workshop on The Interfaces between Agriculture, Food Science, and Human Nutrition in the Middle East, ICARDA, Aleppo, Syria, February 21–25, 1982).

Per Pinstrup-Anderson, "Export Crop Production and Malnutrition," The Ninth Annual H. Brooks James Memorial Lecture, North Carolina State University (October 21, 1982).

Pasquale L. Scadizzo and Odin K. Knudsen, "The Evaluation of the Benefits of Basic Need Policies," *American Journal of Agricultural Economics* (February 1980).

Marcelo Selowsky, "Target Group Oriented Food Programs: Cost Effectiveness Comparisons," *American Journal of Agricultural Economics*, Vol. 61, No. 5, (December 1979).

——. "Nutrition, Health and Education: The Economic Significance of Complementaries at Early Ages" (Paper presented at the Sixth World Congress of the International Economic Association, Mexico City, August 4–9, 1980).

Marcelo Selowsky and Lance Taylor, "The Economics of Malnourished Children: An Example of Disinvestment in Human Capital ," *Economic Development and Cultural Change*, Vol. 22, No. 1 (October 1973).

Amartya Sen, "Starvation and Exchange Entitlements: A General Approach and Its Application to the Great Bengal Famine," *Cambridge Journal of Economics*, No. 1 (1970).

Amartya Sen, "Famines," *World Development*, Vol. 8 (1980).

EXPLORATIONS OF
FOOD CONSUMPTION AND
NUTRITIONAL STATUS:
BANGLADESH

Lincoln C. Chen

A fundamental premise of food policy is the intuitively obvious linkage between food consumption and nutrition status. An adequately balanced diet is considered a necessary precondition to sound health and nutritional status; and conversely, compromised health and nutritional status is associated with a deficient, excessive, or imbalanced diet. Although few would challenge the basic validity of this fundamental premise, there has been, in general, an absence of precision in delineating the subtleties of the relationship and a lack of empiricism in substantiating the presumed linkages. A host of macro and micro variables have been hypothesized to influence food consumption behavior and its effects on nutritional status. Among others, these include socioeconomic status, diet, food-related bahavior, and infectious diseases. Yet there has been a general lack of evidence quantifying the magnitude and direction of these factors in affecting nutritional status.

What We Do and Do Not Know

Since the research breakthroughs on vitamins around World War II, the nutritional sciences have offered few practical, problem-solving advances. A medical approach involving clinical and field studies dominated nutritional thinking in the 1950s and early 1960s. This approach subsequently gave way to a holistic school of systems analysis, wherein nutrition was related to everything, a point of view which prevailed through the latter half of the 1960s and first half of the 1970s. The effort floundered, entangled in massive data containing a paucity of practical solutions. By the latter half of the 1970s, disillusionment thrust forth political explanations for the continuing existence of hunger and malnutrition. While politics may be one cause of a problem, revolutions are not an easy solution to implement.

Yet we have learned something about the complex system of biosocial, economic, political, and environmental interactions which affect and are affected by nutritional status. The most important lesson we have learned is that there are no simple solutions. Malnutrition, like mortality, is as much a net manifestation of these complex forces as it is a cause of these forces themselves. Our experience underscores the following points:

1. The relative signficance of various macro and micro forces probably varies from one location to another. In some subsistence societies, hill and dry land agriculture in India for example, food production technologies may not yet be adequately developed. In the rapidly developing economies of Latin America, political pathology and food malpractices may be more important. Under some circumstances, efforts to improve food availability among the poor will not do much unless the burden of infections is reduced. Thus problem-solving interventions need to be locally-adaptive, flexible, and relevant.

2. Like poverty, malnutrition is an intergenerational phenomenon; nutritional status today is a cumulative manifestation of earlier deprivations, including parental malnutrition. The direct biological component of this momentum is straightforward; that is, malnourished mothers bear small babies. But changes in cultural and social practices and economic behavior which influence nutritional status also have a time dimension. Expectations regarding the impact of interventions need to accommodate this time-lag phenomenon. In nutrition, we should be thinking in terms of a decade, rather than single years.

3. Technological advances may be necessary preconditions for improvements in productivity, quality of diet, and health-care practices, but they are rarely sufficient. Education and literacy and thus the capacity of local people to use new technologies to their best advantage often have a great deal to do with the outcome. Modes of introducing new technologies and implementing nutrition interventions must take into account the historical, cultural, and sociopolitical context in which they are to be applied. Otherwise interventions may sometimes generate indirect and unfortunately negative consequences for nutrition.

4. The nutrition problem illustrates the limits of applying social knowledge toward the solution of social problems. It is one thing to understand the cause of a problem, another to solve it. We now believe that history,

culture, politics, and technology all matter greatly. But we still understand very little of the linkages between macro forces and micro events, ranging from broad international movements of foodgrains to the hunger or anorexia of a child living in poverty.

This chapter begins by presenting a conceptual framework of the hypothesized linkages between socioeconomic, dietary, and health factors in determining nutritional status. Using longitudinal micro-level data generated in rural Bangladesh, the chapter then presents preliminary findings of an analysis of the direction and quantitative relationship between these factors impacting on the nutritional status of children. The chapter concludes by discussing the implications of the surprising and counter-intuitive findings.

Framework

Figure 1 presents a framework integrating current hypotheses on the mechanisms by which various factors operate to affect the nutritional status of an individual child. An individual focus is selected because malnutrition is ultimately an individual phenomenon and because it enables us to build upward to the household, community, and national levels. Children under age five years are selected because of their nutritional vulnerability. The vertical line in the figure depicts the growth and development of a child from conception to birth through the critical first five years of life. The nutritional status of a child at any point in time can be conceptualized as reflecting the cumulative effects of past nutritional events and the net influence of current nutrient flows into and out of the child (in addition to genetic endowment).

The inflow and outflow of nutrients to an individual can be attributed to direct micro factors imbedded in larger, equally powerful macro forces. A child's nutrient intake is determined by the diet of the mother and child. During pregnancy, maternal diet and the nutritional reserve of the mother are important. In most rural areas of poor countries, breast-feeding is nearly universal, although breast-feeding appears to have declined in many urban and periurban settings. Supplements to breast milk (weaning foods) should be introduced between four to six months. Eventually the child will be weaned, becoming entirely dependent upon an adult diet. The nature, magnitude and timing of these dietary practices are related to household food behavior. Such behavior is affected by many factors, including women's time and work, home management skills, food beliefs and practices.

A family obviously can only consume food that is available, obtained through either home production or market purchases. In agrarian so-

Figure 1. **Framework of Malnutrition**

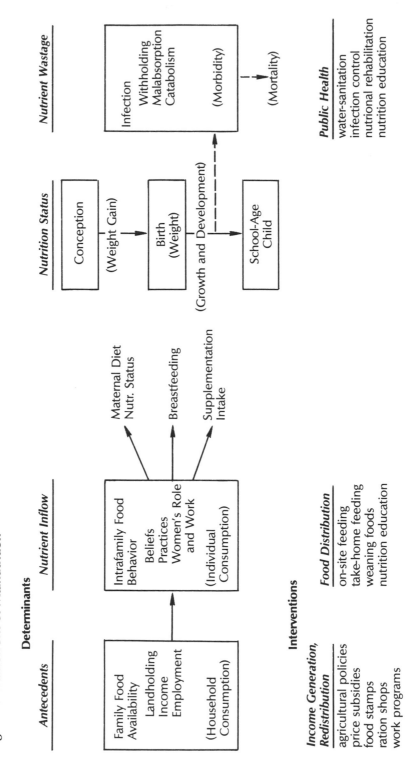

cieties, cash or in-kind income may be generated from assets or from employment. For most of the rural poor who have insufficient land, agricultural labor is the primary source of income. Among the urban poor, stable income is dependent upon employment, and family food availability is determined by a combination of wages earned, preferences, and market prices.

The food inflow is counterbalanced by an outflow of nutrients. Normal usage includes energy and protein required for metabolism, activity, and growth. There are, however, also pathways of unnecessary nutrient wastage. Infections and parasitic infestations (particularly diarrhea, malaria, and measles) have been documented to cause significant acute and chronic nutrient wastage through several sociobiologic mechanisms, including anorexia, malabsorption, catabolism, and direct loss.

Several features of the figure should be underscored. First is the distributive dimension of food among communities, families, and individuals. Adequate national production of food may not translate into adequate family nutrient availability because of maldistribution of purchasing power among families. Sufficient food in a family also may co-exist with individual malnutrition because of maldistribution of food within families. A second dimension is change over time. Although an individual or family intake may be adequate on an annual basis, severe deficiency states may nevertheless result from marked fluctuations of food intake over time, such as during seasonal food shortage. Although the average nutrient wastage due to infections may be quantitatively insignificant, the child who experiences repeated bouts of infection, often in rapid succession, is vulnerable to the vicious cycle of infection-malnutrition and death. Thirdly, although the nutrient inflow and outflow pathways are depicted separately, they are in reality interdependent. Infection, for example, results not only in biologic wastage, but also affects food inflow via feeding practices during and after illness. Other examples are presumed changes of intrafamily food distribution or the dependence of family wage income on the physical health of adult earning members whose capacity to work may be affected by diet and disease.

Summarizing briefly, there are three groups of factors influencing the nutritional status of an individual: (a) family food availability; (b) the efficiency by which these food resources are distributed and utilized by the family; and (c) the level of nutrient wastage due to infections. These three categories are also fundamental to an understanding of approaches to nutritional interventions.

Nutrition policies and programs may be categorized according to their mode of action. There are a host of interventions, for example, that have as their primary aim increasing family food availability, particularly among the poor and disadvantaged. This aim is inherent in agricultural policies, agricultural production programs, food storage, preservation, marketing programs, agro-based employment schemes, food subsidies, food price policies, food stamps, ration shops, guaranteed employment programs, and food-for-work programs. These schemes deal with both food production and distribution, but there is often an explicit aim of increasing food availability among the poor. A second group of interventions aim, not to increase overall food to a family, but rather to improve household food distribution and behavior. Nutrition education and the promotion of breast-feeding are two such examples. Another is child feeding programs. Although child feeding increases the overall food consumed by a family, the primary goal of such programs is distributive, getting more nutrients into only one family member. A third set of interventions relate to reducing the wastage of nutrients. Public health programs, such as clean drinking water, sanitation, immunizations, curative services (such as oral rehydration and antibiotics) improve nutritional status by preventing nutrient wastage. However, evaluations of unipurpose programs have more often than not failed to detect any impact on nutritional status.

Data Source and Methods

To examine some of the relationships among macro and micro forces impacting on nutrition in more detail, the author conducted a longitudinal Food and Nutrition Study in Matlab thana which aimed to elucidate and quantify the effects of socioeconomic variables, infections, food availability, and dietary practices (including food distribution within the family) on the physical growth of children under five years. The study covered 130 Muslim families stratified according to socioeconomic status with each household containing a child under five years of age. The following measurements were obtained from each study household over a one-year period beginning June 1978: initial baseline asset survey, income-expenditure survey, bimonthly; anthropometry (weight, height, mid-upper left arm circumference and left tricep skinfold thickness) of mothers and children monthly and all other household members, tri-monthly; and morbidity surveillance, weekly. Minor illnesses among study family members were treated by a trained paramedic, while severe illnesses were referred to the Matlab central health facility.

The dietary methodology is noteworthy because new field procedures were introduced to measure household and individual food intake simultaneously. The new methodology involved the standard 24–hour weightment method in which all foods consumed by the household in a 24–hour period were weighed before cooking. To ascertain intrafamily food distribution and indivdual food intake, postcooked foods were converted into volume units. Local female dietary workers, using standard teflon volumetric cylinders, measured the volume of postcooked food in cooking pots before and after serving. During meal serving, the workers observed food distribution patterns by counting the numbers of spoonfuls distributed to each individual. Since utensil sizes had been measured in a preliminary round, the accuracy of the observation could be double-checked by comparing the volume lost from the cooking pot with the volume computed by summing the individual spoonfuls of food distributed to individuals. Individual food intake was converted into nutrient intake by applying standard Indian and Bangladesh food conversion tables. Field workers were strictly instructed not to comment upon or interfere with the food distribution process. Study families were informed at the outset that socioeconomic, dietary, anthropometric, and morbidity information were being obtained to assess the factors that influence child health in the community.

For the purposes of this preliminary analysis, the data collected on 101 of the 207 study children for which complete information is available were analyzed. Because the computer software capacity limited analysis to 60 data points, these children were divided into two groups (under age 36 months and between 36 months and 66 months) for regression analyses. Data files were established for each of the 101 children, as follows:

1. Child sex;

2. Child age (in completed months at the midpoint of the study year);

3. Child weight and height (average of 12 monthly measurements over the year);

4. Child anthropometric classification (weight-for-age, weight-for-height, and height-for-age as percent of the Harvard median standard);

5. Child breast-feeding status (none, continuous through the year, weaned during the year);

6. 24–hour child caloric and protein intake (average of six bimonthly measurements over the year);

7. Child morbidity (percent of days ill over the year);

8. Household wealth (three classifications according to the household's landowning status);

9. Number of household members;

10. 24–hour household caloric and protein intake (average of six bimonthly measurements over the year); and

11. 24–hour household per capita caloric and protein intake (with number of household members expressed as adult male equivalents).

Preliminary Study Findings

Internal checks of the data suggest that they are reasonably consistent. With 11 group variables and manifold more specific variables, the data set constitutes a formidable challenge for analysis. Of the myriad of questions which could be posed, this chapter looks at two which appear to be particularly significant. First is the sensitivity of individual child caloric intake to key socioeconomic variables related to the family and certain individual characteristics. Tables 1a–1b present the results of multiple regression with child caloric intake as the dependent variable and the family's wealth, adjusted per capita caloric intake of the household, child age, sex, and breast-feeding status as the independent variables. Table 1a relates to 50 children under 36 months of age, while Table 1b relates to 42 children between ages 36 months and 66 months. Overall, the role of these independent variables in accounting for variability of child caloric intake is disappointing, with a corrected R^2 of 0.64 and 0.50. Of the independent variables, age was statistically significant for both groups of children, while sex and breast-feeding status were significant for only the older children. Noteworthy is the finding that neither family wealth nor adjusted per capita household consumption exerted much influence on child caloric intake.

A second hypothesis relates to the role of individual diets (nutrient inflow) and morbidity (nutrient wastage) on the physical growth of children. These results are shown in Tables 2a–2b. Weight-for-age as a percent of the Harvard standard (representing physical growth) is employed as the dependent variable, but similar results were obtained using other anthropometric indicators as the dependent variable. Of the independent variables examined (child age, sex, caloric intake, and percent of morbid days ill with diarrhea), only the sex of younger children was statistically significant. Regressions, not presented, that examined these relationships using other independent variables (protein intake, number of all illnesses, percent of morbid days due to all illnesses), all gave similarly disappointing results.

Discussion

Our analysis of the Bangladesh data has generated two surprising and counter-intuitive findings. First, there appears to be a weak relationship between socioeconomic factors and child caloric intake. Family wealth and per capita food availability in the household failed to demonstrate significant associations with a child's caloric intake. Also unanticipated was the absence of a clear relationship between child anthropometry and the concurrent inflow and unnecessary outflow of nutrients. In other words, child caloric intake and infectious disease morbidity due to diarrhea were not associated with nutritional status. Similar results were noted when other anthropometric measures (e.g., weight-for-height, height-for-age)

Table 1a. **Child Caloric Intake as a Function of Child Age, Family Wealth, Child Sex, Breastfeeding Status, and Adjusted Per Capita Household Consumption for Children Under 36 Months of Age**

DEPENDENT VAR: AV CAL

RANGE: 0 to 58　　　　　　　　　　　　　　　　　　　#OBS: 59

VARIABLE	COEFF	STD ERR	T-STAT
Constant	−66.445	157.511	− .421
Age	25.424	2.694	9.436
Wealth	−17.180	34.181	− .502
Sex	−17.673	41.581	− .425
BF	−83.518	36.774	−2.271
HHCAL/CUF	.035	.051	.689

R-SQ:	.667	CORR R-SQ:	.636
SER:	154.813	SSR:	1270259.
F (5, 53) =	21.270	DW:	1.619

Table 1b. **Child Caloric Intake as a Function of Child Age, Family Wealth, Child Sex, Breastfeeding Status, and Adjusted Per Capita Household Consumption for Children 36 to 66 Months of Age**

DEPENDENT VAR: AV CAL

RANGE: 0 to 41　　　　　　　　　　　　　　　　　　　#OBS: 42

VARIABLE	COEFF	STD ERR	T-STAT
Constant	605.068	274.404	2.205
Age	8.909	3.705	2.404
Wealth	− 4.821	42.978	− .112
Sex	−185.106	54.782	−3.378
BF	−158.758	44.181	−3.593
HHCAL/CUF	.053	.055	.974

R-SQ:	.564	CORR R-SQ:	.504
SER:	163.066	SSR:	957261.6
F (5, 36) =	9.350	DW:	2.115

Table 2a. Weight-for-Age as a Function of Child Age, Child Sex, Child Caloric Intake, and Percent of Illness due to Diarrhea for Children Under 36 Months of Age

DEPENDENT VAR: WT/AGE

RANGE: 0 to 58   #OBS: 59

VARIABLE	COEFF	STD ERR	T-STAT
Constant	81.120	4.292	18.897
Age	− .217	.254	− .854
Sex	− 5.997	2.459	− 2.438
AV CAL	» » » » » »	» » » » » »	.239
ILL/D/%	− .322	.146	− 2.193
R-SQ:	.160	CORR R-SQ:	.098
SER:	9.252	SSR:	4622.479
F (4, 54) =	2.588	DW:	1.687

Table 2b. Weight-for-Age as a Function of Child Age, Child Sex, Child Caloric Intake, and Percent of Illness due to Diarrhea for Children 36 to 66 Months of Age

DEPENDENT VAR: WT/AGE

RANGE: 0 to 41   #OBS: 42

VARIABLE	COEFF	STD ERR	T-STAT
Constant	60.757	8.730	6.958
Age	.031	.166	.188
Sex	1.120	2.625	.426
AV CAL	» » » » » »	» » » » » »	1.229
DAY/D/%	− .017	.130	− .133
R-SQ:	.059	CORR R-SQ:	.042
SER:	7.245	SSR:	1942.424
F (4, 37) =	.584	DW:	1.634

or morbidity indicators (incidence of illness, percent of days ill due to all causes) were employed.

Two alternative explanations emerge. Either the findings are invalid because of methodological weaknesses or, if the findings are valid, alternative explanatory hypotheses are required. Such hypotheses must necessarily affect current theories on the determinants of malnutrition.

The study illustrates methodologically the hazards inherent in research on this topic. Measurement of relevant variables is extraordinarily difficult. To be sure some measurements are straightforward (child, sex, weight, and height); some others are of moderate difficulty (child age, breast-feeding status); but others still are complex and fraught with pitfalls. Age data in Matlab are known to be reliable because of a vital registration program (in which all births are registered) that has been operating for nearly two decades, but such assurances would not be available in most other developing country settings. Much more uncertain is the reliability of morbidity and dietary measurements. The former was collected through weekly recall and reporting, usually by the mother. Morbidity measures are plagued with difficulties because of varying definitions of disease (between families and even occasionally by the same individual), recall lapses, and may have been biased by the ready provision of free treatment for illnesses. Treatment was considered essential for ethical reasons. The 24–hour weightment method for household food intake has been well-studied, but the use of volumetric measurement and observation to quantify individual intake had not been attempted earlier. An assessment of individual intake measurements through examining the variability of individual intakes over three consecutive days showed a coefficient of variability of 15 percent. The data thus appeared to be better suited to group rather than individual analysis.

A second methodological issue is the choice of relevant variable. With virtually every parameter under consideration, selection of the most appropriate indicator was attempted. In the regression shown in Table 1, family wealth was indicated by classifying families into three equal groups according to reported landowning status. Accurate information on landownership is notoriously difficult to obtain and, moreover, such can only be a crude proxy as it excludes non-land sources of wealth and income; and land quality and productivity may be more important than size. Similarly, in an attempt to standardize household caloric intake, an adjusted per capita intake was computed assigning each family member a coefficient according to age and sex requirements. Such an adjustment was believed to be more appropriate than either total household intake or average per capita intake, which is irrespective of age and sex of members.

The complexity of variable selection is even greater in the regression shown in Table 2. Weight-for-age was used as the indicator of nutritional status and morbidity was defined as the percent of days ill due to diarrhea. Similar results were obtained when weight-for-height and height-for-age were used as the dependent variable. Because data on the number and duration of illnesses by cause were collected, the range of possible morbidity variables was enormous. Duration (expressed as percent of days ill) was selected because recent research suggests that duration, rather than incidence, of morbidity is of greater nutritional consequence. Furthermore, the regressions shown in Table 2 are confined to diarrhea morbidity because of the well-substantiated impact of diarrhea on nutritional status and because similar regressions using morbidity due to all causes showed even weaker relationships than diarrhea alone.

Another methodological dimension is time. Because our study is longitudinal and because single-point measurements are subject to high error margins, this analysis employed mean values of measurements taken over the course of a study year. This has the advantage of reducing erroneous single measurements (e.g., six rather than one dietary measurements). But such aggregation also excludes some indicators which may have generated more fruitful results. One example is the possible superiority of child growth (weight or height gain) over time in comparison to a cross-sectional classification of anthropometry. Another example would be the possible dilution of the effects of illness, since morbidity impact would be expected to be coincident time-wise with growth faltering. When averaged over a year, the morbidity effects may be diluted out by the well-documented phenomenon of catch-up growth and the many illnesses of varying nutritional impact.

The final methodological issue relates to variability of measurements. Dietary measurements are subject to a high degree of variability. Thus, large sample sizes may be required to demonstrate statistically significant relationships. Yet, the multiplicity of types of data required for a multi-faceted analysis of the determinants of malnutrition demanded much effort, thereby effectively reducing the possible size of the sample.

An alternative explanation of the findings is that, even if the data and analysis face methodological constraints, the weak associations may nevertheless be valid. How then do we explain the weak relationship between child caloric intake and family wealth and household food availability and, in addition, the virtual absence of association between child anthropometry and caloric intake and morbidity?

The former finding suggests either that socioeconomic differentiation is weak within this rural Bangladesh community or that child intake may be more dependent on community-wide behavioral or agro-ecologic variables than on household wealth, income, or food availability. The latter hypothesis is consistent with other research in South Asia, as well as with research findings reported by Gençağa for Turkey. Bairagi, for example, reported that mothers' education was more significant than household income in determining nutritional status in another area of rural Bangladesh. Furthermore, he noted that higher family income appeared to be of relatively greater benefit to children of literate mothers and that income was only significant for families below a certain threshold income. Ryan and colleagues working in six clusters of villages in South India also observed that individual nutrient intakes of children were not found to be influenced by the level of not household income after allowing for the influence of other variables.

The failure of anthropometry to relate to child caloric intake and morbidity raises a number of questions. The biggest problem is the standardization and definition of nutritional status. Definition and measurement of food or nutrient intake, while difficult, can be precise; but definition and measurement of nutritional status is plagued by ambiguities. Despite recent efforts at precision, including differentiation of acute versus chronic malnutrition, clear understanding of the physical characteristics which signify malnutrition is still lacking. Moreover, anthropometry or the measurement of growth reflects the net effects of an interaction between environmental and genetic factors with strong ecologic and intergenerational components. And the congruence between anthropometry and other indicators employed to assess nutritional status such as diet, clinical or biochemical symptoms, or functional behavior, is often highly uncertain. Thus it is too soon to conclude that the failure of anthropometry to relate to child caloric intake and morbidity in rural Bangladesh necessarily calls into question the basic premise of the intimate relationship between income level, food intake, and nutrition. However, when taken together with findings from other studies suggesting that income level does not affect child caloric intake except at very low levels and that educational level of the parents has more influence on nutritional status than do other variables, these results do suggest that some rethinking may be in order about the importance of supplying additional food versus other types of health care and public educational intervention in the presence of chronic malnutrition.

EXPLORATIONS OF FOOD CONSUMPTION AND NUTRITIONAL STATUS: TURKEY

Hasan Gençağa

Introduction

A National Food Consumption and Nutrition Survey was conducted in 1981–82 by the Turkish Development Research Foundation (TDRF). It includes measures of food intake for all age groups and anthropometric measures for children up to the age of 17.

The survey is a follow-up of a previous study conducted in 1974 by the Hacettepe University, which reported that 17 to 40 percent of Turkish population was malnourished depending on the definition of malnourishment adopted.[1] The anthropometric measures of children revealed that there was growth retardation in 20 percent of children up to age 5.

The Survey Objectives

The TDRF Food Consumption and Nutrition survey had five major objectives:

1. To identify the determinants of demand for food items;
2. To determine the sources and relative costs of nutrients in the food baskets of different social groups;
3. To identify seasonal changes in consumption;
4. To .dentify malnourished groups; and finally

5. To propose a set of policy guidelines for adoption by national development agencies to reduce malnutrition in Turkey.

Scope and Preliminary Results of the Survey

Until the results of the 1974 Survey became available, the only source of information on national food intake levels in Turkey was aggregate Food Balance Sheets. The results of both the 1974 and 1981/82 surveys show that the actual food intake levels are about 70 percent of those indicated by the Food Balance Sheets. The 1974 Survey results, however, recorded consumption during September only and, as a result, the findings were generally regarded as not being reliable indicators of annual consumption levels. Partially to compensate for this shortcoming, the TDRF survey was repeated three times (September 1981, January– February 1982, and May 1982) to capture seasonal changes in consumption.

The main source of discrepancy between the Balance Sheet and the survey results derives from over-estimated production. Half of total calories and protein consumed in Turkey, for example, derives from wheat (See Table 1). The results of the two surveys and independent estimates place the actual wheat production at only 70 percent of the official production figures.[2] The production levels of practically all other sources of nutrients seem also to be over-estimated. The over-estimated production levels lead to a proportionate over-estimate in intake levels.

The first cycle of the Foundation's survey was conducted during the same month as the Hacettepe University survey in 1974. This allows for analysis of change over time.

In between these two surveys, there was a radical change in national development policies. Beginning in 1980, there was a change of policies from inward-oriented, import substitution policies to export-led growth policies in line with Turkey's comparative advantage. One result of this change in policy was the lifting of restrictions on food exports. The survey provides information on the impact of the new trade policies on food consumption, prices, and production.

The TDRF Survey not only records the sources of nutrients but also records the marketing channels and costs of nutrients from different sources, as well as auto-consumption. Comparisons of the 1974 and 1981/82 Survey reveal patterns which could not be detected from the national price and food production data.

For decades, Turkey has not allowed exports of food items on the grounds of national nutritional needs. Following policy changes in January 1980, there was a major expansion in food exports. Two commodities for which expansion in exports has been most rapid are red meat and

Table 1. The Sources of Nutrients and the Changes in Nutrient Sources Between 1974 and 1981/1982 (percent of all nutrients derived from each source)

Nutrient Sources	Period	Calories[1]		Total Protein[1]	
		Rural	*Urban*	*Rural*	*Urban*
Wheat	1974	47.4%	44.3%	50.6%	44.7%
	1981/1982	46.2	45.5	49.3	47.2
Other Cereals	1974	21.2	15.1	20.5	13.8
	1981/1982	21.0	13.8	20.9	12.5
Meat (red meat, poultry and fish)	1974	2.2	6.3	6.3	18.1
	1981/1982	1.8	5.4	4.8	14.2
Milk and milk products	1974	4.9	5.3	10.7	10.3
	1981/1982	7.7	7.2	14.4	12.5
Fruits and vegetables	1974	9.1	10.5	9.2	10.7
	1981/1982	4.8	6.1	4.3	5.7
Pulses	1974	1.1	1.0	2.5	2.3
	1981/1982	2.6	3.3	5.3	6.7
Oils (including butter)	1974	10.3	12.7	0.2	0.3
	1981/1982	9.6	11.4	0.3	0.4
Sugar and condiments	1974	5.0	6.5		
	1981/1982	6.0	6.6		

[1] Unweighted sample averages.
Sources: The 1974 data are derived from the Hacettepe University Survey; the 1981/1982 data are from the survey conducted by Turkish Development Research Foundation.

pulses. Eighty percent of lentils and 62 percent of chickpeas produced were exported in 1981. The red meat exports accounted for 15 percent of total national production and 40 percent of all commercially traded meat.[3] The nutritional impact of this policy is depicted in Table 2.

While the relative cost of red meat increased by 14 percent between 1974 and 1981, that of milk and cheese taken together went down by more than 50 percent. This change results from the joint-product nature of these commodities. Meat is exported, but not milk.[4]

Second and third quality pulses sold in the domestic market are made available at prices lower than the pre-export domestic prices, and the volume made available domestically exceeds levels when export bans were in force.[5]

Two of the most important links between nutrition and food consumption are generally assumed to be the price and availability of food. The results of both the 1974 and 1981/82 surveys show these relationships not to be as significant as expected.

A. Income and Food Consumption

The relationship between nutrient intake and income is shown in Table 3. There is no relationship between income and consumption of protein and calories for any income group except the top 10 percent. However, animal protein intake has a very strong correlation with income. An extremely important point to note is that even the lowest income groups, on the average, consume more nutrients than is required on health grounds.[6] Therefore, it appears that higher income is not a requirement for the necessary intake. The relationship between poverty and malnutrition seems to be very tenuous.

There seem to be three factors which account for the lack of this relationship. First, rural solidarity manifested in food gifts (which were not reported as income) and exchanges of services for food allow families to consume food valued at more than their total reported income in cash or kind. The urban migrants receive food from their communities of origin which they do not report. As a result, the total value of food consumed per consumption unit for the low income brackets does not differ significantly from that of the higher income units, although the incomes of the latter are more than 10 times higher than the incomes of the former. (See Table 3.)

The second factor is the possibility of substitution within the food basket. Table 2 shows that there are large differences in the costs of calories and protein from different sources. The nature of the food basket, therefore, allows the low income groups to shift to cheaper sources of nutrients and still maintain healthy intake levels. The lowest income

Table 2. **The Quantity of Nutrients which could be Purchased from Different Sources for a Fixed Level of Expenditure**

Nutrient Sources	Calorie Intake		Protein Intake	
	1974	1981	1974	1981
Bread	1.50	1.20	1.40	1.30
Other wheat flour derivatives	0.90	1.10	0.90	1.30
Rice	0.40	0.60	0.20	0.30
Red meats	0.16	0.12	0.35	0.30
Poultry meat	0.12	0.08	0.45	0.30
Fish	0.12	0.09	0.45	0.32
Eggs	0.12	0.14	0.50	0.25
Milk	0.21	0.23	0.35	0.40
Cheese	0.20	0.23	0.45	0.70
Pulses	0.60	0.92	1.10	1.90
Butter	0.26	0.31	–	–
Margarine and liquid oils	0.85	1.15	–	–
Sugar	1.00	0.90	–	–
Potatoes	0.45	0.52	0.30	0.45
Weighted average[1]	1.00	1.00	1.00	1.00

[1] Weighted on the basis of the national proportion of nutrients derived from each source presented in Table 7.

Table 3. The Relationship Between Income, Nutrient Intake and Food Expenditures

	Income Brackets (Turkish Liras)										
	Under 5,000	5,000-10,000	10,001-15,000	15,001-20,000	20,001-30,000	30,001-40,000	40,001-50,000	50,000-75,000	75,001-100,000	Over 100,000	Sample Average
Calorie intake (calories per person per day)	3,273	3,132	3,101	3,174	3,172	3,147	3,235	3,404	3,221	3,192	3,179
Total protein intake (grams per person per day)	99	96	94	97	96	97	101	106	102	102	98
Animal protein intake (grams per person per day)	24	21	21	25	27	30	34	39	41	36	28
Number of Households	114	169	257	262	289	155	87	71	26	29	1,459
Number of adult person equivalents	288	588	846	850	1,063	581	332	248	86	111	4,994
Mean income per household (TL)	1,946	8,208	13,198	17,915	25,048	35,556	45,504	60,721	85,176	236,850	22,732
Monthly food expenditure (TL)	6,236	10,281	10,254	11,366	12,346	15,117	16,109	16,925	13,705	19,555	11,686
Proportion of income spent on food	3.20[1]	1.25[1]	0.78	0.63	0.49	0.43	0.35	0.28	0.16	0.08	

[1] Represents the value of food consumed. Values imputed by taking the local prices, even if some food items are not paid for by the household. Households helped by neighbors or relatives consume food valued at more than their total income. All items in this table are based on the results of three cycles, except for the "proportion of income spent on food" which represents the results of the first cycle only. The food expenditure does not include food outside the home which could be considerable for upper income bracket urban households.

group in Table 3, for example, spends 40 percent less on food per consumption unit yet receives the same level of calories, total protein, and animal protein as the second lowest income group. By shifting expenditures from eggs and red meat to cheese, for example, a family can purchase three times as much animal protein. Such a shift leaves the quality of the diet unaffected.

The high rates of inflation, varying from 60 to 130 percent per annum during the period 1978–81, the stagnation in the economy, and the consequent deterioration in income distribution have not been accompanied by any worsening in the nutritional status of the population, partly as a result of this shift in the food basket. The proportion of population which consumed less than 2500 calories per person daily has declined from 40 percent in 1974 to 30 percent in 1981–82.

The last factor which masks the possible relationships between income and intake is a result of a measurement problem. The survey measures incomes in rural areas as a certain ratio of the gross revenue from animal husbandry and crops. Yet the ratio of the return to land and labor in both activities is closely related to the degree to which the farm activities are commercialized. A modern dairy farm, for example, may have to incur up to 90 percent of its gross revenue as expenses, while this could be as little as 30 percent under traditional practices. Collection of data at that level of detail was beyond the scope of the survey.

Aside from the three factors discussed above, there are serious reporting problems. High income farmers and self-employed individuals are known to under-report their income while the salaried workers and wage earners report their incomes fairly accurately.[7]

There are similar reporting biases between the low and high income groups in the reported number and diversity of meals consumed. The concern with projecting an image is likely to lead the poor to report a richer diet, while the high income households do the opposite. The repetitive collection of information on three consecutive days and in three seasons, however, allows for checks on this by allowing separate estimates of changes in the responses between the first and the following days.

The opposite tendencies in reporting income and food consumption reinforce each other to prevent, to some extent, detection of the variation in intake and differences in the quality of diet as a result of variations in incomes.

B. Food Consumption and Health Standards

In addition to the lack of any apparent relationship between income and intake, levels of average family intake do not seem to determine the health standards of the members of that family.

The emphasis placed on nutrition leads to neglect of resource allocation, income distribution, and employment creation implications of inter-
ventionist policies which adversely affect the terms of trade between
agricultural and other commodities.

Aside from irrigation, almost all public investment resources in agriculture are channeled to commercial enterprises in dairying, fattening, and
poultry. The output of these projects is disproportionately consumed by
high income groups, as depicted in levels of animal protein consumption
shown in Table 2. At the same time, subsidies for these projects are
justified on the grounds of nutritional improvement

Pulses, margarine and vegetable oils, and potatoes tend to be consumed fairly equitably between different groups in the society. There has
been practically no government support for any of these crops either in
the form of direct subsidies or by giving these crops special emphasis for
research and extension.

An important conclusion of the analysis presented so far is that nutritional improvements cannot be brought about by food availability and low
prices. Agricultural development objectives, confined to nutritional improvement, distort the pattern of resource allocation. Emphasis should be
placed on objectives, such as increasing farm incomes and income stability, increasing export earnings from food products, and providing the
necessary raw materials to meet the demands of the processing sectors.

Educational campaigns, improvement of environmental hygiene, reductions in birth rates, and changes in child feeding habits appear to be
more effective instruments in nutritional improvement than increasing
food availability.

The TDRF Survey collected data on height and weight of children by
age groups as well as food intake. The relationship between the average
calorie intake of the family and the weight of children is presented in
Table 4. Table 5 presents the relationship between protein intake and
height of children. In both cases there is no significant relationship, and
this pattern was confirmed by the 1974 Survey as well.

Further breakdown of children into age groups 0–2, 3–6, 7–11, and
11 to 17 year-old does not change this striking finding. Similarly, there is
no change in this pattern when the analysis is conducted separately for
boys and girls. This is a significant finding, as malnutrition is a special
problem affecting children and pregnant and lactating mothers. The high
infant mortality rate in Turkey (140 in 1000 live births in 1980) is generally
attributed to malnutrition.[8]

Malnutrition in general, and in children in particular, seems to derive
from factors other than income and food availability. These include education of parents, frequency of pregnancies and births, weaning habits,
environmental conditions (availability of clean water and excreta disposal

Table 4. The Relationship Between the Average Intake of the Family and the Weight Standards of Children

Average Daily Family Intake of Calories per Consumption Unit	The Ratio of Weight Actually Measured to Standards[1]				
	.79 or Less	.80-.99	1.00-1.24	1.25 or More	Total
	Number of Observations				
2,000 or less	126	180	82	37	425
2,001-2,250	95	152	70	27	344
2,251-2,500	105	167	174	28	474
2,501-2,750	105	180	92	30	407
2,751-3,000	99	172	82	41	394
More than 3,000	336	592	207	130	1,265
Total	866	1,443	707	293	3,309

The calculated value of $X^2 = 10.88$ (Tab. $X^2_{9, .95} = 16.92$)

[1]The smaller the value of this coefficient, the more severely malnourished is the child.

Table 5. The Relationship Between Total Protein Intake and the Height Standards of Children

Average Daily Family Intake of Total Protein per Consumption Unit	The Ratio of Actual Height Measured to Standards				
	.79 or Less	.80-.99	1.00-1.24	1.25 or More	Total
	Number of Observations				
49 or less	16	115	29	6	166
50-69	53	452	141	13	659
70-89	74	694	197	24	989
More than 90	111	1,015	333	34	1,493
Total	254	2,276	700	77	3,307

The calculated value of $X^2 = 5.34$ (Tab. $X^2_{9, .95} = 16.92$)

Table 6. The Relationship Between the Mother's Education and the Weight Standards of Children up to the Age of 17

| | The Weight Standard of the Children | | | | |
Mother's Schooling	.79 or Less	.80-.99	1.00-1.24	1.25 or More	Total
	Number of Observations				
Illiterate	516	798	398	105	1,817
Primary	319	610	287	59	1,275
Secondary	15	40	22	11	88
Lycee	14	34	25	8	81
University	5	16	1	3	25
Total	**869**	**1,498**	**733**	**186**	**3,286**

The calculated value of $X^2 = 38.12$ (Tab. $X^2_{9, .95} = 21.03$; male and female children taken together)

Table 7. The Relationship Between the Mother's Education and the Height Standards of Children up to the Age of 17

| | The Height Standard of the Children | | | | |
Mother's Schooling	.79 or Less	.80-.99	1.00-1.24	1.25 or More	Total
	Number of Observations				
Illiterate	133	1,350	328	6	1,817
Primary	64	903	298	10	1,275
Secondary	5	56	23	4	88
Lycee	–	37	43	1	81
University	3	14	8	–	25
Total	**205**	**2,360**	**700**	**21**	**3,286**

The calculated value of $X^2 = 83.79$ (Tab. $X^2_{9, .95} = 21.03$; male and female children taken together) systems) which lead to infections and parasites, and food preservation and preparation habits which affect the nutrient quality of food intake.

The survey included information on the first three of these factors while information on other factors would have required a major change in the survey approach.

C. Education and Health Standard of Children

Unlike income and intake levels, the education of parents has a very strong correlation with the health standards of the children. Tables 6 to 9 present the relationship between the anthropometric measures of children and the educational level of parents.

The TDRF Survey includes data on some of the factors through which the parent's education would affect the health status of children. These include the duration of breast-feeding, frequency of births, baby food given to children between 0 to 24 months, and the introduction of solid food into the child's diet.

Conclusions

The preliminary results of the 1981/82 and those of the 1974 surveys show that the hypothesis "low incomes lead to low levels of intake which, in turn, lead to malnutrition" cannot be accepted. There is also no apparent relationship between low incomes and quality of diet as measured by the minimum levels of animal protein contained in the diet. The lack of the causal link between income, intake, and nutritional status in Turkey, however, may not necessarily be true for countries less developed than Turkey and in countries where the costs of available foods are not as diverse as in Turkey.

Despite the lack of causal links, all four of the five-year development plans of Turkey take nutritional improvement as the main objective in determining agricultural development policies, including input subsidies, output price interventions, and export and import restrictions.[9]

Appendix: Survey Sample and Interview Methodology

The Foundation's Survey of Food Consumption and Nutrition is based on a multi-stage, stratified, systematic sample of 1480 households, drawn in cooperation with the State Institute of Statistics. The sample is designed to represent not only Turkey as a whole but also regions and settlements of different sizes.

Table 8. The Relationship Between the Father's Education and the Weight Standards of Children up to the Age of 17

Father's Schooling	The Weight Standard of the Children				
	.79 or Less	.80-.99	1.00-1.24	1.25 or More	Total
	Number of Observations				
Illiterate	167	248	138	28	581
Primary	627	1,094	515	139	2,375
Secondary	41	72	55	5	173
Lycee	48	88	38	13	187
University	22	65	33	12	132
Total	905	1,567	779	197	3,448

The calculated value of $X^2 = 24.77$ (Tab. $X^2_{9, .95} = 21.03$; male and female children taken together)

Table 9. The Relationship Between the Father's Education and the Height Standards of Children up to the Age of 17

Father's Schooling	The Height Standard of the Children				
	.79 or Less	.80-.99	1.00-1.24	1.25 or More	Total
	Number of Observations				
Illiterate	40	430	108	3	581
Primary	148	1,724	491	12	2,375
Secondary	10	117	44	2	173
Lycee	7	132	48	3	190
University	6	72	52	2	132
Total	211	2,475	743	22	3,451

The calculated value of $X^2 = 41.87$ (Tab. $X^2_{9, .95} = 21.03$; male and female children taken together)

A. Selection of the Sample

The sample is drawn in stages. In the first stage, urban and rural settlements are the sampling units, and there are three stratification variables, i.e., region, settlement sizes, and the level of development. (The last variable taken into account for urban areas only.)

The sampling units are the districts during the second stage. The districts within a city are classified into three groups according to their level of development. A paired selection is made within each district. The number randomly drawn from each district is proportionate to the relative weight of each group of districts in that city.

In the last stage, households are selected systematically by using the census record books thus grouped for urban and rural areas. Selection in pairs provides two separate estimates for each sample statistic for each region or settlement size group.

B. Survey Methodology

The interviewers were provided by the State Institute of Statistics from among its trained staff of around 3000 interviewers. Following their training in Ankara, 100 interviewers and 18 controllers were dispatched to the field. The first cycle was conducted in September 1981, the second cycle in January/February 1982, and the last cycle in June 1982.

To allow tests of hypotheses on food consumption and malnutrition, the questionnaire contains information on the following variables:

1. Region and settlement size groups;
2. Low, middle, and high income districts in urban areas;
3. Length of residence in the present settlement and migration pattern;
4. Home ownership and rentals;
5. Household structure and size;
6. Education of the members of the household;
7. Occupation of the household members;
8. Female participation in the labor force;
9. The number of income earners in the household;
10. Total household income;
11. Source of income (crops, animal husbandry, wage income and other income);
12. Nutrition measures, such as weight, height, weaning habits, and introduction of solid food into child's diet.

The record of food consumption starts with courses consumed during each meal. Having registered each course consumed throughout the day, the interviewers record the ingredients in each course.

The salaried people are paid at the end of the month in Turkey, and it was assumed that the consumption pattern would vary with the time of the month. The pattern during the weekdays and the weekend also varies, particularly in households where the women work. The interviews were, therefore, staggered throughout the week and the month to record the possible variations.

The changes in the seasonal consumption patterns are recorded by repeating the interviews three times in order to establish the consumption patterns in Autumn, Winter, and Spring. The seasonal interviews are conducted with the same families. Different interviewers are sent to each household for each cycle and the socioeconomic and the anthropometric data is repeatedly collected.

The three independent questionnaires applied to a particular household are compared during the coding phase for consistency. In cases of gross inconsistencies, the interviewer believed to have erred is sent back to the field to check the data.

NOTES

1. Calorie intake of 2000 and 2500 per consumption unit respectively. See, O. Koksal, "Nutrition in Turkey," Hacettepe University, Ankara (1978), p. 239.

2. Total wheat supply of 13 vs. 17.5 million tons per annum, taking into account changes in stocks, imports and exports, seed requirements, waste, and wheat used for animal feed.

3. Republic of Turkey, "Agricultural Development Alternatives for Growth with Exports," Vol. II, Annex II (1983).

4. Both have the same relative weight as animal protein sources (see Table 1).

5. The paper by Gomez indicates that indeed there is a tremendous potential for increasing supplies for the three commodities which he has included in his case study. A similar conclusion was reached in a recent study of the Turkish livestock sector. See, H. Gençağa, "Animal Husbandry Development Strategies for Turkey," Proceedings of the VII National Livestock Congress of Turkey, The Union of Turkish Veterinarians, Ankara (1981).

6. FAO/WHO, "Energy and Protein Requirements," Technical Report Series No. 522 (1973).

7. State Planning Organization, Income Distribution in Turkey: 1973 (Türkiye Gelir Dagilimi), SPO Publication No. 1495/290, Ankara (1976), p. 13.

8. A. Baysal, "Nutrition (Beslenme)," Hacettepe University Publications No. A13, Ankara (1977), p. 362.

9. Republic of Turkey, The Fourth-Five-Year Development Plan (Dorduncu Bes Yillik Kalkinma Plani), SPO Publication No. 1664, Ankara (1979), p. 337.

NUTRITION SURVEILLANCE
AND FOOD POLICY

David O. Dapice

It is by now well accepted that pursuit of policies aimed only at increasing average per capita income and output will result in significant segments of the population remaining in poverty for a considerable period. This realization has led governments to undertake different types of remedial measures to assure some level of basic needs throughout their populations. For planners, the task is to identify the specific problems, the groups who most need assistance, and to design and implement programs and policies that efficiently and effectively remedy the problems which have been identified. There is a growing realization that nutritional surveillance can be useful in a variety of ways. This chapter describes the nature of nutritional surveillance and recent developments in which it has been used for planning purposes.

What Is Nutritional Surveillance (NS)?

While malnutrition can be usefully thought of as a side effect of poverty, it is often productive to treat it as a disease. By using techniques which were developed for epidemiology, it is possible to understand causality better if the demographic and social characteristics of the malnourished are mapped along with regional and temporal variations in malnutrition.

This chapter is based largely on a document prepared by a group at the Division of Nutritional Sciences at Cornell University, headed by Professor J. P. Habicht and Dr. J. B. Mason. Their draft document, *Nutrition Surveillance*, published in February 1982, represents several years of effort supported by A. I. D. and accomplished in cooperation with other international agencies. Dr. Dapice has cooperated with the conferences and discussions that led to the draft document.

However, where patterns of causality are not already known, this approach could lead to a great amount of data gathering with little practical value. Indeed, some critics maintain that early efforts at nutritional surveillance were so diffused and unfocused as to be useless. It is now agreed that priorities have to be established for data gathering and analysis. Only data needed for making important decisions on public policies and programs is now included in the definition of NS. The ability to recognize patterns of causality which are already understood is thus part of NS, but discovering new patterns is a problem for scientific research. The latter requires much more elaborate and careful data collection and must not be confused with the former. Basically then, NS "provides regular information about nutrition in populations . . . in order to make decisions which will lead to improvements in nutrition in populations."[1]

Background

While there are now evident beginnings of useful cooperation between planners and those in the nutrition community, considerable skepticism and ignorance still exists among many experts and policy makers about the utility of NS. Much of this gulf can be explained by the history of nutrition and past efforts to apply it to policy. For a considerable period, nutrition was mainly a laboratory science with practical applications limited to wartime rationing or feeding of institutional or disasterstruck populations. When linkages between growth of children and nutrition became better appreciated, nutrition became a minor part of most health ministries. There were educational and feeding programs for mothers and children which seemed to be associated more with social welfare than with serious issues, such as investment or pricing policies. Many of the height and weight measurements were for individual patient diagnosis and were not gathered for or suitable for use in policy making. The use of NS as a guide to feeding programs during the Sahelian drought only underlined to many its seemingly marginal character. It seemed to be (and too often was) useful only in emergency or individual diagnostic situations. It was quite separated from the needs of decision makers who needed guidance about the design of programs to ameliorate poverty or to provide for basic needs.

During the 1970s, a great deal of intellectual energy was expended on elaborate food and nutrition planning exercises. These assumed essentially that the only or one of the major objectives of national leaders was the elimination of malnutrition. It was assumed that all resources and policies would be brought to bear on the problem. While these efforts did push nutrition experts in the direction of thinking about policy, ultimately they bore little fruit. There was too little appreciation about the trade-offs between proposed remedial measures and other desirable goals. The cost of data and analysis required for undertaking a full-fledged planning exercise was often prohibitive. Again, the message that seemed to emerge was that helpful and realistic advice from nutrition experts was not available.

Fortunately, there has been movement on the part of both camps in recent years. Economists have begun to emphasize the role of staple food pricing and to investigate various types of food subsidy or food stamp schemes as they study consumption from the point of view of adequate family or individual food intake. No longer do they look only at aggregate food demand. There also has been promising preliminary work on the impact of economic projects on nutrition. Nutritionists have seen the shortcomings of many conventional feeding and nutrition programs and have come to understand how important it is to reflect nutritional concerns in project design and pricing decisions. Both sides appreciate that resources are scarce and that careful setting of priorities and efficient pursuit of solutions is crucial. Finally, there is the beginning of a productive dialogue.

Present Uses of NS

There are currently three major fields in which NS is seen as providing relevant data for decision making. The first is its use in planning. This includes adjusting present policies, starting new ones, and targeting both health/nutrition and development programs. It can play a role in planning projects which may have a significant nutritional impact, even if they are not primarily meant to do that. The second use is for program management and evaluation. The third general area is in preventing irregular and temporary sharp declines in food consumption. The types of data needed for supporting each type of activity vary markedly. In addition, the general development strategy pursued by a nation will also constrain and direct the type of useful NS activity. Each of these points needs elaboration.

It should be clear from the outset that if a government has no interest in basic needs, then no amount of information will be of any use. It is assumed here that there is at least some interest in amelioration of the effects of poverty, but also there is concern with other goals and, above all, a fair amount of confusion. NS can be helpful in giving a clear statement of the problems faced and suggestions about the ways to proceed and the probable costs of different levels of effort. But the type of contribution possible will depend on the broad strategy being followed with respect to the interaction between development and satisfaction of basic needs. Any classification of strategies is apt to be imperfect, but one suggested by the Cornell group is the following: asset redistribution; income (usually rent) redistribution; acceptance of structural inequality ameliorated by social services for vulnerable groups; and a mixed approach incorporating a combination of growth and equity goals. The countries suggested for each category are China, Taiwan, and the Koreas for the first; Jamaica and Sri Lanka for the second; moderately high income Latin American countries, such as Colombia and Chile for the third; and a diverse group of lower income countries such as Indonesia, Malawi, and perhaps Kenya for the fourth.

The suggestive division above is scarcely the final word but serves mainly to create awareness of the types of policies which a particular government may consider. Since data gathering is supposed to serve decision making, a first step is to identify the universe of decisions which are or may be acceptable.

The first major use of NS is in providing guidance for decisions on investment allocation and policy. While these decisions have a major impact on the malnourished, this impact is seldom recognized explicitly or anticipated. In order to review these plans for their nutritional impact, some institutional link is needed between those skilled in analysis and the decision makers. This may be a group within a planning or agricultural ministry, or a nutrition group in an academic or research institute. In any case, the group must be attuned to the issues being considered and be able to use analytical methods and data to suggest useful alternatives. For example, consider a discussion about staple food production, consumption, and pricing. In order to introduce nutritional considerations into policy making, it is necessary to define who is malnourished, their socioeconomic and demographic characteristics, and several other aspects of their behavior. Do they purchase or grow their own food? Are they concentrated in certain geographic regions? Do they eat staple foods that are different from other better-fed segments of the population? By combining surveys of food consumption with other data on nutritional status and health indicators, it is possible to identify more precisely the characteristics of the malnourished and to foresee the probable impact of a proposed change in, for example, a staple food price. Alternative or offsetting policies can be explored, such as lowering the price of an inferior staple which is not widely consumed across all income groups, while raising the price of the primary staple.

Another possible example comes from a project to increase the output of cash crops. Often such projects are the only way to increase incomes easily and rapidly. But switching from food to cash crop production can actually increase malnutrition even if incomes rise. Careful observation of different groups, cultures, and practices can help identify probable problems and suggest remedial activities as part of the project investment. In general, prediction of nutritional side effects can lead to prevention of potential negative changes or enhancement of positive ones.

It should be clear that NS draws upon many sources of data including those not usually considered to be nutritional. Consumer budget surveys, agricultural censuses, socioeconomic surveys, and macro data on food disappearance and prices all can be used, in addition to height and weight data or morbidity and mortality surveys. For project and defined-area program analysis, it is usually necessary to go to the regional level; much of the macro data may be unusable at this level.

Attempting to identify the beneficiaries of a project and the extent to which their income and consumption patterns will change is a first step, but this may require special surveys. Much of the same type of information needed at a national level is needed for these projects or area programs. However, is is needed only for a defined region or class of producers, rather than for an entire nation. It is sometimes too difficult to anticipate the impact of a particular project due to a scarcity of data or analytical talent. In that case, a small sample baseline survey and periodic follow-up surveys at least could monitor the impact of a project at reasonable cost. This latter alternative does not allow for modification of the initial project plan, but it does insure that actual changes will be known and does provide a basis for subsequent modification of the existing program or future similar programs in other areas.

This leads to the second use of NS, which is far better established and accepted, at least for health and nutrition programs. However, it can apply to any programs or projects which are supposed to have an impact on the well-being of a target group. Intelligent management of programs with direct or indirect nutrition impact requires some notion of who the recipients should be and whether the program actually is having any impact on those it is aimed at. It is only in the last few years that any comprehensive effort has been made to review the record of past intervention programs. The findings suggest that better and more integrated planning of interventions is needed, along with skilled implementation and funding at realistic levels, if there is to be a measurable improvement in the target groups at acceptable cost.

Detailed planning of these interventions requires, as stated in the previous section, a detailed knowledge of the specific problems and the characteristics of the groups needing assistance. It also requires some sense of what interventions will be productive and how they should be combined with other interventions. When these are not known with precision at the outset, it becomes doubly important to develop management and evaluation tools to allow improvements in ongoing programs. For example, a sensible attack on malnutrition requires some idea of the extent to which resources should be devoted to primary health care, clean water, or food supplements or some combination of the three. Realistically, only field experience may indicate the best mix in a specific situation; NS can assist managers in making that judgment.

This same monitoring of program activities and results will greatly assist the management and evaluation of such programs in other ways. For a variety of reasons, many well-meant programs have little or no impact. Latrines or protected wells might be built but not used. Nutrition education programs may be disseminated but not be understood or acted upon. Food subsidies may simply displace food which would otherwise be provided at home. In general, these programs work better if the selected population is carefully targeted rather than broadly defined, and if the progress realized (or lack of it) is quickly known, allowing modifications in program planning or implementation.

Early Warning and Intervention Systems (EWIS)

The last general field of activity for NS is a relatively recent one. It involves the identification of regions or populations which suffer occasional and temporary shortfalls in food consumption due to a variety of reasons, but often primarily due to fluctuations in food output. This sort of activity tends to be local, is predictive rather than prescriptive, and is tied into a well-understood set of interventions which are triggered by certain findings. In Indonesia, in one area it was necessary to inquire about the past several years of experience with food shortages. The seasonal characteristics and approximate linkages leading to each shortage were identified. In this case, a shortfall in rice population—the major staple—was a good indicator of developing food scarcity. This was best captured by comparing the area harvested in a three-month peak period with total normal rice area. While this worked well for a fairly isolated region with little industry or cash crop production, other indicators are useful in other circumstances. A fairly detailed knowledge of the sources of income, agricultural activities and their timing, and other alternatives such as migration is needed for a successful EWIS.

It is not easy to design and run a system that collects, analyzes, and acts upon data in a period of weeks rather than months or years as in the second and first cases. It is this combination of a local unit of observation, a rapid turnaround time for data analysis, and the integration of analysis with quick intervention that separates an early-warning and intervention system from other types of NS activity. Important points about this are first, that it is not equivalent to a famine relief system. However, if it operates as designed, an EWIS should prevent famine from occurring. Famine relief is reactive—it waits for a problem to develop before intervention begins, and it is usually on a large scale. The EWIS anticipates problems over a considerably smaller area and tries to deal with them before they get out of hand. It encompasses villages or counties, not countries or provinces. Second, the EWIS tends to be palliative rather than curative. It is unlikely to address the underlying causes of these periodic shortfalls successfully and is therefore complementary to program and project planning.

Examples of NS and Planning

In countries as diverse as Costa Rica, the Philippines, Kenya, and Sri Lanka, there are examples of NS in practice. A brief review of some of these experiences may clarify the previous discussion and add some plausibility to its general propositions.

In Costa Rica, the Nutrition Information System was set up initially to help direct the Family Allowances Program. This is a large ($40 per capita of total population) transfer program which was set up in 1975 to reduce poverty and malnutrition. The NIS, working largely with existing data, was able to help the FAP target its beneficiaries and rationalize its programs. The global planning division of the planning office subsequently became aware of the value of the NIS data and has developed an investment-centered basic needs strategy based largely on the NIS data. While the small population, relatively high income per capita, and democratic tradition of Costa Rica make it something of a special case, it is an impressive example of how both short- and long-term basic needs strategies can be assisted by NS.

In Kenya, there was a major strategy question concerning the 1979–83 National Development Plan. Should an increased attention to basic needs primarily take the form of greatly expanded direct intervention programs or of broader economic and rural development measures? With nutritional data available from the Integrated Rural Surveys, a summary of nutritional problems and their relation to economic factors was prepared, and it was decided to concentrate on the broader rural development approach, partly as a result of that study. To insure continuing attention to nutritional problems, a Food and Nutrition planning unit was set up within the Ministry of Planning. There is now also an Interministerial Coordinating Committee on Nutrition which helps consider and implement decisions.

In the Philippines, there has been a widespread weighing program for preschool children for several years. Information concerning the geographic distribution of malnutrition has helped direct resources for nutrition programs in depressed areas and has been used by the National Economic Development authority to help identify regions which receive priority in investment allocation. While there has been little evidence of widespread progress against malnutrition, this information has led to greater efforts to reevaluate activities and programs so that some impact will be produced.

In Sri Lanka, recent changes in the food subsidy system and other feeding programs were assisted importantly by the Food and Nutrition Policy Planning Division. This Division had access to a number of surveys of consumption and malnutrition which allowed policy changes to be designed with some appreciation of their probable impact. Because of the tight resource situation, careful planning of cutbacks was considered essential.

There are many other nations where NS is contributing in some way toward policy management or planning, but some of these cases are in early stages and others are not yet well documented. In Indonesia, for example, a pilot EWIS is being set up in a few counties but should eventually cover a significant fraction of the country. In Botswana, a well-developed system of health post reporting is used to detect changes in basic needs status, but a system to respond when adverse changes are detected has not yet been established. In Colombia, the Food and Nutrition Plan has used data from biannual surveys to target some interventions, and state governments are setting up surveillance systems to provide for better targeting in the future. All of these examples suggest that there can be significant gains from using NS as an additional source of data and guidance for policy and program planning and implementation.

NOTES

1. J. B. Mason et al., *Nutrition Surveillance* (Geneva: World Health Organization, 1984).

POLICY ANALYSIS AND POLICY REFORM: A POSSIBLE NEW ROLE FOR INTERNATIONAL AID AGENCIES

Marcelo Selowsky

For international aid institutions, a question frequently asked is whether external resource transfers can be used to help long-run policy making. Aid could provide a bridging function, softening the short-term costs that appear important to governments until the longer-term gains have time to take effect. Indeed, this might be the very core of what international agencies can do about promoting a longer-run view of policy making in developing countries. Essential to identifying what kind of bridging aid is needed is a clear understanding of how governments perceive the benefits and costs of a particular policy; that is, what determines, in their view, the present value of benefits of a particular policy change.

The question can be posed as follows: If our policy advice is so good, why are governments so reluctant to accept it? To answer this question we must first identify the sources of such discrepancies and how international aid institutions can contribute to narrow them.

Two hypothetical extreme situations can be identified. One is when the discrepancy arises from different perceptions on the effects of the policy changes. In this situation, the government and the aid agency have reached different conclusions about who will be the winners and losers, what the magnitudes of the gains and losses will be, and over what periods of time they will occur. We call these *objective* differences. A second situation arises when perceptions coincide, but governments attach different weights, or premia, to particular winners and losers and discount the future differently than do international aid institutions. We call these *subjective* differences, the differences between the more neutral weight implicit in our standard welfare economics and the political weights relevant to a particular government administration. Obviously in the real world we find a combination of objective and subjective differences, where the mix varies according to political regimes or the particular moment in the administration at which the reform is evaluated (just after an election or just before a re-election).

Two types of activities by aid agencies could contribute to narrowing the objective differences: activities aimed at better informing governments about the costs and benefits of policy reforms when their information is not complete, i.e., better transfer of the *technology of prediction*, and activities aimed at increasing the aid institution's own knowledge on the best way of implementing these reforms, i.e., improving our *technology of implementation*. A specific hypothesis regarding the first type of activities is that governments consistently underestimate the long-run responsiveness of the economy to their interventions; hence the misallocation effects of their policies. There are several instances: countries have consistently underestimated the long-run supply elasticities of agriculture, of exports, and of other sectors where incentives have been adversely affected by policies aimed at short-run gains.[1] Activities aimed at better informing governments about the long-run responsiveness of particular sectors might have an influence in their evaluation of policies.

As argued persuasively by Ralph Campbell in Chapter 21, the technology of implementation is a field where the state of the art is substantially weaker. At what speed and in what sequence should a set of policy reforms be implemented? To the extent such reforms affect significantly the short-run gains and losses, and governments have a large premium on the present, the timing of implementation could greatly affect the acceptability of policy change. It is possible that many policy reforms are being rejected but could be accepted if more was known about the dynamics of implementation.

In summary, a narrowing down of these types of differences requires more dissemination about the know-how of prediction and improvement in the state of knowledge about the short-run strategies of implementation.

How can international lending institutions increase the acceptability of a policy reform which offers positive benefits in terms of the present value of its long-run effects, but appears undesirable to the government because of high political weights attached to the losers, particularly if their losses occur in the short run? If the weights themselves cannot be influenced, the only instrument available is to use lending to allow governments to compensate the losers in the short run. If the policy reform is efficient (it has a positive present value according to the more neutral economic analysis), the government then could tax the winners as the benefits of the new policies begin to pay off and repay the loan with all or part of the additional tax revenue. Everybody could gain from this *reform cum loan.*

An essential element for understanding what kind of bridging aid is needed is a clear understanding of the different weights governments give to winners and losers. In terms of social welfare, sub-optimum economic policies may produce short-run gains while efficiency losses are felt only in the long-run. What is more, the distribution of short-run gains and long-run losses may affect different groups with different political weight insofar as government policy makers are concerned. Analytically, long-run efficiency losses from existing policies and long-run efficiency gains from policy reform are valued at very high discount rates, so that the present value of short-run gains is higher than the present value of long-run losses. Further, if policy reform changes the distribution of gains and losses so that winners under present policies become losers if reforms are introduced, the weights attached to present policies by politicians may be even higher.

The World Bank has traditionally viewed its role as that of a quasi-commercial source of investment capital, and has stayed away from program loans which would support policy reform. However, if policy reform is an essential prerequisite for capital investment in agricultural development, the Bank may view policy bridging loans more sympathetically in the future. The important point is that governments cannot undertake policy reforms if the social welfare gains are felt by relatively weaker groups and the losses by relatively stronger groups, unless the losers are compensated in some way. Innovative approaches to the problem of compensation are a feature of food policy analysis where strikingly little work has been done, but which could have high payoff in the future.

Policy analysis must also take into account uncertainty. There may be a kinked demand curve for policy reform. Often the policy reform asks the country to gamble on its future tax base in order to achieve the anticipated gains. Not only does the government discount these for political reasons, but also it discounts them according to the degree of risk it perceives.

To facilitate action, policy analysis must show how to minimize losses, maximize gains, and provide compensatory transfers where policy reform is recommended. It must take into account institutional factors which weight in favor of solutions which are easier to implement bureaucratically and which weight in favor of solutions which are most visible to beneficiaries and least visible to losers. It must take into account the observed phenomenon that policies themselves induce the formation of pressure groups and that the vested interests in a given policy are much greater *ex post* than they are *ex ante*. This has implication for the sequencing as well as the content of policy reforms.

NOTES

1. Notice that 30 years ago the notion of lack of responsiveness of agriculture was quite widespread. It was based on *a priori* notions that farmers do not respond to economic incentives or to rational economic calculations.

THE POLITICAL FRAMEWORK FOR PRICE POLICY DECISIONS

Robert H. Bates

T. W. Schultz once stated, "Once there are investment opportunities and efficient incentives, farmers will turn sand into gold."[1] Schultz and others are quick to point out that governments in the developing areas often provide distorted economic incentives and that their agricultural policies constitute a major reason for low levels of food production. A major purpose of this chapter is to discuss why governments act as they do.

Agricultural policy can be defined as the set of decisions taken by governments that influence the prices farmers confront in the markets which determine their incomes. The level of farm revenues is determined in part by the prices at which sales are made in markets for agricultural commodities. The prices which farmers must pay for farm inputs helps to determine their costs and thus, in combination with revenues, the money value of their incomes from farming. And the real value of farm incomes, in turn, is determined by the prices which farmers must pay for consumer items.

Research throughout the developing world suggests that government policy tends to be antithetical to the interests of most farmers. Governments tend to lower the prices which farmers receive for produce. They tend to shelter domestic manufacturers from meaningful levels of economic competition originating from both at home and abroad, thereby raising the prices which farmers must pay for consumer items. And while they often subsidize the price of farm inputs, these subsidies tend to be captured by the larger farmers. The incomes of most farmers are thus adversely affected by the agricultural policies of Third World governments.

Government policies thus tend to weaken production incentives for farmers. When governments do emphasize production, moreover, they attempt to secure higher output by building projects rather than by raising prices. And when governments do offer positive incentives for increased production, they tend to do so by lowering costs rather than by increasing revenues, i.e., by subsidizing the prices of farm inputs rather than by raising the prices of commodities.

Why do Third World governments tend to adopt these kinds of policies? There are several approaches to explaining the behavior of governments, and I will review three of them.

Applied Welfare Approach to Food Policy Analysis

The first is most often adopted by economists. This approach treats governments as agencies whose job is to maximize the social welfare; public policy is viewed as a set of choices made by governments to secure society's best interests. In poor societies, this approach holds, the social interest is best served by development, and the behavior of governments is analyzed in terms of its impact on this overriding objective.

There are many problems with this approach. One is its lack of explanatory power. Its basic method is to account for the behavior of governments in terms of social objectives. But a given objective can often be secured through a variety of policy instruments, and noting the underlying objective of a policy program often does not allow one to account for the particular instrument that has been chosen. To secure increased food production, for example, governments could pay higher prices to farmers expending the same amount of resources as on food production projects. Under most circumstances, the former would be the more efficient way of securing this social objective, but the latter is more often chosen. Noting the social objectives of government does not account for this systematic bias in government policy.

Not only does the approach possess low explanatory power; but also, when it does make strong predictions, it is often wrong. For example, governments want low-priced food. In the name of this objective, they often strive to impose low food prices. But this choice of policy instrument weakens economic incentives, resulting in lower production and higher food prices. The instrument chosen thus produces an effect precisely opposite to that desired. The objective thus cannot be cited as its cause.

In response to problems such as these, policy analysts often invoke other considerations. They treat the failure of particular government policies as "mistakes" and call for "more information" or "better training" for decision makers. Or they note that governments often have multiple and often conflicting objectives and so treat the failure to maximize with respect to one set of objectives as evidence of efforts to optimize with respect to a larger and more complex set. Both responses represent efforts to preserve the welfare maximizing model of policy formation.

The deeper problem is that unless one is prepared to treat a government as a single, unitary actor—i.e., to treat it as a single decision maker, be it a planner or a dictator—it is impossible to secure from a government a coherent statement of its objectives which possesses even the most limited set of desirable properties. In this area of policy analysis, the Nobel Prize-winning work of Theodore Schultz should be coupled with that of Kenneth Arrow.[2] And any approach that treats governments as agencies for maximizing the best interests of society should be regarded as a normative enterprise rather than as an effort at explanation.

Policy as a Bargaining Outcome for Private Pressure Groups

The pluralist view of policy formation provides an alternative to the assumption of welfare maximization. According to this approach, governments do not pursue transcendent social interests; rather, they respond to private demands. And public policy is regarded not as a result of efforts to divine the social interest but rather as an outcome of political competition among organized groups.

In applying this approach to food policy, we can note forces that shape both the demand and supply of pricing policies. On the demand side, what is striking is the intensity of the pressures for low-priced food. One reason is clear: because urban consumers in the less-developed countries are poor, they spend much of their incomes on food. In Africa, for example, urban consumers often spend between 50 and 60 percent of their disposable incomes on food. Changes in the price of food therefore make a major impact on the economic well-being of urban dwellers, and they pay close attention to the issue of food prices.

Another reason is that urban consumers possess the capacity forcefully to register their preferences on the body politic. Urban consumers are geographically concentrated and strategically located. Because of their geographic concentration, they can be organized quickly; and because they control such basic facilities as transport, communications, and public services, they can impose deprivations on others. They are, therefore, an influential force in politics.

The demand for low-priced food is powerful, moreover, because it can form the basis for the formation of coalitions. It is not only the worker who cares about the price of food. It is also the employer. Employers care about food prices because food is a wage good; with higher food prices, wages must rise and, all else being equal, profits fall. Governments care about food prices not only because they are employers in their own right but also because as owners of industries and promoters of industrial development programs they seek to protect industrial profits. Indicative of the significance of these interests is that in Africa, at least, the unit that sets agricultural prices often resides not in the Ministry of Agriculture but in the Ministry of Finance or Commerce.

When urban unrest begins among food consumers, then, political discontent often rapidly spreads to upper echelons of the polity: it comes to include those whose incomes come from profits, not wages, and those in charge of major bureaucracies. Political regimes that are unable to supply low-cost food are seen as dangerously incompetent and as failing to protect the interests of key elements of the social order. In alliance with the urban masses, influential elites are likely to shift their political loyalties and to replace those in power. Thus it was that protests over food shortages and rising prices formed a critical prelude to the coup that unseated Busia in Ghana and led to the period of political maneuvers and flux that threatened to overthrow the government of Arap Moi in Kenya.

Many of the factors which account for the potency of the demand for low-priced food suggest as well the reason it is not countered by equally strong demands on the side of the producer interests. A prime factor is the cost of organization: while low for urban dwellers, it is high for farmers who are more numerous and widely scattered. Another is the lack of natural allies, particularly at the upper reaches of the polity. While the ties between governments and rural producers are close in some developing areas, they tend not to be in Africa, and this situation may account for the relatively more adverse set of pricing policies which have been adopted by governments in that continent.

Also important are the factors affecting the supply of public policy. One such factor is the quantity of public resources. A lower bound is placed on low-priced policies by the government's capacity to make up for domestic food shortages; foreign exchange constraints, for example, place limits on food imports. Another factor is the character of the nation's political institutions. Where Third World governments are subject to competitive elections, for example, then, the evidence suggests they are more sensitive to rural interests, for farmers constitute a political majority in many developing countries. Where there are representative assemblies whose members are accountable to constituencies then, once again, political pressures will arise for the provision of favorable policies for farmers, for farm districts tend to outnumber urban constituencies in most developing areas. These representative institutions—elections and assemblies—help to offset the anti-farmer bias inherent in pure pressure group politics, as discussed above. At least as important as representative institutions, however, are bureaucracies, and particularly those agencies that regulate agricultural markets. Once formed, such bureaucracies secure resources to reward politicians and thereby come to perpetuate the programs which they administer. The agencies in charge of markets accumulate political power; and their vested interests in the government's agricultural programs help to perpetuate these policy commitments even after clear evidence of the failure of these policies. Clearly, in understanding agricultural policies, we need to know more about these agencies.

The primary strategy of the pluralist approach, then, is to look at the factors that influence the way in which public demands are processed into public policy. From the pluralist viewpoint, the problem of government is the problem of representation. Viewed in this light, the limitations of the approach become obvious, for in agricultural policy a very small subset of relevant interests receive representation. It becomes apparent that a third perspective is required—one that explains how governments get away with institutionalizing the interests of political minorities. In nations where commonly over 50 percent of the gross domestic product and over 70 percent of the labor force are in agriculture, how can governments remain in power while maintaining agricultural programs which violate the interests of most farmers?

Political Benefits of Sub-Optimum Economic Policies

A third approach thus is necessary. It would look at governments as agencies that seek to stay in power and would underscore those features of agricultural programs that let governments organize political followings and disorganize political opposition, particularly in the rural areas. This approach—which for want of a better term we can label a hegemonic approach to policy analysis—would also stress two general points: that economic inefficiency can be politically useful and that government-controlled markets can be employed as instruments for political organization. Economically sub-optimal programs, in short, can be politically attractive.

An approach that stresses the role of public policy as a means of retaining political power is useful in explaining several otherwise puzzling aspects of agricultural policy. In seeking increased food production, for example, governments often favor project-based policies over price-based policies. We have already seen that price-based policies can be politically costly; they are resisted by urban interests. But what is also important is that price-based policies offer few political benefits to governments attempting to organize support in the rural areas. For the benefits of higher prices can be reaped both by the supporters and the opponents of governments in power. Projects, however, can be targeted; their benefits can be conferred on those who support the government and withheld from political opponents. Project-based programs thus often provide superior resources to those who seek to organize the rural areas.

Another example illustrates the same point. In seeking increased food production, governments appear far more willing to manipulate incentives by manipulating prices in a way that lowers farm costs rather than increasing farm revenues. We have already discussed one reason for this: the high political costs and low political benefits of offering higher prices for agricultural commodities. Another reason is that subsidy programs create resources for organizing. When governments lower input prices, private sources of supply withdraw from the market, levels of demand increase, and there is excess demand at the government prices. Under such circumstances, markets do not clear; and those in charge of the farm input program achieve the capacity to ration. Those in charge can then employ the program to build an organization. They can target the program's benefits to the politically faithful and withhold them from political opponents. They can also use the program to *dis*organize. In Ghana, for example, a chief means of breaking the resistance by cocoa farmers to the government's low cocoa prices following self-government was the politicization of farm input programs and the distribution of subsidized farm inputs through the politically loyal faction of the farmer's movement. Combined with outright coercion, the political manipulation of the supply of farm inputs made it in the private interests of farmers to support a government whose agricultural programs, taken as a whole, violated the interests of agriculture.

Market intervention creates the capacity for political organization in other ways. When governments maintain bureaucracies to lower farm prices, for example, they can use regulated markets to build political machines. Those in charge of the market can selectively grant rights of entry into it, and those who reap the economic rewards from access to the artificially cheapened commodities become their clients and supporters.

In this chapter, I have moved away from a form of analysis which views policy as the result of efforts to maximize the social welfare. I have moved instead to a set of approaches that looks at public policy as a solution to political problems. The general theme of this chapter, then, is that politicians are rational actors, but they are solving problems that do not take a purely economic form. What appear as economic costs, I have noted, may often offer political benefits: non-competitive rents or inefficient projects, for example, may be politically attractive in that they offer tools for building loyal organizations.

What economists may evaluate as bad policy, then, is not necessarily the result of poor training, obduracy, or other deficiencies on the part of policy makers. Rather, policy makers may simply be solving a different problem than are economists. As policy analysts, it behooves us to represent explicitly the political problem as perceived by the policy maker and to use our analytic techniques to solve it, both in order to offer better explanations of government behavior and to advocate better policy more effectively.

NOTES

1. T. W. Schultz, *Transforming Traditional Agriculture* (New York: Avon Press, 1976), p. 5.

2. Kenneth Arrow, *Social Choice and Individual Values* (New York: John Wiley, 1951).

ROLE OF POLITICAL CONTRACTS IN ACHIEVING REDISTRIBUTION OF ECONOMIC RENTS

George Delehanty

There are many perspectives on food policy analysis. The one which this chapter will treat is the idea that policy reform must be carried out through negotiation of political contracts which redistribute the economic rents created by public policy. Economic rents are opportunities to buy for less or sell for more than would be the case in the absence of government intervention. Every existing policy and policy instrument in the food and agriculture area has already yielded a distribution of rents or opportunities for rents. Such rents can be either positive or negative.

Any change in a policy (whether quantitative or qualitative) or in a policy instrument changes the distribution of rents in the society. This is what makes policy change difficult. It also gives the definition of policy analysis: the identification and evaluation of the existing distribution of rents and how they would change as policies and policy instruments change.

The existing distribution of rents in any agricultural economy creates economic and political inertia, and this is one reason proposals for change are so difficult to implement. It must also be frankly recognized that the existence of these rents means political and personal risks even in the evaluation of the rent distribution, let alone prescribing changes.

While a textbook might characterize a policy as an objective enunciated by a person or body in authority, with mechanisms or instruments specified to achieve the objective, this description is too simple. While the distinction between a policy and a policy instrument is important conceptually, in practice it is often ambiguous. Some policies are not so much enunciated as inferred, and some instruments exist so long and serve so many objectives that their existence becomes an inferred policy. The rice premium (an export tax) in Thailand or the bread subsidy in Egypt are only two of many cases that can be cited.

The above discussion is based on use of free markets as the standard of reference for policy analysis. This is often characterized as ideological, representing a Western or capitalistic bias. In fact, however, market prices have a real and important significance for policy analysis, regardless of the sociopolitical environment. To keep a country or regional or urban price different from a world price is almost always costly. This situation is the major economic given of food policy analysis, and it should not be seen as highly ideological. Accepting this condition as given makes more understandable the emphasis in almost all of the recent research on agricultural prices in Thailand on who bears the costs and who reaps the benefits of a policy. Indeed, arriving at a sound understanding of this given is an important component of the training or maturation of policy analysts in almost any developing country.

Related to the issue of using market prices as a standard is another methodological issue. This is the use of the term economic rent instead of economic cost or benefit for evaluating the effects of policies. Economic rents are not synonymous with private or social costs and benefits for the reason that rents are more consistent with a concept of policy as a reflection of one or more political contracts. In the theory of pure exchange, the ideas of contracting and recontracting are familiar. But, in general, the dimension of time in this theory is not given great emphasis. It is ironic that undergraduates for generations have been treated to agricultural examples of pure exchange markets where there is no time dimension. Yet the kind of food and agricultural policy analysis needed now is much more consistent with a recently revived analysis of the process and consequences of contracts and contracting where time is of the essence.

There is a current debate in the theory of both industrial and agricultural economics which might be summed up as the question of whether contracts are efficient substitutes for markets. Without going into detail, one implication is that every food and agricultural policy (or for that matter every policy instrument) may be seen best as a relatively long-term contract. What is essential about the character of this contract is the degree of coercion it contains. It is a natural presumption of the uninitiated (and I include some new Ph.D.s in our own field) that the coercion is all on the side of the agency enunciating the policy or administering the policy instrument. Of course, this is not true. In the United States, for example, the use of pretended regulation as a means of cartelization is, despite some recent changes, almost a habit. While our awareness of the consequence of this habit is growing in developing countries at least among policy analysts, the level of public and even professional discussion is not high.

It is never clear whether regulation, as such, is a policy or a policy instrument. In the minds of the public, it is probably the former, as it is so often called upon to solve real problems and yield net social gains. But for many beneficiaries in agriculture, it is an instrument which yields positive rents. Even in this environment examples may be sensitive. But we can mention maize export quotas, minimum rice export prices, subsidies to the sugar industry, and the small number of cassava exporters in Thailand. Further afield, we need only mention the word "parastatal" with reference to Kenya, and the significance should be clear.

There is neither time nor space to give this subject the attention it deserves. But there may be some merit in setting forth the conclusions of this approach:

1. Policies are coercive contractual arrangements;

2. When contractual provisions (e.g., buying food at guaranteed prices) are not met by the dominant party a policy will not be effective;

3. Coercion beyond a certain point will fail, e.g., there will be resort to smuggling, barter, or a return to subsistence agriculture;

4. Given the basic economic conditions in food and agriculture, policies (contracts) are inevitable, but each should demonstrate, continually, its superiority to the market alternative;

5. A crucial legal and economic component of effective contracting is full access to information: in agriculture this is rare;

6. Information and the reduction of risk are the main reasons for preferring contractual arrangements to markets;

7. Policies, like contracts, affect both the magnitude and incidence of transaction costs, especially storage and transport;

8. Problems of enforcement of both policies (contracts) and the implied property rights they generate are complex, and they are very often extremely costly.

While there is nothing especially surprising or unconventional about this way of approaching food and agricultural policy analysis, I believe a little reflection generates some implications for external agencies. In discussing these implications, I will take up four general points and then focus on our own particular role as policy analysts.

The first implication derives from viewing the policy system as a relatively stable rent-generating mechanism. The economics profession has come to accept as demonstrated the willingness of farmers in developing countries to respond to economic incentives. But all of the other actors in the system also do so. Most of us who have worked for long periods in one country have seen hordes of consultants, visiting scholars, and World Bank missions, and I think most of us agree that they often display a remarkable insensitivity to the actions and reactions of the beneficiaries of the rents generated by the existing policy system. Some agricultural scientists, unfortunately, share this insensitivity. So one implication is cautionary; any agency must be aware of (and beware of) not only those policy issues which are politically sensitive but also those which have very large rent implications. They are probably, but not always, the same.

The second implication may be prescriptive; it is that issues or options or projects that appear to leave the existing distribution of rents unchanged, but may generate new rents, will always be popular. There is a third implication which is both academic and practical. It is that data on policy costs and benefits are badly needed but often very difficult to get because of the sensitivities involved. Therefore, proposals must be creatively drafted. For example, one reason why feasibility studies are so popular is that they do not seem threatening, and they carry the atmosphere of new benefits. A final implication is that changes in the policy system that will be effective in changing the distribution of rents are likely to occur on the occasion of a crisis, a change in government, a dramatic technological change, a mature consensus, or perhaps all of the above together. So external agencies need to be aware of these in the timing of their types of assistance or interventions.

Looking at policies as contracts also has implications for the way in which analysis is done. It may be carried out on behalf of contracting parties who may well be told only what they need or wish to hear. Thailand is one of many countries with the problem of how to do analysis for the government without necessarily being for or against that government. Some external agencies are contracting parties: U.N. bodies, the World Bank, the IMF, and some bilateral country donor organizations. Thus they may wish to exercise leverage over the sponsorship and conduct of sensitive analysis. The Rockefeller Foundation relies now upon its reputation, contacts, and scholars for such leverage. Perhaps the implied role is best described by analogy with the law professor using the case method to teach contract law. He has to ask the right questions to bring out the essential features of the case, and he has to elicit the right answers from among a number of possible perspectives on the significance of his example. Similarly for food policy analysis, there are a number of possible perspectives, and the significance of the policy as a contractual arrangement, with attendant rights and obligations, is often overlooked. But it is a fruitful and practical theoretical idea to explore.

A GLOBAL APPROACH TO HOUSEHOLD FOOD SECURITY

Graham Donaldson

Food security is a basic social objective and a sensitive policy issue. Every society, regardless of material circumstances, faces risks relating to food supplies. Every government, regardless of ideology or administration capacity, seeks to assure its citizens that adequate and reliable supplies of food will be available at acceptable cost. The issue of food security, however, has in recent years become emotional and politicized. Because it has taken on these attributes, the issue tends to generate simplistic remedies.

Many of the responses proposed reflect the experiences of the early 1970s and the back-of-the-envelope analyses that were done at the time of the 1972–74 food crisis. There have been, however, significant changes over the past 10 years—in terms of structural changes in global production and international markets and in terms of a growing body of scholarly work on the many aspects of this subject. Either of these alone would justify a serious reassessment of the prospects for food security, and together they provide a compelling case.

In general, the experiences of the 1972–74 period represent a special case, which is unique in history and widely misunderstood. A longer view and a deeper analysis of the food system as a whole provides a less alarming perspective. The subsequent adjustments in the global food system are further reassuring. Analysis of the dimensions of the food security problem at the global and household levels suggests a broad agenda of possible national interventions that may be necessary or useful in improving the conditions within which individual households must pursue their food security. A review of the experience of households over time suggests the very fragile character of national systems, especially in developing countries. It also reveals the potentially devastating effects of wrong or perverse government actions.

The Role of Households

Food security begins and ends with the household: both production and consumption of food must take place at the household level. No matter how far-reaching or effective government's intervention in the food sector may be, the ultimate responsibilities—and penalties—in the food system fall on people and their families. A nation's food security situation is the summation of the prospects of individual households.

Governments can shape the national and international food system, but it is farmers, tenant sharecroppers, landless laborers, and their families who actually raise and harvest the crops which rise in the fields. It is bullock masters, carriers, and petty entrepreneurs and their households who move the hundreds of millions of tons of produce in rural areas and out towards its final destination. It is, overwhelmingly, small family businesses which sell food to its consumers. Finally, and most importantly, it is the task of households to come up with the money to pay for their own consumption.

Government actions may improve or diminish the chances that food security will be achieved; households can be expected to move in the direction of food security—as they perceive it. A household's efforts to protect itself from adverse relations with the food system require income. Effective demand is articulated within limits set by the availability of household resources, on the one hand, and the cost of nutrition on the other. Thus, food prices affect the provision of goods and services not only within the food sector of the economy but also within non-food sectors as well.

In a changing economy, households experience both economic and biological risks that can never be entirely eliminated. Through individual and collective action in the spheres of production, marketing, and finance, however, an economy's risk structure can be positively altered. Some forms of change are highly desirable; the process of economic development in the Western nations, for example, has nearly eliminated their risk of mass hunger. While moving toward this condition, however, these countries have undergone rapid social changes and progressive waves of economic disequilibria.

Distribution Mechanisms (or Systems)

To manage food risks, it is essential first to identify the means by which households are fed. While there is diversity in the world economy, there are also broad and basic patterns in the workings of the food system.

A large number of people, numbering possibly one billion, rely principally on subsistence agriculture for most of their food. For them, food security depends upon access to resources and the reliability of production systems which are extremely sensitive to weather. Their forays into the market are few and intermittent, though ultimately market focus affects them, if indirectly.

A second, and much larger group—numbering well above three billion—relies heavily upon a food distribution system which is ultimately international. These people are as dependent on the physical capacity to move food from farm field to consumer's table as on the size of local harvests. They are wholly dependent on markets and the forces that affect them.

A group of perhaps 100–200 million has neither access to the resources which would provide self-generated subsistence nor sufficient income to permit purchases from the commercialized system. These households are dependent for this food security on special arrangements—within extended families, village societies, or at a higher level through voluntary or official agencies.

Thus the vast majority of households are dependent for their survival on marketing networks that are ultimately global in nature. This system operates for the most part without detailed planning or direct government participation.

The Global Food Security System

Growth in world food supplies has consistently outstripped population for a hundred years. Because of increased farm productivity, real grain prices are less than half their level of a century ago.

Food production has grown faster in developing countries than in developed countries over the last 30 years, and on a global per capita basis it is 25 percent higher today than in 1950.

Stability of global output has also steadily increased and was more stable in the 1970s than in any previous period. Major regional shortfalls that did occur were caused largely by the unexpectedly heavy demand from the Soviet Union—not from developing countries.

International trade in grains has increased by more than double from 112 mmt in 1970 to 240 mmt in 1980. This trade is handled by a growing number of private and public sector agencies and originates in a growing number of countries. Thus countries wishing to buy grain on a regular or occasional basis have a substantial and diverse pool to draw on.

Increased food imports in much of the world outside Sub-Saharan Africa are related to higher per capita incomes and the resultant growth in the consumption of livestock products in middle-income countries—not population growth or sluggish farm sector performance. Self-sufficiency ratios have actually increased in low-income developing countries since the 1960s.

The middle-income countries as a whole have emerged as major importers, and the fastest growing. About half the total of cereal consumption in their cities is now imported. The middle-income countries have met the income-induced demand for food and feed—the affluence requirement—through increased imports rather than by increased domestic production.

Exceptions to the above overall consumption pattern are the low-income countries of Sub-Saharan Africa and Southeast Asia, (Vietnam, Laos, Kampuchea), where per capita output (and incomes) declined in the 1970s. Causes included the aftermath of war and inappropriate government policies. Poor weather, although sometimes important, was less a factor than often suggested.

Many of these low-income countries are self-sufficient at relatively low levels of consumption. Since at-risk households have little purchasing power, the trading system does not provide as much food security for them as in higher-income countries. The only viable long-term solution is economic growth which will give low-income households and countries access to markets.

About 650 million tons of cereals annually are fed to livestock. Some portion of this—perhaps 20 percent or 120 mmt—could be diverted to human consumption if needed (in 1973–74, grain released from the U.S. feed economy by the effect of rising prices was greater than the world shortfall). This large volume of cereals thus constitutes a ready global reserve whenever needed.

Continued agricultural trade protectionism constitutes a threat to the ready movement of food grains internationally to maintain food security. If internal prices are insulated from the impact of world shortages (as in the USSR, EEC, and Japan), the use of grain for livestock is kept artificially stable, and supplies are not freed to enter the global reserve cited above.

The new IMF Cereal Financing Facility (CFF) minimizes the risk of any country being unable to afford needed supplies. On the other hand, inability to handle additional imports has frequently been a limiting factor in many countries in the past.

Generally, it pays to make up for domestic shortfalls or dispose of surpluses through external trade. Buffer stocks are far more expensive — in the Sahel, using a ton of grain from a buffer stock is estimated to cost $500 compared with world c.i.f. prices of $200. In addition, recent work casts renewed doubt on the stabilizing effects of buffer stocks.

The international Food Aid Convention guarantees that a minimum of 7.6 million metric tons of food grains will be available yearly for shipment to hard-pressed, low-income countries. In 1980 the United States created a 4 million ton special stockpile that can be used only to meet food aid commitments in developing countries. In addition, the international relief agencies (especially the World Food Programme) as well as national and private voluntary agencies, have an established record for effectiveness in responding to crisis situations.

Although the grain import bill in developing countries has increased in absolute terms, the foreign exchange burden of food grain imports, when compared to export earnings, has declined since the 1960s for low-income and middle-income countries. Almost all developing countries—even the poorest—run positive balances on their agricultural trade accounts. In short, shifting to more domestic food production might reduce export earnings and worsen balance of payments positions.

Together, these and other characteristics make it appropriate to assume that there exists a robust global food security system to which governments, and ultimately households, confidently can relate. However, additional efforts to enhance the capacity of developing countries to use this system to their greater advantage are still much needed.

Country Strategies for the 1980s

The prospects for developing country food security in the future depend on how the lessons of the 1970s are applied by national decision makers. Analysis of this experience indicates the following general principles.

Security comes from the ability of households or nations to obtain sufficient food supplies through either production or purchase, the ability to purchase and distribute food being at least as important as the ability to produce it.

Changes in the structure and mechanics of the world food market make it possible for governments efficiently to buffer local dislocations through trade. Taking advantage of international opportunities and being able to manage commercial transactions to the best advantage will remain absolutely essential.

Within countries, it has become clear that households including low-income consumers, rural laborers and small farmers are far better off if they are able to provide for their own food security directly rather than through dependence on outside assistance. Thus, the principal route to sustainable reductions in individual vulnerability is higher production—not with the objective of achieving domestic self-sufficiency in specific foods but in order to strengthen household purchasing power and overall economic stability.

Meeting hunger problems—either where they arise as part of a chronic poverty problem or as a result of acute but short-lived shocks to the food system, such as droughts—depends on the ability physically to move food. Thus, it is critical to increase the capacity, efficiency, and resilience of the internal food distribution pipeline that links supplies, imported or domestic, to consumption requirements. A failure to do so will act as a disincentive to incremental domestic production and increase the likelihood that individual producers and consumers will not be able to meet their food security needs.

Governments should create a standby capacity including logistical arrangements for handling either natural or man-made emergencies. Existing local, private, and official relief agencies have a major role to play in this task.

Stocks play a vital economic and security role in the food marketing system. The capacity of efficient storage, particularly at the farm and village level, must be expanded as the volume of production increases. Governments must ensure that subsidies or regulations do not discourage the holding of food inventories by those best placed to service the overall food distribution pipeline and provide immediate help to those at risk.

The key to the proposed strategy is increasing the ability of individual households to cope with changing circumstances in an efficient and self-reliant fashion. Achieving autarky at a country or local level is neither a realistic nor a desirable option if the aim is to reduce vulnerability. Rather, protecting food security will depend on incremental development of existing frameworks through which households manage consumption risks. Economic policy, regulation, parastatals, and public investments can facilitate this process. Conversely, ill-conceived government actions can reduce household independence and security, particularly when they weaken the food distribution pipeline or pricing mechanisms.

Making Distribution Systems Work

Increasing the reliability and efficiency of mechanisms for supplying local food consumption requirements is the logical starting point for public policy and interventions. It is not a question of private sector versus government responsibility, but rather of making existing systems work better, augmenting them where they are shown to be deficient in meeting the needs of the people actually at risk. To this end, there is a need for additional investments and new activities by profit-oriented and cost-minimizing actors, especially farmers and merchants, as well as by non-profit operations, including state-owned enterprises and voluntary relief agencies.

Specific areas for attention in this area include:
1. Collection and distribution of rural food surpluses;
2. Transport infrastructure and services;
3. Commercial codes, grading, and standards;
4. Stockholding and storage;
5. Processing;
6. Retailing;
7. Rural financial systems;
8. Information collection and access;
9. Using international markets.

Price Policy and Stabilization

Government intervention to buffer prices affecting household consumption from exogenous and domestic shocks is critical to food security of poorer groups. The dual objectives must be to provide minimum needs in the short-run while ensuring secular growth based on production gains. The price of food over the long-run should reflect production, distribution, and risk-related costs in order to ensure incentives at all stages of the food chain. But scarcity is an unavoidable fact and must be reflected by prices if efficient economic responses are to be made.

The best indicator of the economic costs of food is provided by world market prices. This is the opportunity cost in that any country has the option of actually buying or selling at that price. This does not mean that a country should resort to wholly free trade or a totally open agricultural economy. As a rule of thumb, a moving average of f.o.b. export prices and c.i.f. import prices, respectively, provide the lower and upper limits of a range within which food prices might be held. A key to success is the provision of a pricing framework which producers, consumers, and traders can relate to and depend upon.

Any recourse to extra-market pricing should take account of the following:

1. Provide for differentials that reflect the economic cost of holding stocks and physically transporting food;

2. Not be based on strict attempts to project average costs of production and corresponding cash flows for farm operations to be applied throughout the country regardless of subsequent crop developments, local prices, or farmer needs;

3. Distinguish among

a. *Minimum price* schemes that are enforced to protect farmer incomes;

b. *Target prices* that reflect desires to increase the absolute level of production but which are not strictly enforced;

c. *Export taxes* through artifically low procurement prices and the public sector monopolizing exports;

d. *Consumer subsidies* through artificially low producer prices;

e. *Consumer subsidies* through government absorbing marketing costs; and

f. *Reference prices* for official credit programs, such as financing of farmer, co-op, or merchant inventories but which are not maintained through market interventions;

4. Take account of consequences for agriculture when exchange rates are overvalued and it becomes cheaper to import, thereby penalizing farmers through lower prices for domestic foodcrops and higher input prices.

Protecting the Poor

Even the most efficient production and distribution systems do not assure that the poor will have the means to acquire basic nutrition. The problem of poverty is much more than a food security question; alleviating poverty is much of what politics, economic policies, and development are all about. But poverty has unavoidable effects on food risks, and any government attempting to reduce these must come to terms with it. Interventions to ensure food supplies to people at risk range from broad spectrum approaches, such as ration shops, to highly-targeted programs, such as feeding babies and lactating mothers. World Bank studies suggest that the more highly-targeted the program the lower its economic rate of return and the lower its cost effectiveness. Some degree of targeting can be achieved by selection of outlet locations and by use of inferior foods.

In general, intervention programs should be planned recognizing the following:

1. Subsidized marketing of food in rural areas—where the need is often greatest—is not practical on a continuing basis; the side effects in terms of production losses simply outweigh any potential social gains;

2. When large amounts of aid, especially imported food aid, are placed under the control of government officials whose performance is not carefully audited, there is considerable scope for corruption;

3. Governments can often achieve cost-effective distribution by supporting and possibly augmenting the ability of private voluntary and religious groups who manage targeted nutrition interventions which create additional demand and do not disrupt markets;

4. The vulnerable often acquire the bulk of their subsistence from what is left over when markets clear. The "seconds" from fresh fruit and vegetable stalls or grain milling are frequently consumed by the poorest of the poor; hence the welfare effect of modernizing processing or reducing post-harvest losses should be analyzed *before* governments support them.

Public sector agencies have a role to play in assuring that contingency planning is undertaken on a systematic basis to ensure timely responses when needed in the event of disasters, either natural or man-made. Investments in standby logistical facilities and early warning systems are important. In most developing countries, particularly low-income ones, the institutional requirements are such as to imply that the military and outside donor agencies should be assigned a major part of overall responsibility for managing relief.

Production Growth and Technology

The adequacy of the marketing and distribution system and the pricing framework (mentioned above) are two of the three key requirements for ensuring a responsive food production system. The third is the availability of production technology that is reliable, accessible, affordable, and will enhance productivity. This is another area in which governments have a role.

Research and development, together with mechanisms to transfer technology from field trial to the farmer require adequate funding and careful attention to organization. Research must be "applied," in nature and in practice. Many modes of extension exist—dependence on centrally controlled systems may not be desirable. In addition to research and extension *per se*, there is also a need for science services—testing laboratories and experiment facilities to help in establishing and maintaining quantity and quality standards and verifying assessments about pest incidence and other occurrences. This is an element of the system required to support a science-based agriculture which is frequently overlooked.

Technology and infrastructure that will reduce production variability is at a premium. This technology applies not only to biological elements such as drought-resistant varieties of crops but also to irrigation and field mechanization—both of which can reduce production risk in some circumstances. Credit to facilitate access to new inputs, especially those of a lumpy nature, may also require policy attention.

In Conclusion

The key to improving food security in the low-income developing countries lies in increasing the incomes of low-productivity groups and increasing the efficiency of the distribution systems which serve them. In part this will result from improvements in human capital—education, health, and skills. But the macro-environment of incentives, rewards, and risks is equally important, as are physical conditions, both of which can be shaped by government policies even in the poorest nation.

MAKING FOOD POLICY
IN A NEW
INTERNATIONAL
ENVIRONMENT

G. Edward Schuh

Introduction

The range of policies and policy-emphases that one needs to consider in dealing with food and agricultural policies is wide. Incentives, or getting the prices right, represents one important class of problems, one which focuses attention on conventional commodity programs and price distortions.[1] The socioeconomic aspects of nutrition is another. Closely related is the issue of equity, since an important share of the world's hunger is directly related to the problem of poverty. The economics of resource use is still another class of problems, especially in the context of marginal lands, water, and fragile environments.

Without minimizing the importance of any one of these areas, or the importance of developing the analytical capacity to address any or all of them as a means of alleviating world hunger, I want to take a somewhat different perspective. My emphasis will be on the growing importance of international relationships, the growing deficiencies of international economic and policy institutions, and the need to understand why governments do what they do.

This chapter is divided into three parts: a brief review of major changes in the structure of the international economic systems, a discussion of the breakdown and growing irrelevance of international institutions, and a summary of high priority areas needing attention.

This chapter is predicated on an assumption that feeding the world's population in the future will require that we make most efficient use of the *world's* resources. This will require that individual countries realize their particular comparative advantage in production, a process that depends as much on how countries relate to each other as it does on what they do in their own countries and with their own policies. To the extent that individual countries relate more efficiently with each other, total world output of food will increase and the international distribution of income will be more equitable.

I. The Changing Structure of the International Economic System

The structure of the world's economy has changed dramatically in the period since the end of World War II. Unfortunately, policy makers have not kept up with these changes and consequently have failed to devise policies consistent with the changed conditions. Four changes in the structure of the international economic system already have emerged, and three more changes appear to be in the offing.

A. Emergence of Integrated Capital Market

Perhaps one of the most significant changes in the structure of the international economy in the post-Warld War II period has been the emergence of a well-integrated international capital market. At the end of World War II, international capital markets were debilitated. Such international transfers of capital as occurred were from one country to another, and on concessional terms. The Marshall Plan was the outstanding example of such transfers, and in some years it involved transfers as high as three percent of the GNP of the United States. But the United States also assisted countries other than our wartime allies; and as the Marshall Plan phased out, concessional assistance to other countries increased, especially to the less-developed countries.

Over time, government-to-government transfers of capital on concessional terms declined. In their place arose a very effective international market for capital. This market started out as a Euro-dollar market but eventually evolved into a Euro-currency market. Later there arose an Asian-dollar market, and in recent years there has been talk of creating a Rio-dollar market.

The amount of resources that flow through this international capital market is now huge. Countries borrow in this market to finance their development programs. Consortia of banks mobilize large quantities of funds. Compared to the sizeable amounts of capital which pass through the rather unregulated commerical markets, that transferred on concessional terms has become a pittance.

With the emergence of this international capital market, the economies of the world are increasingly well integrated and linked together. While conventionally we tend to think that countries are linked together by means of trade, in point of fact, they are now also linked together by the international capital market. Moreover, as will be explained in more detail below, the capital market links economic policies in ways that they were not linked in the past.

B. Flexible Exchange Rates

The second change in the structure of the international economy was the shift from a system of fixed exchange rates, which had reigned throughout the post-World War II period, to a system of quasi-flexible exchange rates in 1973, forced upon the international community by the United States. Although more properly decribed as a system of block floating, something like 85 percent of world trade still moves across flexible exchange rates.

This shift has a number of important implications for policies designed to deal with the world food problem. First, trade and exchange rate policies have been an important means of taxing agriculture in the less-developed countries. With a system of flexible exchange rates, implementing such policies becomes a great deal more complex.

The current difficulties faced by United States agriculture further illustrate some of the consequences of these structural changes in the international economy. Over the past several years, the value of the dollar has risen dramatically in foreign exchange markets, due in part to tight monetary policies here at home. The strong dollar has made United States exports less competitive in international markets, while at the same time lowering the dollar price of imports. With a strong dollar, United States agricultural exports can be expected to decline, other things remaining equal. Hence, a strong dollar has helped create a serious farm problem here at home.[2]

A persistently strong dollar can be expected to have additional consequences. In those countries that keep the value of their currency tied to the United States dollar, the effect on agriculture will be similar to the effect on United States agriculture. This includes a large number of less-developed countries. The agriculture of these countries will face the same sort of adjustment problem which United States agriculture now faces as the effective price of their exports rises. By the same token, agricultural output will increase in countries whose currencies have declined vis-a-vis the dollar. These countries can be expected to be more competitive in international markets, either importing less or exporting more, as the case may be.

These limited examples point out some of the important consequences of the changes in structure of the international economy. These changes have made the world's economy a great deal more interdependent, and in ways that have important implications for the world food problem and for food and agricultural policies.

C. Changing Trade Patterns

Once the bulk of trade in cereals was among the industrialized countries. During the 1970s this trade took on important North-South and East-West dimensions. For example, from 1971 through 1979, imports of cereals by the centrally planned economies increased over seven-fold, from 6.5 million metric tons to 54.6 million tons. Similarly, imports by the less-developed market economies increased over six-fold, from 8.9 million tons to 54.5 million tons. Imports by the industrialized, market economies increased only 40 percent during this same period, from 27.4 million tons to 38.3 million tons. Most of this increase was due to growing imports by Japan, however, which increased by 131 percent, from 10.3 million tons to 23.8 million tons. Imports by the European community actually declined by 68 percent, from 13 million tons to 4.2 million tons. In recent years, the European community, aided by large export subsidies, has become a net exporter of grains.

These large changes in the patterns of trade have important implications for the relevance of the international institutions created to manage and regulate that trade. Those implications will be discussed in more detail below.

D. Labor Migration

While the problem of the undocumented worker in the United States has received a great deal of attention in the popular press, massive migrations of labor have become significant economic events in other parts of the world, such as in Asia and Africa. These migrations are important for food and agricultural policy, for they help change the comparative advantage of particular sectors in individual economies. For example, the United States is able to remain competitive in labor-intensive fruits and vegetables in part because of the ready supply of undocumented workers.

In addition to these four changes in the structure of the international economy that have already occurred, there are at least three more changes that may be in the offing. First, the comparative advantage of individual countries is likely to undergo further dramatic shifts in the decade ahead. Second, there is likely to be a growing liberalization of economic policies in developing countries. Third, there could be significantly greater integration of centrally-planned economies into world markets. All these developments could have significant impact on the structure of incentives for food and cash crops in developing countries and on their future production performance.

E. Changing Comparative Advantage

The basis for dramatic shifts in comparative advantage are already well in place. The technological base of world agriculture is likely to change significantly in the decade ahead, due to the maturation of the International Agricultural Research System. The capacity of this system to produce new production technology was developed during the 1970s. The payoff for the system should begin to emerge in the 1980s. New production technologies should significantly alter the comparative advantage of individual countries.

Investments by individual countries in their own capacity to produce and distribute new production technology have also increased greatly. The less-developed countries as a group are investing a great deal more in their domestic capability—Brazil and some other countries being outstanding examples. These investments will have a positive payoff in their own right. They also enable these countries to take greater advantage of investments made by the international community.

Similarly, industrial technology is being diffused around the world at a much faster rate and on a broader scale than in the past. The increased speed is due both to the growing recognition of technology as the basis for development and the improvements in educational attainment in the less-developed countries. This rapid diffusion of technological knowledge will probably give the less-developed countries an ever-stronger comparative advantage in labor-intensive manufactured products.

It is too early to say how these various developments will balance out in the decade ahead. It seems clear, however, that they will pose serious challenges both to international trade policies and to the domestic food and agricultural policies in individual countries.

F. Economic Liberalization in LDCs

The autarchic, import-substitution industrialization policies which characterized the developing world in the 1950s and 1960s are now discredited, together with the neglect they implied for agriculture. The potential of export-based development policies increasingly is being recognized. These shifts lead to different perspectives on the role of agriculture in the development process and in the LDC posture vis-a-vis trade.

Throughout most of the post-World War II period the industrialized countries as a bloc have promoted freer trade and greater international economic intercourse. The less-developed countries have been inward-looking and autarchic. Today those positions are almost exactly reversed. The developed countries are becoming increasingly protectionist, while the less-developed countries are beginning to open up their economies.

The implications of these changes in trade perspectives have important consequences for food and agricultural policies. They further illustrate the growing dependence of such policies on international trade issues.

G. Integration of Centrally Planned Economies in World Economy

The centrally-planned economies appear to be moving toward increasingly decentralized, liberal, and market-oriented economic systems. This judgment about the future is somewhat more speculative than the previous two. But changes in the centrally-planned system are already significant. Changes in China, for example, have gone beyond what most people thought possible only a few years ago. The Polish summer of 1982 may be a harbinger of the future, even though that important attempt at liberalization has been sidetracked, at least for the time being.

In any case, it seems likely that increasingly we will need to incorporate the centrally-planned economies into the international economic system. That incorporation will make trade and other international issues a great deal more complex that they have been in the past.

II. The Breakdown and Growing Irrelevance of International Institutions

A. The Breakdown of Major Provisions of the Bretton Woods Conventions

The end of World War II witnessed the birth of significant international institutions: the United Nations, the FAO, the World Bank, the International Monetary Fund. The Bretton Woods conventions were established to guide international monetary relations, the GATT to guide international trade. This period witnessed a significant burst of creativity in terms of international institutions.

A number of characteristics of this period and of the institutions created at that time are worth noting. First, the technical capability to design these institutions was apparently ample and relevant. Second, there was significant political leadership to bring the institutions into being. The United States played a major role in the events of those days, due in no small part to its dominance of the international economy as the only clear winner of the war. And third, the institutions that emerged in that period were designed in large part by representatives of the industrialized West and to serve the interests of the industrialized West. For the most part, they have served those interests quite well. However, they have not, as a practical matter, served the interests of the rest of the world nearly as well.

An important element of the Bretton-Woods convention was the agreement to operate with fixed currency exchange rates. Another element was the agreement that there would be only a limited number of reserve currencies. A third was that disequilibria in the external accounts would be corrected by changes in domestic policies rather than by changes in exchange rates.

This system served the industrialized countries of the world quite well for almost 30 years. However, when the United States forced the world to a system of flexible exchange rates in 1973, the main elements of this system were eliminated. Unfortunately, no formal agreed-upon rules have replaced the old system. Problems are dealt with on an ad hoc basis as they arise. And there are few generally accepted principles to serve as a guide for crisis management when crises arise.

B. The Shift in Trade Patterns Makes the GATT Less Relevant

The General Agreement on Tariffs and Trade has established rules which govern trade relations among countries. It has also provided the leadership for a succession of Multilateral Trade Negotiations which have successively lowered tariffs, and to a lesser extent, other barriers to trade.

However, the signatories to the GATT are primarily the industrialized countries of the West. The centrally-planned and less-developed countries for the most part are not members. Hence, the provisions of the GATT do not apply to them.

At one time, this was not a serious issue since most of the world's trade was among the industrialized countries. With trade patterns shifting more and more towards the centrally-planned and less-developed countries, however, the result is that a larger and larger share of international trade is not governed by any agreed-upon rules.

In the case of agriculture, the situation is even more serious. The GATT in general has provided little assistance in providing a more reponsible, stable trade environment. The industrialized countries have protected their domestic agricultural programs by excluding agriculture from the provisions of the GATT. Hence, agriculture has experienced little direct benefit from the general reduction of tariffs in the post-World War II period. There has also been only limited progress in establishing rules for the use of nontariff barriers to trade, even in the most recent MTN, which gave increased attention to nontariff barriers.

C. The Emergence of the UNCTAD

The failure of the less-developed countries of the world to become signatories of the GATT, together with their inability to gain a voice in the deliberations of the GATT, gave rise to the first United Nations Conference on Trade and Development in the mid-1960s. Designed in the beginning to call attention to the importance of trade to the development of the less-developed countries, the UNCTAD rapidly coalesced into a political movement which has both challenged the trade rules established by the industrialized market economies and pressured for resource transfers from the developed countries.

A series of UNCTAD conferences has followed. An increasingly coherent political rhetoric has evolved and the political cohesiveness of the group has grown stronger. The list of demands from the UNCTAD constitutes the agenda for the so-called North-South debate. Major items on the agenda have relevance for the world's food and agricultural problems and policies. So far, however, the agenda has elicited little or no response from the developed countries.

D. The Emergence of State and Quasi-State Trading Agencies

Trade with the centrally-planned economies takes place on a state-to-state basis, at least on the centrally-planned economy side of the exchange. But other countries have developed state or quasi-state trading agencies as well. Among these are the Canadian Wheat Board, CONASUPO in Mexico, INESPRE in the Dominican Republic, and similar agencies in Japan, Australia, and the long list of countries with marketing boards.

These state trading agencies are typically created to provide the government with a monopoly of either the import or export of particular commodities. In some cases, they are the means of taxing agriculture in implicit ways. In other cases, they are the means of providing implicit subsidies to agriculture or other groups in society.

As vehicles for food and agricultural policies, these organizations have become increasingly important. In the trade context, they create serious difficulties because they make it difficult to measure objective costs and therefore to identify subsidies and taxes. Hence, ultimately they become important sources of distortions to trade.

Despite their growing importance, there are few agreed-upon rules for the regulation of state trading agencies. The GATT has been notably silent on them, as has the UNCTAD. Conflicts over their trade practices have to date been resolved primarily through bilateral negotiations.

E. The Lack of International Arrangements Responsive to International Trade Adjustment Problems

With trade becoming an ever larger component of national GNP and with rapid shifts in comparative advantage emerging on the international scene, the world is faced with serious trade adjustment problems. Agriculture is likely to be in the forefront of these adjustments, especially if the potential of new technology as the basis of developing the agricultural sector is realized.

The world faces something of a paradox when it addresses the trade adjustment problem. Such problems are inherently domestic issues and typically involve tradeoffs between domestic consumers and domestic producers. However, trade problems are typically perceived and articulated as tradeoffs between domestic producers and foreign producers. Under such circumstances, it is not surprising that the foreigner loses out and that protectionism prevails.

A possible way to address this problem is to recognize it as an international problem and devise an appropriate mechanism with international resources to deal with it. Elsewhere I have proposed the establishment of an International Adjustment Fund which would be financed by a tax on countries proportional to their trade.[3] The Fund would provide resources to individual countries to help them in responding to their adjustment problems. Other means might be devised.

F. The Growing Use of Economic Sanctions to Influence the Behavior of Countries

Economic blockades and other forms of economic sanctions have been long used as a means to attain political objectives. But the growing reluctance to use military force in international affairs, especially by the industrialized countries, has led to increased use of economic sanctions. Moreover, they are likely to be of increasing importance in the future.

Food and agriculture are likely to be in the forefront of such sanctions. Moreover, as in the case of the Soviet embargo, such measures may well represent large shocks to the world's food and agricultural policies.

If such practices do indeed become more important in the future, a set of principles to guide and discipline their use is needed. The world long ago agreed on a set of rules for military warfare. It would seem equally plausible that it agree on a set of rules for conducting economic warfare.

G. The Development of the Consultative Group on International Agricultural Research: An Exception to the General Trend

To conclude this section, it should be noted that there has been one important international institutional innovation of relevance to agriculture in the post-World War II period: The CGIAR and the system of international agricultural research centers which it represents. However, this innovation has been the exception to the general rule. The general rule has been a breakdown of international institutions that at one time were effective—without anything to replace them—the growing irrelevance of some major institutions such as the GATT, and a failure to devise new institutional arrangements to address emerging problems. Whether this situation is due to a lack of creativity on the part of social scientists, to political paralysis at the international level, or to some combination of the two is an open question. But the impasse and paralysis have occurred at the very time that the world's economy is becoming rapidly internationalized.

III. Areas Needing High Priority Attention

With the growing internationalization of the world's economy, some of the high priority needs are in areas rather far removed from conventional food and agricultural policy, even though they are of signal importance to the food and agriculture sector. The discussion is cast as if the need were for additional research. To the extent that our present impasse is due to a lack of knowledge, that is a proper perspective. But more than new knowledge is needed, important as that may be. The knowledge needs to be widely diffused among the body politic so that the rapidly changing international economy can be better understood. This is essential to curtailing the malaise that now prevails regarding that system. The knowledge also needs to be fed into the political process so that it can influence effectively the course of events.

A. New Institutional Arrangements

Institutional design questions are critical to the future of the world's economy. Some means needs to be found to focus talent more effectively on this class of problems. As to institutional arguments, two areas in particular merit immediate attention.

1. Control of International Monetary Reserves

The break-down of the Bretton-Woods Conventions and the failure to develop new institutional arrangements have left the world with a rudderless economy. The last decade has witnessed two bursts of international inflation due to the burgeoning of international monetary resources. To the extent that the United States serves as the world's central banker, there is a tremendous cost in this to certain sectors of its own economy, particularly agriculture.

I have argued elsewhere that the world needs an International Central Bank.[4] Such a Bank would manage the growth of international monetary reserves. Stability in the growth of these reserves would add stability to international commodity markets and provide a more stable environment for the implementation of food and agricultural policies.

2. Institutional Arrangements Governing Trade

Either the GATT needs a major reform to take in a wider range of countries and to provide broader coverage of trade flows, or a completely new institutional arrangement is needed. While some sort of marriage of the GATT and the UNCTAD is possible, more likely is the need for a completely new arrangement.

B. Improved Knowledge on International Capital Markets

Because international capital markets are a newcomer on the international scene, little is known about them in a systematic way. Yet they are critical in understanding international commodity markets and what takes place in them. Commodity markets and financial markets have become increasingly linked together, both within national economies and on the international scene. One cannot understand one without understanding the other.

Second, international capital markets are important links among the policies of various countries. Capital flows induce changes in currency exchange rates which in turn can induce changes in monetary and fiscal policies. These in turn can induce changes in domestic food and agricultural policies. There are important yet poorly understood relationships between macroeconomic policies and commodity policies. These relationships are important not only within individual countries but also between the domestic monetary and fiscal policies in one country and the commodity policies in other countries.

C. Improved Knowledge on the International Migration of Labor

The economics profession has given a great deal of attention to the so-called brain-drain. However, it has given a great deal less attention to the migration of unskilled labor. Yet in recent years, the migration of unskilled workers has been much more important than the migration of skilled labor. Not only does the migration of labor act as a substitute for trade, but also it can help individual countries delay further specialization in trade, thereby retaining a more balanced economy.

The availability of a supply of migrant labor has important implications for food and agricultural policies. On the other hand, losing a steady stream of migrants, as in the case of Mexico, can have similar effects. We need to understand better these flows of labor and to devise appropriate arrangements to regulate them.

D. Improved Knowledge on Who Benefits and Who Loses from International Exchange

Central to the North-South debate is a belief on the part of the South that they have been exploited by international trade. Despite the persistence and vehemence of this allegation, there has been little empirical research on the issue.

Improved knowledge will help to resolve some of the issues in the North-South debate and also can help individual countries to devise improved domestic and trade policies. It can be also an important input into devising more rational and equitable international relations. The international capital market as a source of gains and losses also should be investigated.[5]

E. Improved Knowledge on Why Public Policy Is What It Is

Most of neoclassical economics has taken government to be exogenous, nonexistent, or irrational. Yet the government sector is important in most economies of the world and is becoming more important in quite a large number of countries. The effects of government policy tend to be pervasive, ultimately affecting almost all members of a society.

Increasingly we are coming to understand that governments respond to economic forces just like other entities in the economy. This has opened up a whole new field in economics, one with considerable potential for multidisciplinary collaboration.[6]

Recent work on trade policy illustrates the potential for such research. In the past, considerable effort was expended in showing the benefits of freer trade and in analyzing the consequences of distortions to trade. Yet governments continue to intervene in trade in significant ways. The new approach is to try to understand why governments intervene. Improved knowledge on this question should encourage more rational policies.

While this is an exciting new area of policy research, work to date has hardly scratched the surface. Additional work in this area promises a high payoff.

F. The Economics of Foreign Relations

Issues of food and agricultural policy powerfully affect relations between the United States and the European Community, between the United States and the Soviet Union, and the relations among a long list of other countries. To date, political scientists have tended to dominate the field of international relations. Economists generally have ignored it, especially those brought up in the neoclassical tradition. Yet, there is within the corpus of neoclassical theory an ample body of theory useful in understanding international relations and in designing international policies and institutions.[7] It is a fruitful area for creative economic analysis.

In summary, the internationalization of the world's economy is of fairly recent vintage. We do not yet understand in a systematic way the interdependencies which have emerged. Moreover, international institutions have not kept up with the changing times. To the extent that new institutions and new knowledge lead to a more efficient use of the world's agricultural resources, they promise a substantial increase in agricultural output and its more equitable distribution.

NOTES

1. "Getting the prices right" is highly complementary to technological policy in most countries, since farmers will not be inclined to adopt new production technologies if they are not profitable.

2. For more detail, see G. Edward Schuh, "Agriculture in Transition," testimony before the Joint Economic Committee, U.S. Congress (April 28, 1982).

3. G. Edward Schuh, "Positive Adjustment Policies for Agriculture," University of Minnesota (December 1979).

4. G. Edward Schuh, "Agriculture in Transition."

5. Antonio Brandao and G. Edward Schuh, "New Perspectives on the Terms of Trade and the Gains from Trade" (Mimeographed).

6. Gordon C. Rausser, Erik Lichtenberg, and Ralph Lattimore, "Developments in Theory and Empirical Application of Endogenous Governmental Behavior," in *New Directions in Econometric Modeling and Forecasting in U.S. Agriculture*, ed., Gordon C. Rausser (Amsterdam: North Holland Publisher, Inc., 1983).

7. G. Edward Schuh, "Economics and International Relations: A Conceptual Framework," *American Journal of Agricultural Economics* 63(5): 767–778 (Presidential Address).

Part II:
Approaches to Developing National Food Policy Capabilities

FOOD POLICY RESEARCH AND THE POLICY PROCESS IN THE THIRD WORLD

Alberto Valdés

This chapter will first spell out some important issues and premises faced by a policy research institute with respect to the integration of research and actual policy making. It will then describe several mechanisms utilized to integrate research results more effectively into the policy making process and will end with a few illustrations of how the process has worked for IFPRI in recent years. Although the paper draws heavily on IFPRI's recent experience as a new policy research institute, many of the lessons learned are broadly applicable for researchers at both national and international levels.

The primary purpose of food policy research done at international agencies such as IFPRI is to help developing countries in the analysis and improvement of policies for food production, distribution, consumption, and trade. Ultimately, the principal concern is the welfare of the people in developing countries, particularly the low-income people in these countries.

Issues and Premises

There are a number of issues relating to the policy-making process that should be addressed.

1. Who are the policy makers and who comprises the audience? Food policy research work enters the food policy process through its principal audience—the policy makers and policy analysts in developing countries. Policy makers are an amorphous group including primarily representa-

tives of many agencies within a government and representatives of universities and private groups outside government. The process of making food policy is usually an inter-agency one, with the ministry of agriculture serving as the primary actor influencing production policies and other agencies serving as the primary actors on consumption, distribution, and trade policies. The visible policy maker is aided by many others behind the scenes who do important work. While the international agencies must develop strong interactions with national policy makers, policy analysts in developing countries are at least as important a part of these agencies' clientele.

Furthermore, broad macroeconomic policies such as exchange rates and industrial policies, although often not considered part of the set of policies that impinge on agriculture, may have profound effects on the structure of incentives for agricultural production, as demonstrated for Colombia and Argentina in IFPRI's Research Reports 24 and 36.[1] Thus, the dialogue within government encompasses planning, finance, and supply ministries, as well as marketing boards where these exist. Given such a broad clientele within each developing country, reaching all the relevant agencies is a very complex task. Also, the capacity for policy analysis and the routes to policy making vary greatly among developing countries.

Furthermore, the external economic environment within which food and agricultural policies of developing countries are designed is influenced by the agricultural and trade policies of developed countries and by the policies of international financial aid and development agencies. Thus, two other audiences of this food policy research work are researchers (including those in the CGIAR system and other international organizations, and those within the research communities of the developing and developed countries), and the public in general (including specialized journalists, policy analysts, and graduate students in the social sciences). Thus, food policy analysis enlightens not only governments but also the public in more general terms; and therefore, research results should try to reach this broad audience.

2. Policy development is rarely a process in which policy analysts and advisors start with a clear, predetermined national welfare function. The various effects of a policy change on different groups of consumers and producers usually are not known at the outset. The policy making process is dynamic, and clear balances may exist only in an ex post facto sense. For food policy research, this requires consideration of different possible outcomes in forward-looking analysis, trying to make explicit the various trade-offs involved; this also applies for ex post facto interpretations of particular policies.

3. At a high level of abstraction, there is general agreement that an accepted objective of policy change is to achieve economic growth with

distributional equity.[2] However, when faced with necessary trade-offs between growth and equity and the normative aspects of food policy, disagreements arise as to which deserves greater weight. Moreover, among policy makers, there are contending interests, and there are frequently different perceptions as to the true values of the parameters of the system. Through empirical analysis that looks at the facts within a clear analytical framework, economic policy research can inform the policy process by positive analysis, and thereby reduce significantly the scope for subjective evaluation of policies. But in the end, as with other types of policies, making food policy is an art that encompasses a large number of elements, of which research results on the economics of food policy are only one.

4. Therefore, as a research institute, we should not attempt to tell a government what it should be doing. The role of research is to elucidate, not to recommend a specific policy or an absolutely best course of action in a particular situation. However, direct implications for policy change often emerge rather naturally from applied policy analysis. For example, if policy makers in Brazil decide to use food subsidies to increase the calorie consumption of the malnourished, research indicates that subsidizing wheat bread may actually add to the problem of calorie deficiency because the poor substitute the bread for higher calorie foods. Instead, as found in IFPRI's Research Report 32,[3] rice appears to be the best food to subsidize for nutritional purposes in Brazil. But important as they are, nutritional goals are only one of the several dimensions of food and agricultural policies, and in this case a clear-cut policy recommendation could be made only within the context of nutritional objectives.

5. Proper identification of the policy issues to be researched is a critical task. For example, as a research institute, IFPRI's Board and its staff develops its own research agenda. This is a necessary condition for a sustained long-term effort involving specific policy issues. But in the process of doing so, the Institute continuously interacts with policy makers and analysts, and their requests clearly influence decisions on proposed research.

The time horizon is strongly related to the definition of the research agenda. Most policy makers place a high premium on research that addresses today's pressing issues. But research has a rather long gestation period; and with one year's notice, it is difficult to come up with useful results. Thus a research institute should try, in consultation with individuals in government and in the private sector, to anticipate what the policy needs are going to be in three to four years, so that research results will be available at that time to meet the requests of policy makers. Signals that come from the field are crucial. The research institute must evaluate these signals in light of existing knowledge of the problem and of the institute's research framework.

6. There is a need both for broad policy frameworks, which take general approaches to food policy analysis and are adaptable to various local conditions, and for microeconomic analysis of country-specific structures and institutions leading to policy prescription and implementation. The comparative advantage of international research institutes vis-à-vis individual developing-country policy makers and analysts is primarily in developing approaches for the analysis of public policies, both at the national and international levels. This does not preclude the need to use microeconomic data. A problem for both national and international research institutes, if they need to generate such data, is the high cost of doing so, and the difficulty of finding adequate financing to provide a proper information base for policy makers.

A clarification is needed on the distinction between micro and macro levels. There are essentially three levels: the micro, which is the farm and household level; the sector and commodity aggregates; and the macro, which is in the tradition of macroeconomic theory. Public policy analysis related to food involves sectoral aggregates and macro analysis. Research at international institutions is not concerned with giving advice to individual farmers or households.

What matters most is clarifying where the issue lies, not the research method. Thus, even though these institutes' main research thrust is not at the farm level—which has been the bread and butter of agricultural economists at other international centers and local agricultural economists in developing countries—some food consumption and production issues do require that research be done at the household and farm levels because it is essential to understanding how food policy affects poverty, food consumption, and the nutritional status of the poor. Policy analysis on food consumption requires addressing some issues at the household level, both in substance and in method. However, most policy issues, such as those related to food subsidies in developing countries, are not at the micro level, although they require microeconomic data. Similarly, at the farm level, although the issues analyzed are usually sectoral in nature, their analysis sometimes requires microeconomic data.

7. The traditional conflict of how to deal with short-term losses in order to achieve long-term goals is a critical issue in practical policy making (see Selowsky, p. 102). This is a relatively new area in research in economic policy. The optimum path of a policy adjustment—that is, the path of its effects horizontally through various dimensions and through time—seldom has been studied. Yet to understand better the politics of food policy in terms of why governments do what they do, research needs to enter into policy dynamics much more than it does now.

8. A diversity of constraints, real and perceived, determine the feasible boundaries of policy change in a given country. This is one of the most difficult issues facing researchers. The common reasoning that one works within the constraints of the local policy-making process does not really solve the dilemma. In many countries there are several policy issues perceived to be untouchable because changing them would offend powerful local interests. These issues often include exchange rate adjustments, pricing policies by parastatals, reorientation of consumer subsidy programs, and others. How does one achieve the right balance between analytical rigor, policy relevance, sensitivity to the local situation, and intellectual integrity? For example, should economic research really look for a first-best solution, or should it instead explore what is possible within the prevailing policy environment, which might be an nth-best solution from a welfare economics point of view? Whichever approach is followed, researchers should have the independence to speak frankly, albeit sensibly and with good documentation, in addressing the policy implications of research results.

9. Recognizing that food policy is a dynamic process and that research results necessarily cover only some dimensions of the process, an important question nevertheless remains: what kind of follow-up work should be done after research work has been published? It is usually hard to decide at what stage in the work to close the books on a study with policy implications. There are, of course, several complementary mechanisms that can be used to disseminate and foster discussion of research results.

Follow-up work by the research institute after one of its research reports has been completed should be examined as a new proposal, examining the nature of costs and benefits but not necessarily attempting to quantify them. The important point is that the institute's priorities should be assessed as substantive policy issues, and not as country-specific issues. Ideally, country economists could pick up from this research report and expand it and integrate it more fully into the local policy framework. That has happened, for example, with several of IFPRI's research projects. But not all developing countries have the capacity to do this, and thus there are some explicit requests for IFPRI or other research institutes to follow up on a project. But given the desire to limit the expansion of the total size of staff of most research institutes, however, it would be unrealistic to attempt to satisfy these demands unless the new project can be defended in terms of its potential contribution to clarifying policy issues high on the institute's own research agenda.

10. In a broad and very real sense, research at international institutes helps to expand the national capacity for food policy analysis in developing countries, and thus it is a form of training. All outreach activities are usually aimed at fairly high-level policy makers and analysts. The research

work determines what training opportunities may arise. Given its usually small size, a research institute has to be very selective in offering training opportunities, and training will have to be somewhat ad hoc, basically determined by opportunities provided by research activities.

Formal training programs in the more traditional sense of bringing groups of relatively junior policy analysts to the research institute for classroom activities should not become a primary activity at such institutes. But training opportunities in food policy research, related to specific research projects, could be offered occasionally for individuals at the master's or doctoral level in economics, who are involved in research in developing countries.

Outreach Mechanisms

1. Publications are fundamental to a research institute; they force rigorous analysis, and they reach many interested people who then initiate interactions with the researchers. Publications take various forms. In addition to research reports, a complementary set of abstracts, short reports, journal articles, and other publications are keyed to the policy-making process. IFPRI's experience shows that research publications can generate considerable public debate. For example, two recent reports on agricultural production instability in India focused on a subject of policy interest which then was debated at some length in India.[4]

2. Personal contacts between research staff and policy makers is difficult to document, but many ideas and research results circulate through this informal mechanism.

3. Visiting researchers from other institutions also help foster dialogue and exchange of new ideas. When researchers in developing countries are involved, either as hosts or as visitors, this process can represent, through time, a substantial contribution to the process of building capacity for policy analysis in LDCs.

4. Policy seminars are perhaps the most direct instrument for the transmission of research results. Through such seminars the research institute can play an important catalytic role in bringing policy makers together in order to share their experiences and learn from each other as well as from the research itself. The fundamental role of the organizing institute is to identify the agenda and to provide an analytical framework within which discussion can be productive. Such a framework draws on generalizable worldwide experiences resulting from research. It provides a structure within which policy makers can make cross-country comparisons.

Conferences are most appropriate when an institute has accumulated through research a substantial stock of knowledge in one policy area. The conference becomes a forum to present research results and to evaluate their policy implications.

Two Illustrations from IFPRI's Experience

At IFPRI some research work has moved quite rapidly into the arena of public policy debate without any explicit outreach activity. For example, this was the case of IFPRI's reports on the effect of commercial policy and exchange rates on Colombian agriculture by Jorge Garcia, and on Argentinian culture by Domingo Cavallo and Yair Mundlak, respectively. The novelty and relevance of the topic, the contacts and the position of the authors in Colombia and Argentina, and the existence of a substantial group of well-trained economists in these countries all helped to aid in the rapid appreciation of these reports.

In contrast, an illustration of a rather comprehensive outreach effort in promoting debate and contribution to policy action was the case of financial schemes for food security. This is a case where research by individuals in several institutions on one particular aspect of food supply strategy filled a crucial gap in the knowledge and policy-making areas. Through publications, meetings, seminars, and conferences, IFPRI engaged in a comprehensive effort designed to assess the relative merits of several initiatives in the food security area, the results of which were printed in book form.[5] Once our conclusions were firm in terms of the advantages of a food financing facility, IFPRI collaborated with the World Food Council and FAO which, as inter-governmental agencies, were the appropriate vehicle to convey to policy makers the need for and feasibility of such an initiative to increase food security.[6]

These examples serve to illustrate the point that research results move into the policy-making process in diverse ways. Part of the art in making food policy is using imagination in bringing research to bear on political decisions in ways which are suitable to the specific issue and the specific environment within each food policy decision necessarily is taken.

NOTES

1. Jorge Garcia Garcia, *The Effects of Exchange Rates and Commercial Policy on Agricultural Incentives in Colombia*, Research Report 24. Washington, DC: International Food Policy Research Institute (June 1981); and Domingo Cavallo

and Yair Mundlak, *Agriculture and Economic Growth in an Open Economy: The Case of Argentina*, Research Report 36. Washington, DC: International Food Policy Research Institute (December 1982).

2. The relationship between research and the policy-making process and its objectives could be the subject of an essay on the philosophy of science. This short chapter is certainly not an attempt at such an essay.

3. Cheryl Williamson, *Food Consumption Parameters for Brazil and Their Application to Food Policy*, Research Report 32. Washington, DC: International Food Policy Research Institute (September 1982).

4. Shakuntla Mehra, *Instability in Indian Agriculture in the Context of the New Technology*, Research Report 25. Washington, DC: International Food Policy Research Institute (July 1981); and Peter Hazell, *Instability in Indian Foodgrain Production*, Research Report 30, Washington, DC: International Food Policy Research Institute (May 1982).

5. Alberto Valdés, ed., *Food Security for Developing Countries* (Boulder: Westview Press, 1981).

6. Richard Adams, *IFPRI Research and the Creation of the IMF Cereal Import Facility*, Washington, DC: International Food Policy Research Institute (August 1982).

DEVELOPING POLITICAL SUPPORT FOR FOOD POLICY PLANNING

Maurice J. Williams

Too little attention has been given in the past to food policy and to the training of people in its requisite skills. Assistance organizations have emphasized projects, without sufficient attention to the need for accompanying economic policy reforms. These issues have become more important since the 1974 World Food Conference, when governments undertook to increase priority efforts to solve food problems.

The Basis of Political Action within Countries

The thesis of this chapter is a fairly simple one, namely that policy reform is brought about by political conviction of the need for change. Such a conviction is often the result of crisis and pressures on a society, including rapidly rising demand for food due to population increase, insecurity of food supplies, and an adverse economic environment. Certainly these pressures are growing in many of the world's poorest countries today. In a real sense, the problem of food shortages is less a global problem than it is a problem for the low-income countries.

Political will is also influenced by a response to human needs. As the food and hunger gap between the affluent nations and the poorer countries continues to widen, there is political pressure within affluent societies to respond more effectively to the situation in poorer countries.

While conviction that change is necessary lays the political foundation for reform, action is made possible only by specific knowledge of what can be done. Without knowing what the options are for addressing a problem, the conviction that it needs to be addressed may not result in any particular action. Indeed, the initial conviction may be lost. Understanding realistic policy options requires knowledge. Given the knowledge, then its diffusion throughout the society and its sustainability through training are important aspects of maintaining political will.

To summarize, the elements of political action for reform are: conviction of the need for change, knowledge of how to respond to the problem which necessitates change, diffusion of that knowledge to policy makers and to the people who will be affected by the reform, and its sustainability through training and public education.

A South Asian Example

In the 1960s, India and Pakistan were pursuing a development strategy based on what has been called the Russian model of rapid industrialization, which meant relative neglect of food and agriculture. The idea behind this strategy was that industrialization offered the best hope for rapid economic growth and that taxing the rural sector would benefit the country as a whole. This policy was made possible by the fact that rising food needs could be met from United States surpluses through PL480. However, the monsoon failure in India in the mid-sixties, and the shipment of 10 million tons of grain to India in a single year highlighted the crisis of growing dependence on food imports. To the governments of India and Pakistan, the United States became less reliable as a supplier when it began to demand performance in political terms in return for continued food aid. As then President Johnson said, "if you sup at our table, you mind your manners." And there was some political specificity behind that observation.

So a major change in development strategy took place in the Indian sub-continent. Political concerns coincided with the availability of new varieties of grain, and South Asia had the management skills for the diffusion of that knowledge and its sustainability. Thus food policy reform in India and Pakistan in the late 1960s was brought about by conviction under duress and was made possible by the knowledge then available and by the diffusion of that knowledge within society. The World Bank and other development agencies played a key role in that process.

The World Food Crisis 1973-75

Another example development strategy is the response to the world food crisis of 1973-75. Although this crisis is now seen as having been caused in part by a market aberration, the crisis was real enough at the time. There was panic behavior on the part of developed and developing countries. In particular, developing countries were deeply concerned about the security of their imported food supplies, and there was a feeling that the food gap was likely to continue to grow unless immediate actions were taken. This sense of crisis led to the 1974 World Food Conference.

The focus of the World Food Conference was on the need to increase agricultural production, as well as to meet immediate emergency measures. Conviction of that need to act led to an increase in agricultural investment, and the level of aid doubled in real terms in the period 1973-78. Nevertheless, this sense of urgency and conviction for change and reform lasted only three to four years. By the end of 1977, with the recovery of world cereal production, the impetus for change had been largely dissipated.

The idea of food policy was not much in evidence at the World Food Conference itself. Indeed, most of the initial impetus for reform was on institutions rather than on issues of substance. The developing countries wished to see the creation of a World Food authority—which was a measure of their concern. Instead, several inter-governmental committees with very broad mandates but very little power were actually established. Thus the initiative for a World Food Council to serve a coordinating function came from Third World countries.

Another of these new inter-governmental organizations was the Consultative Group on Food Production and Investment (CGFPI). Its major focus was to be on policy reform and investment for increasing production. Robert McNamara, then President of the World Bank, promoted the idea that the CGFPI should work on food plans. His concept was that it should be possible for a country to figure out its current food needs, project those needs into the future, and adopt the programs necessary to meet them.

However, the CGFPI did not do very well, perhaps because it was torn between trying to work out the new concept and trying itself to develop the projects that would lead to stepped-up investment. Whatever the reasons, the agencies that financed that Consultative Group—the World Bank, the United Nations Development Program, and FAO—abolished it at the end of 1977. However, there was still some sentiment among developing countries favoring food plans, and they supported the assignment of this activity to the World Food Council.

During 1978-79, the World Food Council resolved, by means of a series of meetings with developing countries and assistance agencies, that national food strategies should be encouraged in order to translate effectively the general priority for resolving food problems into national programs. The objective was to encourage a more integrated policy approach rather than the fragmented project approach and to relate food production to consumption objectives, more or less along the lines that McNamara had stated initially for food plans.

This recommendation was endorsed by the World Food Council at its 1979 meeting in Ottawa, and the developing countries responded beyond any expectation. During the months immediately following the Ottawa meeting, some 30 countries requested the World Food Council to arrange technical assistance for national food strategies. That interest by the developing countries has continued; the number which has requested assistance from the World Food Council is now 50 countries, 30 of them in Africa. Much of the interest was certainly a conviction that food strategies would satisfy a need for more integrated planning, please donors, and thereby generate additional assistance. But it was more than that.

As they realized four years ago, the low-income food-deficit countries are facing an increasingly harsh international economic environment with adverse terms and reduced trade earnings. They do not have the discretionary foreign exchange to continue the food imports they need, and dependence on food aid is rising. Consequently, they must give higher priority to domestic food production. By the same token, the donor countries are interested in food strategies as a means of stimulating more effective production policies and reducing food aid dependence. Hence, more integrated national food policies are of concern to both developing and developed countries.

Food Issues at the Top of the Global Agenda

During 1980-81, the issue of food went to the top of the global agenda. This concern came as a surprise to many because in the proposed United Nations agenda for global negotiations, food was not mentioned. Previously, food was regarded as subsidiary to issues of finance, trade, energy, and commodities. This change occurred in part because of a general feeling that the stalemate in global negotiations might be broken by focusing on an area in which there was the widest possible agreement among all countries that more should be done. Also, more emphasis on food problems might help to sustain aid programs which were beginning to falter. As a result, wide support for food strategies was expressed by many countries during the course of 1981.

The Cancun Summit meeting concluded that "developing countries should define and put into operation, with the aid of ample and effective international support, national food strategies" as a first measure to overcome world hunger, and the Ministers of the European Community in early 1982 affirmed that assistance to agricultural development requires a stable framework of supporting policies and structures, "and above all a food sector strategy." Thus a number of development assistance agencies undertook to support the food strategies of interested countries as a basis of improved food policies and mutual commitment of necessary resources.

What is the role of the World Food Council in mobilizing political will and initiating change? First of all, it has a small secretariat, 12 food specialists. It has a mandate from the UN General Assembly for policy guidance and general coordination, but not for implementing programs. What we have therefore sought to do is to match developing-country requests for food strategy assistance with interested international agencies and bilateral donors. These agencies then provide technical assistance for the preparation and implementation of the food strategies. However, the World Food Council Ministers at their annual meetings have sought to set guidelines, using the results of regional workshops which reflected specific country experience. And we have undertaken to monitor the results.

Thirteen African countries have completed the initial phase of their food strategies (Cameroon, Cape Verde, Gambia, Kenya, Mali, Mauritania, Morocco, Niger, Nigeria, Rwanda, Tanzania, Zaire, and Zambia). In some cases, such as Nigeria, the results are being embodied in the national development plans. In others, such as the Philippines, elements of the strategies are being implemented. So far the results are not too striking. Countries have been proceeding at their own pace, which is often slow because of conflicting and vested interests. But there has been progress. The priority for food has been raised, and there is a clearer understanding of the need for more integrated policies. Many governments are still feeling their way in the area of food policy reforms.

There are certain minimum conditions for involvement by the World Food Council. The developing country should request help at the ministerial level and assure high-level support for the strategy effort. Whereas policy analysis and planning is a fact-finding process, food policies are politically sensitive and the essential decision must be made by developing-country leaders. The Council facilitates direct policy dialogue between the developing country and assistance agencies to gain essential technical and financial support. Inevitably this dialogue involves elements of bargaining and persuasion. For its part, the World Food Council tries to avoid telling governments or agencies what to do, although its involvement has some influence.

The Importance of Food Policy Analysis

While there is now fairly broad acceptance by governments of the need to deal more effectively with their food problems in terms of policy adjustments, knowledge of the means for doing so is often inadequate. Food policy planning is an area in which experience has been limited until recently. Today, food policy staffs are being built up by the World Bank, members of the European Community, and the United States. IFPRI has stepped up its work on food policy. The Japanese have expressed great interest. Although there is conviction of the need to address food policy issues, the knowledge for doing so is not entirely in place.

Certainly there is a conviction of urgency, particularly in Africa and in other low-income areas, and there is a consensus that there must be better use of aid and other resources. Also, there is agreement that more of a program approach is needed, rather than solely a project approach, and that the incentive structure for production needs to be improved in many countries in relation to consumption needs. Several bad policies have been followed in the past, and many specialized interests are built into those bad policies, so that proposals for reform also have to take into account the political problems involved.

Food sector strategies represent a recent response to a sense of crisis. The process of using them to develop political support and sustained economic assistance for policy reform in a number of countries is only beginning. Part of the process is to create a built-in capability within developing countries to facilitate decisions and the implementation of food policies. The development-assistance agencies have the means to train people in food policy analysis. More needs to be done here. As developing countries gain the requisite skills and greater experience with food strategies, the political base for tackling food policy issues and reforms will be strengthened accordingly.

In conclusion, conviction of the need for reform generates political support, but this support must be buttressed by relevant knowledge, and that knowledge must be diffused to policy makers and consolidated through education and training. The knowledge base on food policy issues must be extended through further analysis and experience.

A good deal is known about incentives for food production, about the introduction of new agricultural technologies, about the ways to take into account the weak market position of the poor and the marginalization of disadvantaged, small subsistence producers, including women. And a good deal is known about the income and food distribution effects of aid — what works and what does not work in projects — at the local level. But much less is known about how to relate micro-level issues to food policy on the country level.

If we could relate more effectively projects at the local level to sensible national food policies, I think we could mount a major effort to reduce hunger. There is tremendous political interest in doing so, but there is also hesitation as to whether the knowledge is adequate to carry through effectively on such programs.

While more research is important, it should not be used as an excuse to delay assistance in helping to relieve food deficits and hunger. There is an immediate need to bring forward what is already known from past experience and to capitalize on the high political concern with food problems in the developing regions. People who are living on the margin of subsistence need help now. Can we draw on what we know now about what works effectively to move forward with new, imaginative programs, while working simultaneously to build and strengthen the knowledge base? Unless we do, mobilization of political support in itself will not be enough to get the job done in the area of food policy and the alleviation of hunger.

THE FOOD POLICY ANALYSIS PROJECT IN THAILAND: AN OVERVIEW

Snoh Unakul

Thailand, being a food surplus country, faces a different set of food policy issues than do other developing countries. For instance, attainment of food self-sufficiency is not a policy issue in Thailand. The threat of famine, the vulnerability of food imports, and the role of foreign food aid are not central to our food policy formulation. Food, far from being a drain on our foreign exchange earnings, is *the* major source of our export earnings. Thailand has been for several decades a major world exporter of rice. Other food and feed items exported are maize, sugar, tapioca, fruits, and fishery products.

The existence of food surpluses for export, however, does not imply that all food-related problems have been solved. While hunger as such is not a problem in Thailand, malnutrition persists both in urban slums and in backward rural areas. Production of increasing food surpluses does not necessarily mean that agricultural productivity has been rising, nor that farmers' incomes have been improving. Nor does the existence of exportable surplus prevent the consumer prices for food from rising; far from it, food exports tend to pull the domestic food prices to world price levels which might be both unacceptably high and disruptively unstable. Moreover, it is not uncommon, even in food surplus countries, for the consumers to pay high prices for food and the farmers to be receiving low prices, the large discrepancy being accounted for by high marketing costs and excessive marketing margins due to inefficiencies and market imperfections. Last but not least, we cannot claim that we always make the best of our export opportunities. Export of large quantities of food at the right time would benefit both Thailand and its customers. There is a certain sense of responsibility which goes with being a major world food exporter; Thailand would like to live up to that.

Food policy analysis can make a substantial contribution towards a more effective policy formulation by analysing the issues and predicting the qualitative and quantitative effect of alternative policies. The policy maker can then consider the various policy options presented by the policy analyst and make a choice based on their cost effectiveness in achieving the stated objectives as well as on political considerations.

While food policy analysis on an *ad hoc* basis has been practiced for some time in Thailand, one of the first attempts to conduct systematic policy analysis on a number of related issues has been the Food and Agricultural Policy Analysis Project, undertaken jointly by National Economics and Social Development Board and Kasetsart and Thammasat Universities, under the sponsorship of the Rockefeller Foundation, with technical input from both the Foundation and the Agricultural Development Council.

The Food Policy Analysis Project is of considerable importance to Thailand because it comes at a time when the government is planning a new strategy for sustainable growth and a more equitable distribution of income against a background of both serious problems (such as the deterioration of basic natural resources, depletion of land frontier, low yields, etc.) and unique opportunities (such as the improved energy and fertilizer situation and a critical mass of intellectual resources).

The Food Policy Project is a response to these problems and opportunities, a forum for articulating the needs for policy changes and evaluating policy options. We regard it as a catalyst to establish a link between analysts and policy makers, to facilitate the flow of information and to demonstrate the usefulness of policy analysis in decision making. It is a small effort, but we hope an exemplary one.

The overall objectives, targets, and strategies are broadly established in the Fifth National Economic and Social Development Plan (1982–1986):

> The Fifth Plan calls for restructuring the production process, improving efficiency in the utilization of land, water and forestry resources, and fishing grounds, and improving the agricultural marketing and pricing system in order to create greater justice for farmers by emphasizing the target to "raise agricultural productivity" as an essential principle. This target is based on the fact that the future expansion of cultivated area will be very limited. The Plan also intends to increase the standard of living and income of farmers, and thus simultaneously reduce the problems of rural poverty (p. 47).

The role of food policy analysis is to assist in the formulation of specific policies and programs to achieve the overall targets. We expect that each of the studies will be both good economics and good policy analysis. Further, we expect that the process of the research, the quality of the results, and the wide dissemination of the implications in a form comprehensible to the policy makers will be compelling enough to affect not only the commodities and processes studied but also the design and standards of future studies. The time is right, the opportunities are here, and the resources we have gathered, with the help of the Foundation, are appropriate for the task. Our expectations are that by the end of this Project, we will have made considerable progress towards the attainment of our targets:

1. Awakened interest and expertise among Thai scholars in agricultural policy analysis;

2. Increased awareness among policy makers of the usefulness of policy analysis in decision making;

3. Strengthened linkages between policy analysts and decision makers;

4. A number of high-quality analytical studies that will have some effect on policies, as well as form paradigms for future policy analysis and research;

5. A group of experienced policy analysts with strengthened analytical capabilities who have conducted these studies and can continue working in the field, as well as instruct others in the techniques; and

6. Substantial progress towards institutionalizing policy analysis in Thailand.

As we are approaching the completion of the project, it is appropriate to take stock. That progress has been made towards the project's objectives there is little doubt. The question is: *how much* progress? It is true that policy analysis was not unknown and some analytical capability was available when the Project started two years ago. It was not uncommon for policy makers (government departments, NESDB, etc.) to commission policy-analysis studies to University staff. In fact, a number of the participants in the Food Policy Analysis Group, prior to their joining of the Program, have carried out policy related research for NESDB and other government agencies. However, this practice was more the exception than the rule. The Project's role is to provide momentum through research on a wide spectrum of issues of interest to the policy makers and to provide them with understandable and implementable policy options. Whether this has been accomplished is too early to say, since the policy makers have not yet been presented with the Group's final research output.

What can be said at this stage with confidence is that there has been considerable improvement in the participants' analytical capability as evidenced both by the sophistication of their research output and the growing demand for their services from government agencies and international organizations. Still, we have a long way to go before a sustained dialogue between policy analysts and policy makers is established and food policy analysis in Thailand is put on a sound institutional basis.

THE INTEGRATED RESEARCH PROJECT APPROACH AND ITS RESULTS

George E. Delehanty and Laurence D. Stifel

A small but significant effort to develop food policy analysis capability in Thailand reached a milestone, of sorts, with a workshop held in Bangkok on 7th and 8th October, 1982. The milestone was the discussion and criticism of eight papers on different aspects of the Thai food and agriculture policy system. This chapter, along with those of Drs. Panayotou and Kosit, summarizes the development, both intellectually and practically, of that project and sets forth some generalizations which may be worth the consideration of any agency contemplating related programs.

The project grew out of and builds upon earlier Rockefeller Foundation-Thai cooperation, particularly the Education for Development programs at Thammasat and Kasetsart Universities. Dr. Snoh Unakul observed that much of Thailand's best analytical talent was engaged in well-paid but relatively unimportant and unrelated research tasks. He proposed to the Foundation a project that would draw together a food policy research group which could focus their attention on some of Thailand's most important problems. A series of separate research projects would be designed within a unifying, overall framework, and the group's work related closely to the policy-making process.

The general features of the Thai policy context within which the project was carried out are as follows:

1. Frequent changes of government with military figures playing a key role in directing a stable and increasingly sophisticated bureaucracy;

2. Reliance on exports of food and agricultural crops, especially rice, sugar, cassava, maize, and rubber.

3. Recent awareness that frontiers of expansion into new lands rapidly are being approached;

4. Generally low productivity per unit of land in virtually all agriculture, particularly in rice;

5. A strongly skewed income distribution, with Bangkok as a relatively wealthy City-State and the most populous region, the Northeast, subject to poverty and serious nutritional problems. The food and agricultural policy system can be characterized, until recently, as reinforcing this structural difference through many policy instruments;

6. A recent but relatively strong consensus at high levels in government that the welfare of the poorest rural people must be improved; substantial resources have been devoted to promoting this objective, under the guidance of the planning agency;

7. A policy-making system and policy for agriculture that is highly diffuse, and, in Thai style, highly personalized;

8. Balance of payments problems, coming later than they had to most LDCs, but acute enough to stimulate reappraisal of many agricultural policies;

9. Pressures from the IBRD and the IMF to improve the policy process as part of structural adjustment;

10. A rapid growth in the number of Ph.D. level economists in the country as a result of Rockefeller Foundation and other fellowship programs; most of whom are in academic institutions, and poorly paid;

11. A rather poor research environment in which university budgets could allocate a maximum of five percent to research expenditures.

In this context a program was organized, coordinated by Dr. Snoh Unakul (at that time yet to become head of the planning agency). The program's aim was to focus on major commodities and problem areas, and it was staffed by faculty members from two universities and by specialists in rural development from the planning agency. Particular projects were developed by researchers along the lines of their own interests but within the general program focus. A major consideration was that each researcher should be able to specialize, develop his or her skills in policy analysis, interact with the other researchers as well as scientists, and (not incidentally) supplement his or her income. For reasons of necessity and strategy, a substantive objective was to complete, within two years, a set of monographs which would be professionally sound, aimed at policy options and be "required reading" for any analyst or policy maker dealing with that topic in the future.

There was real and substantial demand for the research undertaken by the project. A vigorous agriculture was widely seen as being a condition of economic growth. The fact that Thailand is a food exporter makes this no less important.

While there was strong interest in what we have defined as food policy, it was equally clear that the Thai research and academic community was not structured to look at the range of interrelationships which characterize this approach, particularly viewing food and agriculture as a system of interacting markets. Moreover, the community of economists is small and fragile in Thailand, though increasing with each generation. The first generation in Thailand after World War II had only four or five Ph.D. economists, most notably Dr. Puey. In Dr. Snoh's generation, there are perhaps 10 to 15. Now in Mr. Kosit's generation, there are over 50. Nonetheless, the supply is still insufficient both because this new generation has replaced expatriates and because demand for economic analysis is increasing rapidly.

The food policy project experience showed that talent in analysis is still scarce. In Thailand too much money is chasing too few good people. This situation both raises the prices and lowers the quality of the product. Moreover, a Ph.D. in agricultural economics does not guarantee that an individual will be good at doing policy analysis. In this respect, the experience of doing analysis has had, for project researchers, tremendous benefits. It is hard to describe this in a single dimension, since the gains were maturity, confidence, subtlety, skepticism, technical skills, and many other things, in addition to knowledge. At the final workshop, the researchers were scarcely recognizable as the same people who had silently and glumly sat through the early working meetings. Perhaps this development of human capital is the most important result of the project. It carries with it, of course, the implication that the participants *needed* the experience. Furthermore, there are and have been very few opportunities for comparable experiences. Some reasons for this lack are unique to Thailand; others are found in almost every LDC. A sketchy list is as follows:

1. Incentives for doing high-quality research are not well developed;

2. Status considerations have such unfavorable effects as inhibiting peer review and collegial cooperation; in particular Thais are quite reluctant to admit ignorance, ask for help, or even ask for advice;

3. Legitimacy of the university as performing a role as constructive critic is not well developed;

4. There is a clear bias toward independence, that is, single-person rather than multidisciplinary research.

5. Graduate study in agricultural economics appears to have some bias toward studying processes (marketing, management) rather than analysis of the complete system that affects a particular commodity;

6. Projects which pay the highest honoraria are those with the shortest time horizon;

7. Consultancy pays more per day than research;

8. University lecturers are civil servants; when they do analysis for the government, they are normally paid only for attending official meetings.

Although rare, some opportunities for similar experiences do arise. The World Bank sponsored a group study of agricultural marketing, and USAID financed a major study of off-farm employment as well as the long-term Iowa State University Crop Model Project. On the criterion of human capital development, the food policy project compares very favorably with such examples.

The project has three major characteristics. First, while basically an academic research group, there was clear and strong linkage with the National Economic and Social Development Board through both Dr. Snoh and Dr. Kosit, Director of the NESDB's Development Studies Division. Although the pressures of their duties restricted how much they could interact with the group, this relationship with the policy-making process was important to the project. Among other things, it has resulted in some of the project insights being incorporated into the five-year plan.

The second characteristic is the early development of a conceptual framework which provided an important focus for the work. This was both a useful analytical and pedagogical device which helped the group to think through the linkages among the various sub-projects and with major government objectives. While the framework was not identical to the one proposed by Timmer (pp. 17–25), it served a similar purpose. With the separate groups working on various aspects of the framework, the plan was to draw them all together at project end into a grand synthesis. One problem in this regard is the difficulty of incorporating a wide variation in quality within such a unified final product.[1]

The third key characteristic is the fact that the research agenda was set by Thais. This was a critical point distinguishing this from other research. It had the effect of shifting the intellectual balance from the developed country to the developing country side of the table. Such a shift can alter fundamentally the nature of the policy debate. For example, for over 20 years there has been a vigorous debate on rice-tax policy. The interests of the Thai farmer traditionally have been championed by expatriate economists, arguing against the misallocation of resources caused by the so-called rice premium. Only recently their place has been taken by Thai economists, several of whom are former Rockefeller Foundation Fellows, writing persuasively on the function and structure of the domestic rice market. Their public stance on this issue is another example of the growing professional self-confidence of the Thai economist community.

Turning to the substance of the project, the approach and therefore the results have been biased towards the micro side. In retrospect, this approach appears to have been correct. The Thai economy is very open, and trade economists have been working on macro issues for many years. Yet the serious micro-analysis for many areas simply has not been done.

Early in the program, we all shared the presumption that we could carry out meaningful analysis with secondary data. Yet in each project it became clear, within the first year, that many kinds of data had never been collected or produced because micro-studies had not been made. A second reason will make all present or former teachers of elementary economics smile. We continue to be surprised at how rare is the belief in allowing market processes to allocate goods and services. It is not only rare among students, it is often not found among important figures in policy making. As to the researchers, the project work enhanced considerably their understanding of markets. They had received rigorous technical training in the United States (linear programming, introductory supply and demand elasticities, production functions), but they were inexperienced regarding fundamental food policy relations and the role of process and markets. The basic principles of efficiency, opportunity costs, and how policies affect these variables were unfamiliar to them, and they lacked knowledge of how decisions are made. A large part of the dynamism of the Thai agricultural economy is due to a vigorous competitive market operating within tight contractural constraints. (See Delehanty, pp. 113–16). The project experience facilitated a critical learning process by the researchers about the nature of this dynamic.

In addition to the substantive aspects of the project experience, there are procedural implications as well. One set has to do with stipends and honoraria and the need to investigate the possibility of more direct incentive schemes. A perennial problem is the location of the program. The Rockefeller Foundation made a grant to one university with the Rector delegating administrative responsibility to the local Foundation office and substantive responsibility to Dr. Snoh and his deputy. We still see no better alternative. But there were problems. The Rector of the grantee university was not re-elected, and his influence was lost, particularly with his own staff members. Individual researchers made clear very early that they really wanted control over "their" money. Whether they would have worked harder under such an arrangement is an interesting question. Finally, the logistical problems of researchers in three separate locations, given Bangkok traffic, cost much in efficiency.

To maximize human capital effects, we planned for each project to have one Ph.D. researcher and an associate, intended to be at the Master's level. Researchers chose their associates, who in two cases were also at the Ph.D. level. Our experience with this system was mixed. In at least one case, the associate did most of the work, while in another the associate did very little. Again, as a feature of the Thai system, changes in these relationships proved very difficult.

In retrospect, it might have been useful to include biological scientists along with economists in the process. More interaction with agricultural and planning practitioners would have improved the realism of the analysis. While this was increasing as the project went along, there still is not a great deal of involvement with practitioners.

Although we believe all of the researchers are now capable of preparing a good research proposal, initially none of them were good. This situation is not uncommon, but it requires a great deal of negotiation between the funder and the prospective researcher to achieve a respectable proposal draft. Consequently, start-up costs are high and must be expected in any food policy project of this type.

Workshops were used to enforce deadlines, inform others of the work done, and get outside comment on the analysis and policy implications. We believe they are essential and that ours were quite successful. The major difficulty lay in achieving enough pressure to get the right people to attend. For maximum effectiveness, a briefing session is needed when the final papers are completed, with executive summaries polished and condensed for those who most need the information.

An implication of the scarce talent conclusion is that the greatest demands are for the rental of human capital, once it exists. The demands for the services of our researchers are high and rising. But willingness to invest in the *production* of the human capital is low and falling. The issue is how to design a system of research financing that contains a component of contributions to fixed costs or at least toward replacement of that very scarce factor, analytical talent.

As to institutionalizing the talent created through this project, both Dr. Snoh and Mr. Kosit report that the NESDB has learned enormously from the experience both in terms of specific results and in terms of how to use the process for other policy issues. Several other projects will use this one as a model. It has given confidence to government officials as well as researchers to speak more forthrightly. It has provided a different perception of the nature of the food policy problem and suggested a different agenda for research than would have been proposed three years ago. It has encouraged intellectual interaction instead of the more customary tendency of Thai researchers to work alone.

The researchers have acquired more intellectual maturity and have been established on paths of professional development where they can make a continuing contribution, if they remain on the course set. They can now defend their own findings and competently challenge others. The main question is whether they will be drawn off course by the reward system, which pays so much more for short-term work, and by the heavy demands for researchers' time.

The Rockefeller Foundation has learned several lessons: food policy analysis projects must be country-specific; they are people intensive; their value becomes embodied in the participants; they build importantly on prior investments in human capital, in this case the heavy RF investment in faculty development at Thammasat and Kasetsart Universities. The future sources of replenishment of this stock of capital are a matter of concern.

As to the monographs themselves, their quality and potential impact, it is too early to reach firm conclusions. There is a fairly wide range of quality: they will not all merit respectable publication. All need revision, particularly in drawing out all of the policy implications from the analysis and making them explicit. A paper to synthesize the studies would be useful; there are plenty of findings to stress and relate to each other. Such a paper should also try to compensate for what is insufficient attention to linkage issues in individual papers. Despite many frustrations, the average quality is higher than it would have been in the absence of Foundation and A/D/C technical help.

Like most human efforts, the program has had problems and the results have imperfections. Yet the conclusion is clear that both Thailand and the Rockefeller Foundation got good value for their efforts and resources. For the future, Dr. Snoh seeks to create an autonomous policy institute similar to the Korean Development Institute, but the creation of this institute does not seem likely to come about soon. However, the Thais have enormous capacity for organizational innovation; and if they want it badly enough, some means will probably be found to sustain and build upon the initial investment represented by the food policy project.[2]

NOTES

1. See Theodore Panayatou, ed., *Food Policy Analysis in Thailand* (Bangkok: Agricultural Development Council, 1985).

2. Attesting to the accuracy of the latter observation, the Thai Development Research Institute has since been founded with food and agricultural policy high on its agenda.

THE CONCEPTUAL FRAMEWORK FOR THE FOOD POLICY ANALYSIS PROJECT IN THAILAND

Theodore Panayotou

Introduction

Conducting food policy analysis in a country which consistently produces exportable surpluses of food in some ways is a more challenging task than analyzing policies in food-deficit countries striving for self-sufficiency. In a food surplus country the *raison d'etre* for food policy analysis is not evident; the attainment of a food surplus is seen as evidence of already successful food policies.

The existence of food surplus provides room for complacency. Without a real, perceived, or potential crisis, there is little pressure or justification for change.

Yet while substantial quantities of rice and other foods are being exported every year it cannot be claimed that the domestic food problem has been adequately solved. While hunger as such is not a serious problem in Thailand, malnutrition persists both in urban slums and in the rural areas of the Northeast and the North. Moreover, the absence of hunger as a serious problem in Thailand is due more to the wide distribution of land ownership and the control of the domestic price of rice than to the production of food surpluses. After all, surplus is a relative term depending on both supply and domestic demand for food, which are functions of producer and consumer prices, respectively. In principle, any country can generate a food surplus for export by raising the domestic price of food sufficiently to choke off a large portion of the demand and to induce additional supplies. In the last century, a Russian minister of finance concluded, "We must export, though we die" or as Robert Cassen has been attributed with interpreting it, "I shall export, though you die."[1]

The Fundamental Food Policy Issue in Thailand

One of the fundamental problems of food policy in Thailand is the determination of the exportable food surplus, that is, the allocation of food production between domestic consumption and exports. Moreover, the quantity of food produced is not independent of its allocation. For instance, were the rice export taxes to be eliminated and domestic rice prices allowed to rise to the world market levels, both more rice would be produced and a larger proportion would be exported.[2] In fact, the free market solution is the easiest way to determine this allocation, but it is also the least acceptable outcome to policy makers because of its social welfare and political implications. While the producers of food and the economy as a whole would be better off, the urban poor and the rural laborers will be worse off because they would have to pay higher prices for food.

In theory, those who gain can compensate those who lose, but in the absence of actual compensation (and redistributive mechanisms are often inoperative in LDCs) the problem remains. (On this point, see Selowsky, pp. 102–105.)

On the socioeconomic side, among those who would suffer from higher food prices are those who are already malnourished and close to the margin of hunger; on the political side, among the losers would be the urban consumers who are geographically concentrated and politically organized. There are several other reasons why a free market solution would be unacceptable, including the instability of the world market, the variability of production, and government's desire to exercise control using food as a strategic commodity.

Policy analysis can help to answer the question of the allocation (and hence the determination) of food production by considering food as seen from the standpoint of different socioeconomic and political agents. The commercial farmer sees food mainly as a source of income; the subsistence farmer sees food as a means of subsistence and survival; the urban consumer and the rural laborer see food as a wage good; and the policy maker sees food as a source of foreign exchange, of government revenues, and as a strategic commodity which can be used as a means of control, as a political weapon, or as an instrument of social welfare.

Food prices are policy instruments to the government, returns to the farmer, and costs to the consumer. Agricultural input prices are also policy instruments to the government, costs to the farmers, and returns to the owners of factors of production/consumers (e.g., wages for agricultural labor). The configuration of input and output prices, factor endowments (land, labor, and capital), agricultural technology, and consumer preferences largely determine the input and output mix and its distribution; that is, the amount of food (and non-food) produced, its domestic consumption, and export—largely, but not entirely—because the social and institutional framework, infrastructure, and weather variability also play a role. The government can change the input and/or output prices, improve agricultural technology, redistribute factor endowments, provide more infrastructure, alter consumer preferences, or modify the institutional framework. Redistribution of assets is the most radical policy and hence politically the least palatable, as the efforts at land reform have shown. Similarly, the institutional framework and consumer preferences are not easy to change, at least not in the short run. For these reasons, governments have focused their policies on (a) manipulating prices, (b) providing infrastructure, and (c) improving and extending agricultural technology. The first is a short-term instrument, while the other two are medium to long-run instruments. (On the relative political utility of these approaches, see Bates, pp. 106–12.)

Objectives of Government Intervention

In intervening in the production and consumption of food, governments aim at certain socioeconomic and political objectives. The socioeconomic objectives are basically agricultural growth, alleviation of poverty/inequality, and improvement of nutritional status of the population. Agricultural growth is understandable in the context of overall economic growth to improve the levels of living of a growing population. Increased agricultural production means more food consumed and/or exported. If prices do not fall much, it means also higher farming incomes and more foreign-exchange earnings. On the other hand, to the extent that domestic food prices are reduced and food consumption is responsive to prices, the real incomes of consumers (including the urban poor and rural labor) will improve, and hunger will be alleviated.

Malnutrition, however, may persist if the wrong type of food is being consumed. Whether inequality will be reduced or increased depends, among other things, on the relative percentages of the increase in production and the fall in prices and on the price responsiveness of the food consumption of low-income groups compared to that of higher-income groups. For example, it is important whether the food item (whose production has increased and price dropped) is rice or meat.

The concern with the alleviation of poverty and inequality as a specific objective arises from disillusionment with agricultural and general economic growth as the only means of alleviating poverty and improving income distribution. Agricultural growth, whether measured in volume or value terms, is too aggregate a concept to reveal what happens to individual income groups as the input-output mix changes. Even as the per capita income in the farming sector rises, it is possible that certain groups become poorer. For instance, a change in relative prices in favor of a crop grown in one area and against the crop grown in another may register as agricultural growth if the former offsets the latter; nevertheless, the farmers in the latter group are now worse off if they cannot switch to a more profitable crop.[3] Naturally, poverty and distributional considerations require disaggregation of data down to specific areas, crops, and income groups. The effects of each policy (or exogenous change) on each group must be studied separately and compared to those on other groups to determine both absolute and relative changes in income position. Where agricultural growth and poverty/inequality reduction are in conflict, it is necessary to determine appropriate trade-offs.

Finally, the concern with nutrition arises from a presumption that the additional income brought about through poverty/inequality reduction is not sufficient (in magnitude, speed, or effectiveness) to improve nutritional status to the desired extent because of bad food habits, lack of nutritional education, unavailability of nutritious food, and so forth. Here, there is an effort to change consumption patterns through direct or indirect modification of consumer preferences.

The political objectives of the government include remaining in office and retaining control of the country and the economy. In this context, the government will pursue its socioeconomic objectives to the extent that its political objectives are also realized. For example, a government would resist a policy which calls for a substantial rise in urban food prices, even if this policy might be the most cost-effective means of achieving its socioeconomic objectives of agricultural growth with equity. It is also important for policy analysts to recognize that the policy makers are facing budgetary and administrative constraints, as well as demands from different pressure groups with varying influence.

The Scope of Food Policy Analysis

The objective of policy analysis is to determine a set of policy options (of varying cost-effectiveness and political acceptability) for the attainment of the acknowledged socioeconomic objective of respectable growth with a more equitable distribution of income, with less poverty and better nutrition. While it is not clear how much growth is respectable or how much improvement in income distribution and nutrition is desirable, it is clear that only policies which lead to improvement in these indices are relevant, and hence alternative policies should be evaluated in terms of their growth (efficiency), distributive and nutritional outcomes. There are four broad categories of policy instruments relevant in the short to medium-run: (a) input and output prices, (b) infrastructure, (c) agricultural technology (research and extension), and (d) social services and special welfare programs. Redistribution of assets and direct income transfers are not considered for reasons explained earlier.

It is explicitly recognized that the food problem is partly a problem of income distribution and partly a problem of food production. From the observation that people who are not poor do not go hungry nor are they severely malnourished, one may conclude that the food problem is a problem of distribution of wealth (assets or income). However, given the prevailing distribution of wealth and the difficulty of effecting substantial changes over the short-run, food prices determine the ability to buy food. And here lies the role of food production, in that the larger the food production the lower the food prices, assuming a closed economy (no exports or imports of food). Other things being equal, ability to produce more means ability to consume more.

Once the opportunity for exports is introduced, the connection between domestic food production and domestic food prices is weakened, unless government intervenes to break the link between domestic and world food prices. This fact raises the question of how much and what type of government intervention is appropriate, given the objectives of equitable agricultural growth and improved nutrition. Because of the complexity and interdependency of the system, such a question cannot be answered without an analytical framework which serves to highlight the key relationships in the system or to organize the relevant information and to trace the effects of different policies through the system. An analytical framework also helps to identify linkages and minimize inconsistencies.

In formal terms, the framework consists of technical (agronomic) relationships, behavioral (socioeconomic), and structural ones describing the workings of the system. While the interdependence in the system is fully recognized, for manageability the analysis may be conducted in two stages: (a) the study of technical and behavioral relationships of different components (production, distribution, consumption, and export) of the system, and (b) the synthesis and structural analysis. Below we describe the first stage of the analysis starting within the production component.

A Framework for Policy Analysis

To attain the objective of equitable growth in the predominantly agricultural economy of Thailand with its dwindling land frontiers and wide income differentials between rural and urban areas, it is imperative that agricultural productivity (both per man and per unit of land) be raised.

Thus, the crucial policy issue is to make available and induce the farmers to use those inputs and farming practices which will bring about a sustained increase in land-and-labor productivity. To accomplish this goal, it is necessary to identify the objectives and constraints that shape farmers' behavior and hence their response to incentives and penalties introduced by governmental policies. Then the most effective set of policies will be that which rearranges the alternatives facing the farmer in such a way as to make most attractive to him the alternative that serves best the national objectives. This rearrangement involves reconciling the farmer's interest in assured subsistence and relative profitability with the society's concern with average agricultural productivity and total food production.

The individual farmer may devote part of his land and labor to the production of sufficient food for his family and part to the production of cash crops. What quantities of purchased inputs (fertilizer, seeds, insecticides) he uses depend on their productivity and relative prices, as well as on the availability of prerequisite inputs, such as irrigation and credit. These factors, along with the relative prices of the various crops (and the risk associated with each), determine the farmer's crop production, which when summed over all farmers gives rise to the total agricultural production and its composition.

Government policies may induce an increase in agricultural production or a change in its composition by extending new production technologies, by effecting favorable changes in input and output prices, by providing infrastructure such as irrigation and credit facilities and, in general, by making more profitable to the farmer the cultivation of crops and the use of inputs which bring about sustainable increases in productivity and incomes.

Among the factors necessary for increasing agricultural productivity, irrigation is of particular importance not only because of its direct role in increasing yields but also because of its indirect contribution in making possible the use of other productivity-augmenting inputs, such as fertilizers and high-yielding varieties, as well as the introduction of new farming technologies, such as multiple cropping. The analysis of the costs and benefits of existing irrigation facilities and of their distribution has policy implications for their management (e.g., water pricing), as well as for the construction and apportionment of new irrigation systems.

While agricultural growth may raise per capita incomes, it may not improve, and in fact it may further polarize, income distribution. For agricultural growth to contribute to a reduction in poverty, policies for increasing agricultural productivity should be matched by policies for increasing rural employment to absorb the surplus labor and keep rural-urban migration in line with the absorptive capacity of the industrial sector. Agricultural areas of relatively high productivity have been providing employment opportunities for labor from low-productivity, low-income areas. Analysis of the determinants of labor demand and supply will help formulate policies to encourage this linkage, to improve the efficiency of rural labor markets, and to provide more on- and off-farm employment. Such policies may prevent further polarization of income distribution between regions, but they would not eliminate the need for land reform and for correction of capital-market distortions if a sustained improvement in income distribution is to be attained.

The extent to which improvements in agricultural productivity benefit the consumer and the farmer—inducing further productivity improvements—depends largely on the efficiency and competitiveness of the intervening marketing channels. Policies to improve the marketing of agricultural crops require knowledge of market structure, of traders' behavior, and of marketing costs for each commodity. An effective marketing policy is one which promotes a system that carries crops and agricultural inputs from the producer to the consumer at minimum cost; for certain commodities this might be accomplished by encouraging competition among traders, while for others, by establishing marketing organizations to take advantage of economies of scale or to ensure quality control.

Since the prices consumers are willing to pay vis-à-vis production and marketing costs determine the relative profitability of various crops, hence the farmers' output mix and total agricultural production, it is equally important to understand consumers' behavior and response to incentives and penalties introduced by government policies. For instance, subsidizing food prices or raising consumers' incomes may or may not significantly increase food consumption, the outcome depending respectively on the price and income elasticities of demand for food; analogously, higher prices for subsistence crops may or may not induce farmers to consume less and sell more of their own crops. Hence, forecasts of future demand for planning purposes must be based on understanding of consumer behavior as well as on income and population projections.

In Thailand, a country with some comparative advantage in the production and export of food and a dire need for foreign exchange, food production is allocated between domestic consumption and export, as noted earlier. If the commodity is not considered a necessity (e.g., shrimp), exports are left free to pull up the domestic price to world price levels. In the case of necessities, such as rice and sugar, a variety of policy instruments, such as export taxes, reserve requirements, and quotas have been introduced to break the linkage between domestic and world price and to attain the dual objective of low domestic food prices and high foreign exchange earnings. A less acclaimed but equally important function of export policies is to tax away the agricultural surplus for development (and recurrent) expenditure, since taxes are most conveniently collected at the export point.

A number of policy analysis questions arise. What are the most efficient/least distorting policy instruments for accomplishing these objectives without nullifying farmers' incentives to improve productivity? How can Thailand maximize its foreign exchange earnings from export crops which account for a relatively large share of the world market (e.g., rice, rubber and sugar)? Should the country withhold supplies, enter international agreements, or attempt to increase its share by undercutting such agreements?

To sum up, a multiplicity of factors, such as production technologies and consumer preferences, farmers' and consumers' behavior, and market structure and government policies interact within the Thai sociopolitical context to bring about the observed magnitudes and distribution of agricultural production, farm income, and food consumption. This outcome may or may not be compatible with the national objectives of increasing agricultural productivity and reducing income inequalities. The objective of the Food Policy Analysis Group is to conduct the necessary analysis of agricultural supply and demand factors which will enable it to assess alternative sets of policies in terms of their effectiveness and efficiency in accomplishing the national objectives.

A component of the national objectives of growth and distribution is the improvement in the dietary standards of the Thai society. However, while income levels largely may determine food intake and nutrition, improvements in incomes alone may not eliminate malnutrition for such reasons such as unavailability of nutritive foods at affordable prices, ignorance of nutritional requirements, and poor dietary habits. (E.g.: Chen, p. 67ff., and Gençağa, p. 80ff.) Moreover, the solution to the pressing problems of malnutrition cannot and should not await the slow process of income growth, particularly because malnutrition adversely affects labor productivity. For these reasons, correction of nutrition deficiencies and general improvement in dietary standards should be sought not only indirectly through general agricultural policies operating through the market mechanism, but also through an explicit food and nutrition policy. (See Timmer, p. 25.) The formulation of such a policy will be based on (a) analysis of current nutritional status (its level and determinants) for various socioeconomic groups and regions, (b) the estimation of optimum nutritional requirements, and (c) identification of the most effective and cost-efficient instruments for bridging the gap between nutritional status and optimum requirements.

By means of this general framework, we have identified six areas for analysis before existing policies can be evaluated and alternative policies formulated:

1. Demand and supply of farming inputs;
2. Demand and supply of agricultural crops and animal protein;
3. Marketing structure of inputs and outputs;
4. Irrigation and agricultural productivity;
5. Employment and income distribution;
6. Food and nutrition.

In order to limit the scope of the project to manageable proportions, among the hundreds of agricultural commodities whose demand and supply or market structure and nutritional aspects could be studied, three related groups of commodities have been selected as the focus for analysis: rice, upland crops, and animal protein.

Rice in Thailand is an obvious choice, as rice policies directly affect the welfare of the entire population. Furthermore, since Thailand exports one-third of the world's traded rice, its role in world food supply is significant. Since intervention in the rice market is the most important policy affecting the relative prices of agricultural products, its study is expected to yield conclusions of both direct and illustrative relevance to policy making for other crops.

Upland crops, such as maize, sugar, tapioca, and kenaf, call for attention not only because of their own significance as the most important crops and export items after rice but also because of their relationships to rice cultivation. Unlike the heavily regulated rice sector which has experienced a slow growth over the last few decades, upland crops (relatively free from government intervention until recently) expanded rapidly both in terms of cultivated area and production. A comparative study of the rice and upland crop policies will provide an explanation of their differential growth as well as policy implications for the government's diversification program.

Animal protein is chosen as the third composite commodity for attention because protein deficiency is the most serious nutritional problem in Thailand. The per capita consumption of fish protein, the traditional source of animal protein, has been declining as a result of population growth, dwindling supplies (due to past over-fishing), and rising prices. The Thai government has an explicit policy to conserve wild fish stocks while improving diets by promoting livestock development and fish culture. Moreover, with Thailand's feed-grain exports facing increasing restrictions in world markets, livestock appears as an alternative (indirect) means of exporting feedgrains to a protein-hungry region.

The rationale behind this choice lies not only in the importance of the above commodities to farmers, consumers, and policy makers, but also in their functional interrelationship: rice competes for land, water, and other farming inputs with upland crops; upland crops compete for land with (as well as provide inputs for) the production of animal protein; animal protein competes with rice for the consumer's income while it is a complement in terms of nutrition. Moreover, the choice of these commodities has implications for regional income distribution. Rice is a purchased staple in the urban areas, a cash crop in the Central Plain, and a subsistence crop in the Northeast, hence the income distribution implications of rice price policies. Livestock and tapioca are of great importance to the Northeast, fisheries to the South, sugar to the Central Plain, and maize to the North. Regional income distribution is affected both by differential crop policies and by uniform input policies because of differences in input requirements among crops.

For manageability, the analysis was divided into six subject areas according to commodities and policy issues involved. However, a logical extension of the exercise (but beyond the scope of the Thailand Project) would be the synthesis of the analytical results of the individual studies, for general policy formulation. Such a synthesis would seek to integrate the individual study findings (and their partial policy implications) in the context of contemporary policy concerns. It would try to evaluate alternative sets of policies in terms of their (direct and indirect) contribution to the attainment of the national objectives: to raise agricultural productivity and real incomes and to reduce inequality and malnutrition. Non-quantifiable effects should qualify the quantitative evaluation of each set of policies. Their relative cost and constraints to their implementation should also be assessed.

Concluding Remarks

While the project's analyses do attempt to understand and incorporate the behavior of the farmers, traders, and consumers of food, one may ask how is the behavior of the policy makers themselves being incorporated into the system. This is done, first, by using the policy makers' expressed socioeconomic objectives as the yardstick by which alternative policies are evaluated; second, by calculating the budgetary requirements and cost-effectiveness of alternative policies; and third, by presenting policy options (rather than policy recommendations) as the outcome of policy analysis. These multiple options allow the policy makers to accommodate their political objectives in the final policy choice. The contribution of policy analysis is seen in the narrowing down of the choice to a set of fairly cost-effective policies, in highlighting inconsistencies, side effects and linkages of policies, and in making policy makers aware of the socioeconomic costs of their policy choices.

NOTES

1. P. F. Bartlett, "Introduction: Development Issues and Economic Anthropology," in *Agricultural Decision Making: Anthropological Contributions to Rural Development*, ed. P. F. Bartlett (New York: Academic Press, 1980), p. 4.

2. This statement assumes that Thailand is a price taker in the world rice market and that the marketing system is an efficient transmitter of price signals.

3. An example is the increase in rice production in one area due to the provision of irrigation which depresses rice prices, adversely affecting rice farmers in the rainfed areas whose production and productivity remained unchanged.

THAILAND
NATIONAL FOOD POLICY
AND THE ROLE OF
EXTERNAL AGENCIES

Kosit Panpiemras

This chapter focuses on some analyses of various aspects of national food policy in Thailand. The chapter will first review some of the major characteristics of the food and agricultural situation in Thailand and the need for more comprehensive food policy. It will identify major problems associated with existing food policy analysis in Thailand and highlight priorities in food policy research within the context of the present food policy system. It will then examine the role of external agencies in food policy formulation and implementation in the light of Thailand's experiences. Finally, it will draw some conclusions as to how to strengthen the food policy system with the aid of external agencies.

Features of Thailand's Food Situation

While Thailand has always been a food exporting country, by no means has it solved all problems related to hunger or malnutrition. There remain several pockets in the rural area where a large number of people in the villages cannot produce sufficient quantities of food, including such staples as rice. Evidence suggests that malnutrition remains an important

The views expressed in this chapter are drawn primarily from the experiences gained by the author in his capacity as a member of Food and Agriculture Policy Research Group, a research project assisted by The Rockefeller Foundation.

problem in backward rural areas particularly in the Northeast, North, and South.

Although Thailand's agricultural growth rate during the past decade has been quite impressive (an average rate of four percent per year), this high growth rate has been achieved largely through expansion of cultivated land. Average yields of most major agricultural products remain low compared to other developing countries. Since the average yield statistics suggest that there is still ample room to improve agricultural productivity, many experts have given a great deal of emphasis to easing marketing and pricing constraints as a means to improve agricultural productivity. However, these statistics in part reflect the low-yield marginal land which has been brought into agricultural use. This area presents difficult technical problems which require much more serious attention. It is difficult to expect average yield to increase substantially without resolving problems related to rain-fed agriculture, particularly in these marginal land areas.

Another challenging problem now is how Thailand can continue to diversify its agricultural production. Fifteen years ago, Thailand depended heavily on rice and rubber as the major source of foreign exchange. Since then a large number of agricultural products have emerged as significant foreign exchange earners, including maize, sugarcane, tapioca, fruits, livestock, and fishery products. In view of today's volatile world food market, continued progress in diversification is important.

Finally, evidence suggests that soil erosion and continued decline in soil fertility have become increasingly serious obstacles to increasing long-term productivity. In some rural areas, productivity has actually shown a declining trend. Any important improvement in this situation will require not only appropriate technology but also improved management capability of millions of farming families.

Framework for Food Policy Analysis

Based on the above picture of the Thai food situation, it is clear that the major objective of Thailand's food policy is not simply to feed adequately its population. Major aspects of traditional food policy, such as productivity and marketing, although very relevant to the Thai situation, are not sufficient to provide a framework for policy decision. Such a framework should address both the short-run and the long-run and take into account environmental, distributional, and foreign trade concerns, not production alone.

In constructing meaningful food policy analysis, one of the major complicating factors is the dynamism of Thai farmers. While this has contributed significantly to the success in the agriculture sector, it creates a situation rendering a traditional commodity approach to food policy analysis much less useful. Farmers in Thailand do change their cropping pattern in response to change in the marketing system and market potential. Although most researchers prescribe reduction in governmental intervention in the market, it is uncertain how much these interventions encouraged the very agricultural diversification which itself is a major success in the agriculture sector. To find out, it is necessary to make the food policy analysis more comprehensive through emphasis on the interaction of a wide range of commodities, rather than focusing on a few particular commodities. It is possible to conceive a system which emphasizes more the role of farmers and less the role of government.

In emphasizing more the role of farmers in food policy analysis, the non-homogeneity of Thai farmers presents a problem. Because of the importance of this factor, the Fifth Five-Year Plan clearly recognizes the dualism existing in the rural economy. Rural areas are therefore divided into backward and progressive in each of our regions. This division permits addressing food policy questions in an area-specific manner. For example, what will be the impact of a specific food policy upon a given area? How would this influence other policy objectives, such as poverty reduction or economic growth? In other words, from a policy standpoint, it appears desirable to be able to analyze food policy with respect to specific areas and other national objectives. Policy makers in reality have to deal with these complex interactions.

A final area of concern is the importance of non-food policies to food policy analysis. This, of course, is one of the more difficult areas, one in which past attempts have been inadequate. In the context of Thailand's national development, emphasis on industrialization and utilization of our new-found resources, such as oil and natural gas, is likely to require substantial financial resources. To the extent that this diverts resources away from food and agriculture, policy makers need to be aware of the serious consequences for the food and agriculture sector. Other countries as well are facing this problem, and Thailand needs to be fully aware of their experiences.

Priorities in Food Policy Analysis

Having described gaps in our present food policy analysis, we can turn now to the question of establishing priorities for our future food policy analysis. Several major attempts already have been made to reduce these gaps. To name just a few, the Rockefeller project gives much emphasis to seasonal employment and migration as a means to link the traditional commodity approach to the area approach. Another major attempt is the work going on at IFPRI to determine the impact of change in food prices on distribution objectives.

In addition to the required synthesis of all these on-going works, additional work is required in at least three areas. First, more emphasis is needed to analyze the impact of a given food policy on different areas and different objectives. Moreover, a prescription related to a single given commodity is unlikely to attract policy makers' attention and thus will be only an academic exercise. Secondly, there is a need to continue to probe the inter-relationship among various factors affecting the food and agriculture sector. Without a comprehensive understanding of the working of the total system, it is unlikely that policy research will be effective. Finally, increased attention is required to the institutional and management aspects of food policy. Realism dictates that any prescriptions should be both manageable and attractive to practitioners. Failing to recognize the importance of these factors will cause careful and costly analyses to go unheeded.

All of the above suggestions are by no means simple. Furthermore, they imply a somewhat different approach to food policy analysis. One minimum requirement for success is that the suggested work be carried out in an inter-disciplinary manner. Continued dialogue among various people of all disciplines related to food policy analysis is very important since it helps to steer numerous, sometimes conflicting, contributions into a useful direction. The yardstick for measuring food policy success is not simply to ask whether or not policy recommendations have been followed. Rather, it is also the extent of the contribution to the promotion of continued interest in food policy.

Role of External Agencies

For the purpose of this chapter, foreign agencies will be classified into agencies chiefly interested in research and study and those whose chief interest is to provide development assistance to Third World countries. For the first category of foreign agencies, the Thai experiences clearly indicate that the more useful role which an external agency can play occurs when its efforts are made at a broad program objective level, rather than at a sectoral or sub-sectoral issues. The danger of ignoring specific problems does not seem to be serious once a broad framework for analysis has been provided. In addition, it appears that the inter-sectoral approach to food policy or to other policies can produce results more meaningful to policy makers.

The organization of external agencies' assistance represents a major factor determining the success or failure of their contribution. In our experiences, external agencies have played a significant role in our institutional building. This approach, however, requires a great deal of financial input as well as a long period of time. A new approach has been tried in Thailand whereby several external agencies are invited to work together to assist one institution. At present, the U.S. and Japanese governments are working together to assist Khon Kaen University, a regional university in the Northeast region. This project has just started, and thus its results still remain to be seen.

Another useful approach concerning foreign agencies' contributions is to have the foreign agency work with a number of institutions under a broad program objective. The food and agriculture policy analysis group assisted by Rockefeller represents one such case. One interesting characteristic of this project is that the national planning agency has been given a role together with a few academic institutions. This approach is very useful, particularly since it opens up opportunities for wider participation in policy formulation and for continued dialogue between academicians, planners, and practitioners. This same approach has been applied to our rural poverty, industry, and land resource programs, and it is being expanded to include human resources and employment programs. Experience indicates that this approach has great potential and should be further encouraged.

For the developmental assistance foreign agencies, serious problems still exist. As Thailand moves from requiring financial assistance in capital construction projects to the soft side of human and organizational development, the role of the foreign agency has not been adjusted accordingly. Everyone knows that it is simple to finance a dam or road or other construction project. However, problems arise when foreign agencies try to use the same approach for the soft side of development. Increasing rapidly in recent years are problems such as unnecessary foreign components, ineffective consultancy service, unnecessarily high construction standards, transfer of inappropriate technology, and ineffective relationships with the local people and organizations. Constraints, of course, exist both within the receiving country and within the donor agency. Insufficient efforts have been made to remove these constraints. This problem threatens to reduce the usefulness of project assistance in non-construction projects in Thailand. At present, efforts are being made to explore the possibility of expanding the so-called program type of assistance. It is too early to say whether or not this relatively new type of assistance is capable of reducing the present problems.

The name of the game between Thailand and foreign agencies in future project assistance should be "quality" and not "quantity." It is difficult to imagine how the quality of project assistance can be improved without having both sides closely collaborate in reducing constraints existing on both sides. In many instances, for example, borrowed technology through consultancy services can do more harm than good. Since consultants have long been the backbone of financial assistance of so many agencies, including the World Bank, this point deserves particular emphasis.

A possible way out of this dilemma is perhaps to link the roles of agencies interested in research to those interested in financial assistance. This approach should be proposed for further consideration for all agencies involved in the development process of an LDC at Thailand's stage of development. Without effectively linking attempts to strengthen policy analysis in the national planning agency with the financing of projects and programs, it is likely that the dilemma will continue and create unnecessary waste in Thailand's resources. This new approach deserves a chance to be put to the test.

Concluding Remarks

In conclusion, the approach used in the food and agriculture policy analysis project represents a move in the right direction. In addition to strengthening the capacity of individual researchers and encouraging a continued dialogue between planners and researchers, inclusion of more institutions and practitioners into the food policy analysis team—with the national planning agency acting as a focal point—will be more effective than creating a new specialized institution dealing with food policy matters. In substantive terms, as mentioned earlier, future food policy analysis should focus on different areas and objectives: on interrelationships among various factors in the food and agricultural sector and on institutional and managerial aspects of food policy. In addition, there is a need periodically to synthesize whatever works are available in this field.

The strengthening of food policy analysis should be viewed as a part of an effort to strengthen the capacity of local institutions and generate more effective local participation in general. There is an urgent need to gear the improved local policy analysis capacity toward a more operational approach. In order to move in this direction, external agencies specializing in project and program financing should become a part of the whole movement. This approach will reduce conflicts between borrowers and donors, reduce waste in unnecessary foreign consultants, and open opportunities for wider participation in policy matters. In order to achieve this goal, the role of the national planning agency needs to be strengthened in such a way that it can act as coordinator of all these efforts. More and more emphasis should be placed on the quality rather than quantity of assistance. In the end, it is easy to see that quality cannot improve without the strong participation of local people and local institutions.

BRIDGING THE GAP BETWEEN ANALYSIS AND ACTION

D. Ralph Campbell, Nairobi

Peter Timmer's food policy framework chapter suggests the complexity of the problems facing decision makers as they seek to improve the effectiveness of the food system to meet national needs. There is widespread recognition that a nation's food policy is determined by the interactions of decisions and actions taken in many ministries and organizations, not just those within ministries of agriculture. Attempts to bring greater consistency to national food policy often result in the locus of decision moving upward in the government bureaucracy to levels which can oversee and mediate the actions of numerous ministries and organizations. In Kenya, the Office of the President plays such a role in attempting to bring consistency and focus to the nation's food policy. It has been my pleasure to work within this Office, in the process learning much about the day-to-day challenges facing my capable Kenyan colleagues as they seek to improve the effectiveness of the food system.

Most of the chapters of this book focus mainly on the analytical process involved in determining *what* to do within the food and agriculture sector. My experience suggests that we should give far more attention to *how* to do it, once decisions have been taken. Countries, like individuals, often know roughly *what* to do but find it terribly difficult to do it. In developing countries, bridging the gap between analysis and action is probably the most difficult and yet the most essential of all activities.

Like building a bridge over a river, the bridge between analysis and action should start at both ends and meet somewhere in the middle. Like a civil engineer's bridge, the two ends (analysis and action) have to be in line, of about the same strength, and with the same purpose. Too often the analysis end of the bridge is broad and well-buttressed, but the action end is narrow and rickety and maybe even some distance downstream. Under these conditions, it is no wonder that a traveler (in this case an idea) has problems crossing. He proceeds to the analysis end, finds a broad sweep of concrete until he reaches the middle, then searches around for a ladder or other *ad hoc* means of getting onto the remaining section. All too often he falls off and floats away shouting, "If they would only listen."

Analysis

Analysis may be of several dimensions. In this chapter, we shall concentrate on analysis at the level of a nation; it could be global or regional, or provincial or sectoral. Of course analysis at the national level should not be done in isolation of the other dimensions because the shortages or surpluses of world markets will affect national plans and programs. The same applies to the impact at the national level of provincial or sectoral analyses and plans.

Food policy analysis should not be undertaken in isolation. Food competes for land and other resources with crops, such as coffee, tea, and cotton which are often the major sources of foreign-exchange earnings. Given the fact that for many developing countries balance of payments rivals the supply of homegrown food as a problem, it would be improper to concentrate on one to the exclusion of the other.

Let us consider the steps in the formulation and implementation of a national program in regard to some aspect of food policy. First we shall deal with what may be called the usual process and then with a case which qualifies under the rubric paralysis-by-analysis.

The usual process involves the following steps:

1. Recognition of a problem or potential problem or recognition of an opportunity;

2. Analysis of the problem or opportunity probably in an exploratory way;

3. Research and in-depth analysis, probably involving technical people and economists/sociologists and, if substantial resources are involved, a feasibility study;

4. Consideration of the outcome by the ministry responsible for the subject area, along with economic planning and probably other ministries;

5. A proposal developed in conjunction with Treasury;

6. Presentation of the proposal for discussion with a donor agency, if outside funding seems feasible;

7. Detailed action plans, schedules, and funding requirements;

8. Approval by policy makers and donor agencies, if relevant;

9. Implementation. I shall have more to say on this subject below.

By and large, steps 1 to 8 are usually reasonably well done (with occasional lapses) in regard to new projects, such as a study of grain marketing, building of a sugar factory, or a new policy for providing seasonal farm credit. One or more people, probably in government, recognize a problem or opportunity, do some exploratory work, and bring it to the attention of their senior officers. At this point, research-oriented persons are diverted from within government or employed from a university or consultancy firm to examine the subject and produce a report. Sometimes the report fails to take into account such broader issues as the effect of diverting land from current usage to a new use, for example in creating a sugar complex in a largely subsistence area. Invariably, the researchers/planners fail to recognize the snags which are possible—I would say inevitable—at the implementation stage. In their enthusiasm (and sometimes self-interest if they are consultants who hope to be involved later in the project itself), they indicate output responses which turn out to be above average, costs which are far below those realized later, and assume a level of administrative efficiency which has yet to be achieved in the operating ministries.

Consideration of the report/proposal by a number of ministries takes more time than anticipated and discussions with the donor agencies (if any) may be protracted. The result is that projects start considerably later than the proposal/feasibility study has indicated, and inflation takes its usurious toll on costs.

In case I sound too pessimistic, let me note that not all projects follow this pattern. The Mumias Sugar Project in Kenya was a beautiful example of a first-rate feasibility study, realistic in regard to yields, costs, conversion rates from cane to sugar and so forth, and it made its way through the decision-making process of government most expeditiously. It became one of the most successful projects in Kenya.

Not all analysis relates to projects, of course, but often to policies or programs which are on-going, perhaps on an annual basis. The Price review of 1981 (Kenya sets the prices of many farm products) had excellent documentation, many rounds of informed discussion among ministries, and the results were announced early enough to permit farmers to decide what to produce. Given the over-riding condition that it is government policy to set the prices of many farm products and that there was limited input from farmer organizations, it worked well. In retrospect, only one component was seriously out of line.

From time to time there are instances of paralysis-by-analysis, usually involving a donor. One case involved four consecutive studies all insisted upon and financed by one donor and extending over a period of five years. One of the reports consisted of nine volumes which explored what many

people would call the obvious, but did so in painstaking detail. All of
these studies were expensive and were credited to the donor as part of its
contribution of foreign aid to the host country. They involved a substantial
investment of time on the part of host country personnel. The final result
in terms of an actual project was miniscule.

At the other extreme are occasional instances of substantial investment
on the basis of intuition or policies without adequate analysis. These avoid
the delays of pilot projects, prefeasibility studies, feasibility studies, and
project evaluation, but often result in serious problems later.

Implementation

We come now to implementation and thus to the gap between analysis
and action. In spite of the fact that experience with other projects indicates that progress in implementation invariably lags behind the rate
scheduled in the annual work plans, planners tend to assume that "this
one will be different." I suppose all of us do the same in our daily lives—I
have found myself looking at my bank balance at the end of each month
and ruefully concluding "It was those big items—they won't occur next
month." Indeed *they* did not, but others did, just as in all preceding
months.

It is not just government analysts and planners who are overoptimistic
about what implementers can do. The donor agencies are often equal
offenders. The Smallholder Coffee Improvement Project (SCIP) of Kenya
is a fine example of unbridled optimism by IDA and Kenya. In four years
it was expected to renovate 400 cooperatively-owned coffee factories,
build 14 new ones, make loans to upgrade 15,000 hectares of smallholder
coffee, buy and install 50 mechanical driers, and several other things.
Factory technicians had to be recruited and trained before renovation
designs could begin. Many of the cooperatives were without adequate
accounts or organization; coordination had to be developed between the
cooperatives and two ministries and the Cooperative Bank. If Treasury
had provided funds at the rate called for in the schedule, there would
have been a disaster in an industry which earns twice as much foreign
exchange as any other. As it was, even at a slow pace of implementation,
six factories were only partially renovated when the coffee was ready for
processing, and the product had to be taken to other factories. Thanks to
innovative action, the project will be a success, but it will take seven or
eight years to complete, not four.

Implementing agencies have to share some of the responsibility for
over-ambitious schedules in a project work plan. Naturally they are
reluctant to say to the planners, "We cannot get things done as fast as you

are proposing," because such a statement might appear to be a confession of incompetence on their part even before the project has begun. Furthermore, they want the project to be accepted by Treasury and a donor agency, and so they agree to more than they can possibily achieve. Coordination among ministries and parastatals is always a problem—for some projects the major problem. Usually, in a so-called Integrated Project, several ministries, one or two parastatals, and a number of cooperatives are involved. In the IDA/Kenya Integrated Agricultural Development Project, there were no fewer than 10 agencies involved, plus numerous co-operatives. Ministries submit their estimates to Treasury, receive a good deal less than they ask for (just as well or we would be buried in deficits), and other agencies work out their budgets considering the sums available. Some have enough funds to do what is scheduled; others do not. An action by A must occur before another by B, and if A does not act B is frustrated and the schedule becomes chaotic.

There are four possible solutions to this problem. One is to avoid Integrated Projects and to proceed within each ministry/agency independently. This is not much of a solution because many of the most worthwhile projects cannot succeed without the involvement of a number of bodies.

A second possible solution is to create a miniature Tennessee Valley Authority which takes over the roles of ministries in specified areas of activity. This can work in certain geographical areas (as with TVA). The East Ghor Canal Authority in Jordan was a successful example of one agency providing all of the government services in a clearly delineated geographical area which differed greatly from the rest of the country. In general, however, this approach has dangers because it can segment a country into a number of uncoordinated and perhaps competitive units and undermine the performance and status of national ministries. In Kenya, the role of area Development Authorities has, wisely, been restricted largely to integrated planning and monitoring of programs and projects which are operated by the national ministries.

An alternative to area Development Authorities is a product or commodity authority. The Kenya Tea Development Authority has been one of the most successful bodies to be found in any developing economy, providing research, extension, credit, inputs, collecting the product, processing and marketing it, and making timely payments to thousands of smallholders. Under its leadership, the quality of tea produced by smallholders exceeds that of the large estates. With such a successful model as KTDA, one has to ask why it has not been duplicated for other products whose production and marketing requirements are somewhat less demanding. The answer seems to be not only that superior management capacity is the key, but also that the product has to be processed through specialized factories and cannot be sold into a local market, that demand for the product is stable, and that it is a multi-year crop. These latter conditions are not present for a crop like maize and only partly present for others like cotton and pyrethrum.

The third possible solution is to make one of the ministries *primus inter pares* for a particular project. Among operating ministries this is unlikely to work. It would involve two centers of authority—the coordinator in the "directing" ministry and the normal line authority in the other bodies.

The fourth possible solution is to appoint an "expediter" in Treasury or other non-operational ministry, not to direct the others, but to keep on top of what is going on in each (or not going on), to cajole, remind, press, and generally make a nuisance of himself in a congenial way. He has to be from Treasury or other non-operational ministry to avoid rivalries and, let us face it, to appeal occasionally to his own senior officer to exert pressure on the operating ministries or agencies which are lagging in implementation. This has been the option chosen in a number of successful projects, such as Mumias Sugar, and I have come around to the view that this is probably the most workable of all techniques in projects which involve the integrated efforts of a number of ministries and agencies.

Personnel

In what has been said to this point I have indicated that analysis is usually quite sound, that planning and programming are often unrealistically optimistic, and that implementing is the Achilles Heel of developing countries. How could it be otherwise? Analysis is the preserve of host country graduate students, whether in natural or social sciences, backed up by local university persons, consultants, and expatriate advisers. They are experts in what-to-do. In planning and programming, the graduate students, university professors, and expatriate advisers are out of familiar territory. Here they need some experience with the difficult role of how-to-do-it. Moreover, they work with persons of similar background in the donor agencies. Few of either group have suffered through the frustrations of administrative snags, and they just cannot anticipate fully the problems that confront implementers.

The latter are the troops on the firing line in contrast with the headquarters and ordinance staff. They have to contend with a host of seemingly minor problems—shortage of gasoline, xerox machines which do not work, vacations at inconvenient times, rapid turnover of key personnel, meetings that start 30 minutes late, delays in processing forms—not matters exclusive to developing countries but more difficult to overcome. More important though, the implementers—themselves products of the same type of training as the analysts and planners—often lack two essential and related qualities: a sense of urgency and successful operational experience. Their own university experience as students and professors has fitted them for statistical analysis, for considering all sides of a question, for developing and testing hypotheses; but they seldom have had the experience of meeting a payroll or of producing a cash flow or running a business office. Amateurs in a role that requires professionals, they do their best, and (I congratulate them) they learn as they go. Learning, though, is a trial-and-error procedure producing many mistakes which can be ill-afforded in a developing country.

The most important asset for development that any developing country can have is a vibrant, experienced cadre of administrators/managers. Foreign aid cannot provide them in any substantial numbers, for this is not an area appropriate to expatriates. Development of indigenous administrators takes time and involves many frustrations and losses. It also requires patience and forebearance on the part of donor agencies. In my own experience in Kenya, probably the most gratifying development that I noted on returning after an absence of nine years was that my understudy had become number three in Treasury with a capacity for getting things done in such a systematic way that now I can learn from him. It is on people such as he that the development of his country depends, and it speaks well for the administration that his capacity and performance have been recognized.

Education/Training

As one whose career has been largely in social sciences in developed country universities, I do not wish to downgrade the importance of sound analysis and planning. Econometrics and advanced economic theory have an important place in the requirements for advanced degrees. In developing countries, however, the Ph.D. holder with specialization in such esoteric subjects is at a loss as to how to apply the techniques over which he labored at great length in graduate school. The basic data are questionable, computer hardware and software are seldom available, and even if they were, there are other matters which are at least as relevant. Is it possible to make institutional arrangements which will accomplish the objectives which the analysis dictates? Do the implementing agencies have the capacity for prompt decision making on those items which cannot be predicted or spelled out in fine detail in the analyses? These are questions unanswered in the curricula of graduate schools.

A Permanent Secretary (Treasury) needs to have a grasp of two simple First-Year Economics concepts: supply and demand, and opportunity cost. He needs to be able to evaluate the validity of a cash-flow projection and to grasp the essentials of a balance sheet and an income and expenditure statement. Unfortunately, these latter techniques often have to be learned on the job. Otherwise, his preoccupation is with people and organizational structures. Is the Ministry of Water Development capable of doing what is proposed? Are the accounts of the cotton cooperatives such that loans will be properly accounted for and repayments assured? Is the Pyrethrum Board wise to retain huge stocks rather than to cut prices, suffer losses, but dispose of its product and pay farmers promptly? Unfortunately these subjects are not part of any university curriculum. They can be learned only by experience tempered with good judgment.

Two kinds of education/training are essential in developing countries. One is in technical fields, such as engineering or plant breeding. These people are fortunate in that much of their graduate work can be applied to their tasks at home without extensive modification. The other group is composed of the analysts, planners, and administrators. We have already pointed out that planners and analysts must be familiar with the implementation capacities of those to whom they prescribe courses of action. This kind of education is the product of experience and judgment; successful achievement takes time and involves potentially costly mistakes in the process.

Bureaucracy

The major problem of developing countries is how to get things done, not deciding what to do. All too often, decision making during implementation is concentrated in the hands of a small number of senior civil servants whose approval must be sought at every turn. The bureaucratic system of forms and signatures wastes time and interferes with the growth of responsible attitudes on the part of intermediate personnel. This approach inhibits the private sector, raises costs, and contributes to frustrations. When a potential exporter of Kenyan beans (in vast oversupply) has to have six approving signatures, working up from lowest to highest civil servant levels, it is only natural that he becomes discouraged and next time looks around for a less bureaucratic source.

Public Versus Private Sector

I have chosen this heading deliberately, for often in developing as well as developed countries the appropriate word is *versus*. For successful development to occur, the public and private sectors must work in harmony, listening to each other's problems and aspirations, rather than operating in an atmosphere of suspicion and lack of understanding. Proper analysis must consider not only government policy but also how the implementation of that policy will affect, and be perceived by, the private sector. Since government analysts have normally had little experience in the private sector, they are at a special disadvantage. This can be overcome only by communication between the two, rather than by a group of civil servants hypothesizing as to the problems and aspirations of those in the private sector. Too often this communication is absent, and the two sectors appear to each other to have been working at cross purposes.

The presence of donors sometimes aggravates the problem. Their discussions and negotiations are with government officers and government projects and only indirectly if at all with the private sector. In these circumstances, it is only too easy for civil servants to be so preoccupied with negotiations and "conditions of effectiveness," and all the other terms of a donor agreement that the private sector's role and perceptions may be overlooked.

Perspective

Those of us from the so-called developed countries often fail to regard developing countries from the right perspective. For several hundreds of years, we have tried different approaches, some succeeding and some failing. Our private sectors have become sophisticated, and our general level of education has advanced remarkably. In the developing nations of Africa, the people have converted themselves from simple unsophisticated economies to quasi-modern ones in the course of 80 years or so. One could not expect that errors and prejudices could be avoided in such a short period. When we criticize, as we do too often, concerning administrative know-how, we are not being fair. No one should expect the same level of administrative competence after 80 years as after 400.

We can provide assistance in analysis and planning, but implementation is largely a responsibility of the developing country. Beset by mistakes which often seem obvious, they have made remarkable progress, and I for one have confidence that with our support they can overcome most of the problems which confront them.

THE ROLE OF THE UNIVERSITY

David N. Ngugi

This chapter deals with training and research and how they can be linked to improvement in food policy. It draws upon my experience from the University of Nairobi, in particular the Faculty of Agriculture, which is at the center of the whole food production system, agricultural extension programs in the country, research, and actual administration within the relevant ministries.

There are many factors involved in the food production equation. Therefore, it is quite a difficult task for a trainer to be able to satisfy such a diverse array of individuals. To take Kenya as an example, for a long time we had one Ministry of Agriculture which was responsible for crops and livestock. Two years ago, this responsibility was divided between two ministries, Agriculture and Livestock, making two entities charged with a responsibility of looking after food production.

We also have the Ministries of Finance and Planning, two separate ministries whose activities affect the trainers and also affect the policies that the Agriculture and Livestock Ministries would like to pursue. We have another very powerful ministry—the Ministry of Cooperative Development—under which there are several hundred cooperatives. As my colleague, Ralph Campbell observes, these cooperatives handle many crops, aiding in processing or marketing and sometimes actually distributing inputs. Then, we have the other big array of parastatals. Some of them are production parastatals, others are semi-government credit-giving agencies. Added to these are the private firms whose actions can affect the plans of the ministries with respect to production.

The trainers come into this complex system with the main objective of producing technicians who can go out in the field as extension agents to advise the farmers on various packages which can improve production.

They must also produce researchers who will man very extensive research divisions, particularly within the two ministries of Agriculture and Livestock. In addition, we also have to train our administrators who oversee the overall activities within these ministries.

To address this problem of training agricultural extension officers, administrators, and researchers, there is a large undergraduate program based in various faculties in the University, mainly the Faculties of Agriculture, Science, and Arts, which include the economists. The major feature of our training programs is that various aspects of food production are covered in compartmentalized subjects: Crop Production, Animal Production, and so forth, and only occasionally is there reference to economic or policy implications. Agricultural economics again will be covered as a subject, but we find lacking an ability to integrate subjects with one another. Therefore, when the student graduates, he goes out as a crop production man, another as an animal production man or agricultural economist. When it comes actually to talking about a policy, food policy for example, where one wants to see the interrelationships of the actions of each of these individuals, one then has to bring them together, almost as strangers.

Until many East African countries started experiencing famines, everything appeared to be fine. Then famines started coming with increased rapidity. The three East African countries, particularly Kenya, started thinking seriously about what had gone wrong with our food production. We had taken food production for granted for quite some time. Alarmed by the difficulties in the last two years, the country came up with a food policy statement which tried to distill and define the problems and suggest how they might be alleviated.

At that juncture, we found that the University in a meaningful way came into the picture because considerable consultation with the relevant government ministries took place. This has been very significant. As a result of the government's food policy planning, the University has been involved in writing policy papers on agricultural research, food marketing, and related subjects. From that work, the University has learned to start looking at the curriculum in an effort to improve it so that at the policy level, the graduates can react more effectively and adapt to changing problems.

There are limitations, of course. When it comes to training, there is abundant goodwill from the government, e.g., from the Ministries of Agriculture and Livestock Development. But much as the trainers like to go out and interact with the policy makers or with the executors of policy, many faculty members are feeling the pressures which this added training imposes. The training programs continue to expand, resulting in increased demand for teaching manpower. Yet the ministries which seek more trained people do not always, when requesting aid, recognize the need to train high-level manpower to staff the University. Granted, every now and then in various World Bank projects, expansion programs have been supported within the University; but these efforts have not gone far enough. As a result, with the extra demands being made on the few experts within the University, the academic program may also begin to suffer.

One would have hoped that this interaction would enrich the experience of a trainer so that at this stage he would be able to know what the problems are within the field. This is happening; but on the other hand, it is difficult to strike a really happy balance between assisting within a ministry while at the same time trying to prepare the graduates before they themselves go out to start developing or executing policies.

So we have the undergraduate program, which is a major one, carrying the main brunt of training effort. The way to make an impact on food policy is by turning out first degree holders who are well exposed to technological aspects of food production, to extension methods; then to have them specialize in particular areas by bringing them back to the University later as in-service trainees to take master's degrees and, in a few instances, to take Ph.Ds.

From my point of view, the University has a golden opportunity at the graduate training level to integrate the knowledge that the first degree holders gained earlier. At that time, such integration was not possible because of the many areas to which students needed to be exposed, considering the diversity of challenges they faced once they had left the University. It is in this context that postgraduate programs have been developed in the fields of agricultural economics, agronomy, crop protection, animal production, and plant breeding in the Faculty of Agriculture. Our experience with these programs has been very enriching because we have been able to bring back to the University government officers who have been out for two or three years. Into the University, they bring back experience either from a planning division or from the agricultural production ministries. They take nine months of course work, followed by an examination. Upon passing the examination, they go out to conduct their research. As far as possible, they are encouraged to draw the research project from the particular field in which they have been working. In this way, we are able to penetrate the ministries and also establish a vital link which, over time, has helped our relationship with the policy makers. It has removed the suspicion which sometimes has prevailed, depending on which faculty one comes from. If one comes from the socioeconomic faculties, for example, it has not been easy to be accepted in certain ministries because (a pardon to the economists) one expresses his views too strongly, and sometimes they are misunderstood.

The World Bank, international agencies, and the governments can help to strengthen the training capacity, particularly the postgraduate programs. There is a golden opportunity here, where through training, through extended participation of faculties in government projects, the trainer takes as much risk as the government regarding the success or failure of a project. This arrangement avoids the feeling which exists not only in East Africa but also in other countries that academicians are only interested in short-term consultancies that allow them to make money and then leave.

We should try to devise a way for academicians to participate in a substantial way, for one year, two years, or three years, within ongoing projects in the government sector. If such a project succeeds, it becomes a big plus to the participants. If it fails, of course, one takes the risk, but the lessons will have been learned. This approach would counter the feeling that academicians, particularly because of their well-known, very competitive salaries, are being mercenary, interested only in short-term gains. This idea of longer-term relationships is something that those of us in the University, particularly in the Faculty of Agriculture, are trying to encourage. And we think we may meet with some success.

Another subject with which we have had experience concerns working relationships with parent ministries, in our case the Ministry of Agriculture and Ministry of Livestock. Because of our good working relationship, they have gone before the Treasury on our behalf. They have managed to get some money for what we call cooperative research. This arrangement worked out quite well until the Treasury started running short of money; then it was discontinued. But it was a very useful relationship because the government would usually say, "We would like to work in this area but we don't have the expertise. You have breeders, so why don't you start working on this." This support has helped institutions, such as ours, where research funds have not been sufficient. In the past, we have used a considerable amount of donor money, but our experience lately has taught us that this source of funds is drying up very fast. Therefore, it is important to see if there is any way to tie into a parent ministry who sometimes, because of a shortage of personnel, may have some extra funds. By so doing, we can initiate useful research and additionally develop a workable understanding between the University and the government. At the same time, the cooperation will secure credit and recognition for the University.

To illustrate the fruits of this kind of association, we have recently run two seminars on national food policy in Kenya. In each of these, the government very willingly brought in University personnel. These seminars took place on a national level; to each of these, University and community people were invited. They contributed, and we believe that in this way we will be able to bring feedback into our programs. Over time, these methods will allow us to reorganize the programs and as a result make a better impact on all aspects of agricultural production problems.

To conclude, I would like to recall the point that was raised by Ralph Campbell concerning research analysis leading to paralysis (p. 184). I believe that analysis of food policy issues in Kenya has been good, that management has been examined, but that a more fundamental problem is a too rapid turnover of manpower. Thus by the time one has finished analyzing the problem and making recommendations, one finds that the people who would be managing any particular implementation exercise have oozed out of the organization.

The University now is experiencing this kind of problem. One starts with a strong program, and the government brings in suppport through its sponsorship of students. Before very long, however, the experienced members of the staff leave for more lucrative jobs in the private sector. Consequently, because there are so few qualified faculty members, an insufficient number of people are being trained. To make matters worse, there are not enough fellowships to lure the bright students into staff development work before they go out into the private sector, where they are attracted by the good salaries. Under these circumstances, our faculty never stabilizes, experience never congeals. As a result, one is left with young people all the time. For example, in international conferences, very young people are right up there at the top. It's not that experienced people are unappreciated; rather it's that there is not a large enough manpower pool from which to draw. This condition is due purely to the fact that the mechanism for quantifying the numbers of people required in the particular disciplines has not been refined, nor are there adequate resources to back the already well-established training programs, e.g., agriculture and other fields. The situation becomes more complicated when, due to political changes, people are transplanted across ministries. With so few on the ground, the burden of carrying out programs rests in very inexperienced hands.

In conclusion, one can say that a University such as ours has a major role to play in the development and implementation of a national food policy. Through the undergraduate and postgraduate training programs, food policy issues can be tackled and emphasized. In particular, postgraduate research should be exploited to address food policy issues, and the link between the University and policy makers in government should be strengthened. Short-term and long-term cooperative research, including consultancies between the faculty and government ministries, should be encouraged so as to exploit expertise both in the University and in government. In order for the University to be able effectively to play its role of training and research, adequate resources both in terms of personnel, equipment, and research funds should be provided. Finally, attractive terms of service for University staff should be given so as to ensure the stability and dedication of the staff members.

SOME PRELIMINARY OBSERVATIONS ON MICROCOMPUTER USE IN DEVELOPING COUNTRIES

David O. Dapice

Introduction

There has been a sense among many practical and experienced people that computer technology is ill-suited to less-developed countries, especially insofar as food or agricultural policy is concerned. A number of objections reflect these feelings, but perhaps the most important reservations can be expressed in four main points.

1. Data are weak and oversimplified manipulation leads to impressive tables or equations which mean nothing: "Garbage in, garbage out";

2. The costs of the hardware, upkeep, and difficulty in getting programs to run make the benefits not worth the costs;

3. The technology itself is inappropriate; it uses scarce foreign exchange and reduces the use of plentiful labor;

4. Very few consumers or producers of computerized analysis are available; the upgrading needed to make computerization work is little short of a complete overhaul of the entire system, and that can take years and years of training.

All of these objections have had some weight in the past but are increasingly invalid as a new technology based on cheap and easy to use

This chapter greatly benefited from the HIID discussion paper cited in Note 2. Personal communications from Carl Gotsch, Charles Mann, Dirck Stryker, Dan Sisler, and John Cohen have also helped the author.

microcomputers begins to spread. There are now a number of LDCs where officials are finding their life easier with these machines than without them. From Tunisia to Kenya to Madagascar, groups that never thought about or gave up using large central computers have found the micros to be quite a different story. A recent USDA study found 76 ongoing AID funded projects in 33 countries where microcomputers are being used.[1] Many users beginning to report are quite enthusiastic, and new applications are being discovered with disconcerting rapidity. This brief chapter does no more than open the topic of how micros can be used and what early lessons have been drawn. The evidence is still coming in, but it does appear that many procedures will change as a result of this new technology.

The Technology

The writer of this chapter is 38 years old and finished graduate school in the early 1970s. At that time, the Harvard mainframe computer was an IBM in its own building and air conditioned room. Users submitted data and a program on punched cards and waited a day or, if lucky, several hours for the results of a regression. The machine cost several hundred thousand dollars and needed a full time staff to run it. Today, he has an Apple II Plus with all the fixings in his rather dusty study. With printer, screen, software, and all the rest, the system cost under $4,000. Programs are largely prewritten, with choices clearly available. Data is entered through a typewriter-style keyboard, and results of calculations are displayed immediately on the screen. The programs purchased allow the machine to do the following:

1. Word Processing—Writing papers is considerably easier as each page is shown on a screen, mistakes are corrected quickly, and entire words and paragraphs can be deleted or switched about. A single floppy disk about the size of a 45 rpm record holds over 100 double-spaced pages of text. Printing a page takes only a few seconds, and proofreading labor is much reduced since only the changes made result in changes in the new draft.

2. Electronic Spreadsheets—These versatile programs all feature an electronic matrix of rows and columns. Each row or column can contain entered data or an equation based on some combination of past rows or columns and arithmetic or algebraic manipulations. Changing a row or proportion automatically recalculates all values in the entire sheet. This feature has proven to be very popular for management, budgeting, and some research applications.

3. Regression Analysis—Among others, a version of Time Series Processor (TSP), a powerful regression package is available on micros. The system capacity is quite large with the variables times the observations per variable equal to over 4,000 in one calculation. A far larger data set can be stored on floppy disks and called into the internal memory when needed. Standard output includes the corrected R-squared, t and F statistics for coefficients and regression, Durbin-Watson statistics, and other normal summary statistics. Residual plots are made, and methods, such as two-stage least squares and Cochrane-Orcutt estimation, can be called. Graphs of the estimated and actual values can be printed out.

This brief rundown of one small system gives the reader an idea of the capabilities of a rather old but well-proven machine. The micros are cheap, quite durable, versatile, and easy to use and service. A recent and excellent study of microcomputers in Kenya's Agriculture and Planning Ministry found that secondary school leavers could quickly and easily learn how to use canned programs, while somewhat higher level clerks could, with some training, learn to do simple programming.[2]

Applications and Lessons

What can the micros do in LDCs? The previous listing is suggestive, but a more detailed discussion of the variety of applications may be helpful. Carl Gotsch[3] identified five types of tasks in Kenya where micros could be of use. They included:
1. Improving the ability to forecast crop yields;
2. Improving the assessment of food security;
3. Provision of more systematic and timely budget data;
4. Improving information on project implementation; and
5. Word processing.
Other examples of use are record keeping of small rural banks, on-site cleaning and analysis of farm and rural survey data, monitoring of input availability for crops, and agricultural planning and analysis.

The Harvard study[4] drew several lessons from the experience in Kenya based on the three authors' observations. One important finding was that a full-time specialist was needed for about a year to get a micro system fully introduced and accepted. On the other hand, experiences from Tunisia suggest that even without much technical assistance, the micros can be quite productive in a variety of uses. It may be that the depth of trained people willing to learn is a significant variable in determining the proper level of technical assistance. In most cases, it is likely that some transfer is needed, though possibly in a short course for the local user rather than through a full-time expatriate. The Harvard study, based on

Kenyan experience, suggested an economist with a bit of computer training as ideal for the teacher. He or she should be able to set up models and forecasts for the users and get them over their initial fears. They also pointed out some familiar problems—fascination with the machines led to undue faith in them, both because of poor data or actual errors which they made. This same fascination led to use of the micros for every possible application, rather than those where it was really needed. Control and restraint was needed to focus use where it really paid off. Another pertinent observation was that where an organization had a desire to change, the micros made it easier and faster. But they couldn't force change on unwilling bureaucracies.

The near future holds several other possible applications that should be at least mentioned. Micros can now tap large data banks over telephone lines, thereby giving the user access to the equivalent of a large library. They can also access data and messages in each others' data banks, setting up a network of users. This is cheap and quite easy with existing hardware and software. Messages can be stored and sent at slack periods automatically. Taken together, these capabilities could tie together otherwise isolated researchers or could create data networks for reporting crop conditions, agricultural inputs, or other management data of interest over an entire country.

In New York State, most dairy farmers have micros and are connected to a larger Cornell computer. They punch in the daily production of each cow and get weekly recommendations on feed rations, insemination schedules, optimal slaughtering times, and other management suggestions. This connection suggests a way to stretch scarce expertise.

Training, using computers with educational software and even voice chips (the computer actually talks to the student), is just beginning. The advantage over ordinary teaching is unclear, but the ability to save on scarce teaching resources, set a proper pace, automatically check on progress, and cover almost any topic once a course is worked out has obvious attractions.

The creation of realistic simulation games (not video games) is another application which has proved promising. Desk-bound bureaucrats can play a game called "farmer" in which they have to make economic and technical decisions in the face of bad extension advice, floods, drought, and pest attacks. These have been used successfully in Kenya and at the World Bank.

Concluding Observations

The ability to buy ready-made software for micros considerably enhances their usefulness. As LDC applications increase, it is likely that programs specifically tailored to LDC needs will emerge. However, some effort to accelerate the transfer and availability of these programs is justified due to the fragmentation of the market. Because they reduce the need for scarce programmers and are low in cost, the rapid spread of micros for practical problem-solving is likely. Investing in a clearinghouse and newsletter may be a low-cost, high-payoff activity which can make their use more productive.

The Harvard report correctly observed that hardware is in a state of flux and that flexibility is needed in procurement. Internal and external computer memories are growing in size and shrinking in cost. The brains of the machines are getting bigger and faster. The next generation will be much more able to talk to other computers for problem-solving, not just for messages. The newer micros rival mainframes from just a few years ago and can handle significant amounts of data processing. High speed printers with graphics capabilities are also now available in the $500 to $1,000 range. However, reliability, access to service, and ready availability of software are often decisive considerations. Most of the machines, at least excluding their display screen, are quite portable. Some with smaller screens fold up into portable suitcases.

It is not clear where the best sources of expertise are for micros. Corporations are uneasy with them. Universities have scarcely admitted their existence except where they will form the basis of a network, still very much in the future. Governments have typically ignored their importance in day-to-day operations. Consultants are busy and enthusiasm is uneven. There is a clear need for short (a few days to a few weeks) training courses so that existing experts can get on top of this new technology. Particularly promising for the developing world is the creation of short courses tailored specifically to problems and conditions there.[5]

NOTES

1. Noel Berge and Marcus Ingle, *Microcomputers in Development: A Manager's Guide* (West Hartford, CT: Kumarian Press, 1983).

2. Thomas Pickney, John Cohen, and David Leonard, "Microcomputers and Financial Management in Development Ministries: Experience from Kenya" (Harvard Institute for International Development Discussion Paper #137, August 1982).

3. Carl Gotsch, "Managing Food Security Systems," (Project note prepared for the U.S. Agency for International Development, 2/22/1980).

4. Pickney, Cohen, and Leonard, "Experience from Kenya."

5. For example, Stanford University Food Research Institute's "Workshop on Microcomputers and Development."

IMPROVING THE PRODUCTIVITY OF FOOD POLICY ANALYSTS: A TALE OF TWO COMPUTERS

Charles K. Mann

Efforts to strengthen national food policy capability usually focus on improving human capital. Generally, The Rockefeller Foundation and others pay relatively little attention to the physical capital with which this human capital is augmented. This chapter argues that there is an important interactive aspect between the quality of the human capital and the quality of the physical capital with which those individuals work, particularly physical capital in the form of microcomputers.

While computers have been with us for a long time, the combination of user-friendliness and power of the microcomputer represents a qualitative difference from earlier computers—a difference which is changing the way people conceive and implement both analytical and managerial tasks. With mainframe computers, there were tremendous barriers discouraging individuals from taking advantage of available computer power. Without programming knowledge themselves, they had little idea of just what the computer could do. The programming staff itself represented a formidable human barrier between the potential user and the machine itself.

While timesharing theoretically has been possible for many years, the usual computer installation in the developing countries is the university or government mainframe doing batch processing. This arrangement provides little opportunity for timely feedback between the user and the computer. The computer is used more for large-scale, one-time projects such as survey analysis, rather than for ongoing management tasks.

As noted by Dapice in the preceding chapter, there is evidence now that microcomputer use in the developing countries is growing rapidly. With AID and the World Bank encouraging more use of microcomputers this trend promises to accelerate.

The effect of this physical capital infusion on human capital development will depend in large part on whether these microcomputers are viewed as miniature mainframes or as tools in the direct service of analysts and managers. For example, the bulk of the day-to-day, analytical work which goes on in planning and programming offices is relatively unsophisticated, generally done with a desk calculator, pencils, and accounting spreadsheets. Here is an area where the microcomputer can make an enormous improvement in productivity. One of the programs which sparked the microcomputer revolution was VisiCalc, the electronic spreadsheet for the microcomputer. Its format is immediately familiar to anyone accustomed to working with a row and column layout. Original entries and user-supplied formulas can be used to generate new rows or columns of data.

This ability to create simple models and manipulate data opens up whole new realms of thought; it becomes simple to test out all sorts of what-if questions. What if there is a drought? What if herbicide shipments are delayed? What amount of extra food can be produced by importing more fertilizer?

Once a user becomes comfortable with the basic framework of VisiCalc or similar programs, his or her own imagination begins to see ways to carry out far more elaborate and realistic analyses than can be done with pencil and paper. It is this gradual realization of the power of these spreadsheets that expands the person's concept of the kind of analysis he or she can do. This form of independent learning represents a totally new and important dimension of human capacity development. The same process goes on with other software packages as well.

While this sort of mind-expanding process in theory could take place with a mainframe computer, it is less likely because such activities have to be moderated through a buffer of programmers and often administrative buffers as well. With such programs as electronic spreadsheets, people begin to see that they themselves can design information systems to monitor project performance, to monitor the delivery of inputs, to compare plan objectives with realized performance. A substantial expansion in the individual's own analytical capacity takes place as the framework and power of these programs begin to be internalized. People begin to realize that they can handle large matrices of information, can manipulate it at will, revise it, update it, extend it. The availability of this physical capital in the form of the microcomputer improves the quality of the human capital through continued interaction between the two.

Not only can more elaborate and timely analysis be carried out, but also word processing and graphic packages allow analytical results to be interpreted and clarified and quickly placed before senior officials for decision. Trouble spots can be identified in time to take corrective action. Opportunities for improving food production can be identified more effectively. The scarce analytical and managerial talents of these countries are freed from routine tasks to concentrate on truly important issues.

Against this background, I would like to contrast briefly two fundamentally different approaches to the use of the microcomputer. Both of these took place in Tunisia and the relative progress of the two installations sheds important light on the introduction and use of microcomputers. The first major installation there was within a rural development project using an Apple computer to assist with a baseline survey. The project design called for sophisticated statistical analysis of a large number of variables. Two sociologists/programmers from Cornell worked to develop the necessary software, investing several thousand hours in the task. There was a training program for the technical people to learn how to run the programs and equipment but little local participation in the software design. While I have not had the opportunity to review the progress of this installation recently, the reports of others suggest that the project functioned effectively during the times when the expatriate consultants were there but that not much happened when they were gone. To the extent that the equipment was used, it was used for such things as managing the payroll rather than the intended analytical purpose.

Through circumstance rather than design, there is a second Apple computer installation in Tunisia representing the polar opposite in terms of the outside support given to the installation. In this case, the computers were provided by The Rockefeller Foundation as part of a food policy field project in Tunisia.

The main objective of this particular project was to assist the Tunisians in analyzing the reasons for the sharp decline in their cereal production which had occurred in the several years prior to the project's start. Originally, the project had nothing to do with computers. It had a focus on helping to improve analytical capacity in the agricultural planning office. However, one of the main difficulties was the great amount of time required of the most talented analysts in conducting routine spreadsheet analysis and projection. Moreover, they lacked any means of developing a rapid feedback information system on the realization of planned objectives, such as fertilizer and herbicide deliveries.

Facilitating these analysts' work by enabling them to perform some of these more routine tasks on the computer seemed to offer a way of helping dramatically to improve their productivity. There seemed to be less need for training the individuals in analytical technique than for improving their productivity in the sorts of analytical tasks they were already carrying out. This meant that the objective in providing computers was to improve productivity. We were less concerned with the nature of the particular tasks to which they chose to apply the computer. Whatever way they could use them to make more of their own time available for thinking through the problems of the cereals sector was a positive outcome. This contrasts with the Apple installation in central Tunisia where the diversion of the computer from its intended data base collection to payroll calculations was considered a negative outcome. The Rockefeller Foundation had a more experimental interest in seeing how the computer could improve the productivity of the analytical staff without a particular concern as to what sort of tasks it did.

While the Foundation supplied two Apple computers and a variety of off-the-shelf software, it was made clear that there was no possibility of training, follow-up maintenance, or repair support. A professionally-crafted CARE package was put together with the original shipment, including materials to supplement the normal equipment and software manuals. This included a series of introductory videotapes which became "The Powersharing Series."[1] Beyond this, the Tunisians were on their own. The Rockefeller Foundation field staff person Ms. Chris Mock, had already finished her assignment there when the equipment arrived, although she had helped them to prepare for it. Things went very slowly at first. One of the machines proved to be inoperable. However, once they put their minds to it, the members of the group were able to find resource people within Tunis.

They began simply by transferring the work they had been doing previously with pencil and paper spreadsheets to VisiCalc—primarily provincial cereal production data. While they recognized that they were using the machine at a fraction of its capacity, they were enthusiastic. As they came to learn better the equipment's capacity, they began to see ways that they could improve their analytical and managerial capabilities. They began to ask for timely local reports on plan implementation because they could now digest, analyze, display, and print the consolidated results. Changes in plan assumptions or performance were examined to assess their current and future impact. In particular, analysts could now respond rapidly to what-if questions from their Minister, who has become one of the computer's strongest proponents.

Because the Tunisians have had to teach themselves how to apply the computer to their problems, they have developed self-confidence in their own abilities. At their request, we have provided them with increasingly sophisticated off-the-shelf programs for such applications as time series analysis and linear programming. Simply taking the same individuals and giving them a course in analytical methods would not generate the same outcome as giving them a tool with which they can interact on a day-to-day basis. The interactive process of learning how to use a powerful analytical program is a process which builds the analytical capacity of the person involved. While classroom work and reading can augment this, a major dimension of learning by doing is injected by the microcomputer that simply is not possible without it. In theory, you *can* learn how to do the same thing with a mainframe computer, but if you have to go through programming and administrative intermediaries, in practice you will not.

The substantially different performance in the two Tunisian Apple computer installations illustrates this point. The rural development Apple, for all practical purposes, was conceived and set up as if it were a mainframe. There were computer specialists and a custom program created by an outside group. The main respect in which the computer got integrated into the work of the institution was in doing payroll and budgeting work.

The Planning Office installation, in contrast, had no outside source of expertise. While progress was slow at the start, it accelerated rapidly as the users began to discover the power of various off-the-shelf programs supplied with the machines. The analytical capacity of the individuals has grown; both the quality and quantity of analytical work done by that office clearly have improved. The Minister has better staff work to inform his decision-making.

In developing human capital, the quality and quantity of physical capital is important. However, as this tale of two computers illustrates, simply putting the microcomputer into the place of the mainframe is not enough. What determines the real impact upon human capital formulation is the extent of engagement and interaction between the people and the machines. People can be empowered by microcomputers or they can watch the new computer power flow to the same hands which controlled the earlier computers. The outcome is partly a function of how the microcomputer is conceived by donors and outside consultants. They should highlight rather than obscure the difference between the micros and the mainframes. While specialists are still needed, the computer is no longer their exclusive province.

The microcomputer with some standard off-the-shelf software can play a central role in building analytical and managerial capacity. The possibilities are expanded further as professionals of many disciplines adapt such standard programs as VisiCalc to a wide range of economic analyses. For example, in 1982 Dr. Carl Gotsch—an agricultural economist at Stanford University—graduated the first class of 15 developing country analysts from a six-week course where they were taught how to apply standard microcomputer programs to a wide range of practical agricultural sector analyses. The group included two Tunisians from the planning office project and one from the Turkish survey project described in Chapter 8 by Gençağa. As this and other such courses develop a network of graduates, they can help each other to discover still more ways to improve management and analysis with adaptations of off-the-shelf software. Increasingly, the microcomputer will be helping nationals from the developing world formulate their own questions and seek their own answers.

NOTES

1. *The Powersharing Series,* An Introduction to the Microcomputer (Martha Stuart Communications, New York, New York, 1982, Videotapes).

PEOPLE-CENTERED DEVELOPMENT TO BUILD RURAL INSTITUTIONS

Gabino A. Mendoza

This chapter introduces the Asian Institute of Management, describes some of the work it has been doing with government agencies to help them manage the implementation of policies, and presents some observations on developing policy analysis capacity.

The Asian Institute of Management is a 13-year-old management institute. It was established by two private universities in the Philippines with the help of the Harvard Business School and was set up essentially as a private enterprise management school. About three or four years after its establishment, we realized that to be relevant to Asia, we would have to address the really key problems in our part of the world. We believed these to be in the rural areas and that it was only government that could move the rural areas because it had all the necessary resources. We also believed that within the rural areas, we should pay close attention to the small farmer because he's really what development is all about.

Acting upon these ideas, we put together a small team of faculty members drawn from this private enterprise management faculty. We said to them: "Go into the rural areas and find out what's going on and see what we can learn there about management."

Our first brush with reality in the rural areas had to do with the Ministry of Agriculture. During the late 60s and the early 70s, the Philippines was a rice-importing country. Because government could not import enough rice, we were having all kinds of trouble in the cities. People had to line up in order to buy rice and, after a while, there were riots and demonstrations. When President Marcos took charge of the government, he decided that one of his priorities was that the Philippines

209

should be self-sufficient in rice. That's the mandate that he gave to the Minister of Agriculture, an outstanding strategic manager from the private sector. The Minister took a look at this task and asked himself, "What do we have to do in order to become self-sufficient?" He realized that he would have to get the improved seeds that the International Rice Research Institute (IRRI) had developed and somehow would have to get the farmers to adopt them.

With the improved seeds came a whole new technology. It required more inputs: fertilizer, insecticides, and pesticides. Because our farms are so very small and the farmers very often are tenants, he had to do something with the land reform, and he had to make sure that credit became available to the farmer, otherwise that program would not move. He decided that the strategic element was credit which could serve to bring together all the elements of the improved production package. A central feature of program implementation was to set up a special, more flexible organization separate from the Ministry of Agriculture. Into this organization he co-opted people in the Ministry. Thus, he had two organizations going—one to which the Congress was allocating funds and another for which he got some donor money—and brought in the people to work under the new organization.

When the program had become a success, he came to us and said, "Could you be my consultants? I now want to take a long-term view and reorganize my Ministry so that it can work the way it worked for rice." The Ministry essentially was a series of bureaus which extended all the way down to the farm. He wanted to put all the people at the grass roots together as a force upon which he could build, in effect, to cut up the country into regions with each region having a small Ministry of Agriculture. He would take the existing bureaus and turn them into staff bureaus, which would then support this line organization.

Before agreeing, we set one condition. We said that most reorganizations start from the top and work down. We said that we would like to do it differently; we would like to talk with the farmers and with extension agents. We would like to see if we can structure your Ministry so that we start from the bottom—what the extension agent needs to have, what he has to do with the farmer, and, therefore, what kind of support he needs from the top; then look at how you put the whole thing together.

We worked on this project for about a year. We finally came up with several alternative reorganization structures for him to look at, and we spent another few months discussing these with his people to find out which were the options that were possible.

It took him another two years before he could get the President to agree to it, partly because he had too many regional managers. He had four regional managers for each region, one from each of the bureaus. He had to pick out one to be the regional manager, and the others would have to become deputy regional managers. He also had to get rid of some of the deadwood; it took him two years to retire some people, ease out others, and in general, arrange it so that when he went to the President he could say: "Mr. President, if you approve this, there'll be no trouble. The governors won't kick, nobody's going to fight." It took two years to accomplish that.

Once he had the regional managers in place, he realized that they were not really managers. They really were regional heads of these bureaus, essentially technicians. He needed regional managers who could look at the regions, analyze what was going on, the kind of resources available, the needs of the people, then in light of these factors, come up with a strategy for the region.

We worked with him on trying to develop these regional managers. We ran a training program for them. We did workshops with them. We had them do analyses of their own regions and then sat down in workshops to assess the results. As there are 13 regions in the Philippines, this effort involved a considerable amount of work, some of which is still going on.

He also had to change the budget system so that instead of funds going to the bureaus, they went to the regions. That shift caused some struggle, but finally he has been able to bring the money directly to the regional manager so that the locus of power now has altered. While the bureau directors are still fighting about it, the trend has been established.

But his problems were not yet over. As I've mentioned, he was able to achieve self-sufficiency in rice. As a matter of fact, we have been of late exporting some rice. However, as the plan worked out, most of those who benefited from this push were the bigger farmers. The smaller farmers were not getting reached by the credit he had made available. And so, we're now looking at how the Ministry reaches those small farmers and how we can help the regional manager set up a strategy so that the small farmer gets the benefits and therefore gets the income. We are still struggling with this with the Ministry.

Because of our concern for the small farmers, we started looking at some of the work that the private voluntary organizations in the Philippines have been doing with the small farmers. One of the realities of the Philippines is that our small farms are so very small: one or two hectares at the most. Many of these are farmers who only recently have participated in the land reform and, therefore, nominally own the land. However, they can't do very much with it in terms of getting capital. These small farmers are at the brink of disaster all the time. Because of this, they owe favors to the elite, to the educated, to the rich; they cannot talk back. They cannot go to the government and demand their rights; they do not know how. They are prisoners of their own minds and of their history.

The private voluntary organizations have been trying to liberate them. The process of liberation involves trying to mobilize them into communities where they give support to one another, where they can now talk to government not as individuals but as groups. They can say, "You're supposed to give this to us, give it to us now." To establish such a condition requires extensive work because there are many ways in which the elite can break the community up. But we have been able to find examples of success in the work done by the private voluntary organizations.

One of our agencies, the National Irrigation Authority (NIA)—under pressure from the World Bank, I think—decided that they would have to charge the farmers for the irrigation dams and systems that they were setting up. Their experience was that they would plan an irrigation system for a thousand-hectares. They would achieve an effective coverage of only about 700 hectares and after a couple of years this was down to about 250 hectares, because the farmers didn't really pay attention to it. The farmers did not feel that they had very much to do with it. So the authority decided to go in and mobilize the communities even before they set up the irrigation system. They wanted to consult with the farmers about how they should design it, where the canals should go, et cetera. In effect, they wanted to bring the farmer into the decision-making process in setting up the irrigation system.

This approach connected with our concern for mobilizing communities. Accordingly, we've been working with the authority in helping first to decide how they should work with the farmers, how to organize and mobilize them and make them effective organizations that could deal with the NIA.

A committee was formed at the national level and was made up of management people, anthropologists, agronomists, and others. This became something of an advisory committee to the manager of NIA. As we worked with them, one of the things that we found was that even with a strong desire within the agency to work with people, one had to do something about the agency itself to enable it to work with these people. Many of their procedures, many of their policies, were not suitable for working this closely with people. As soon as the farmers were organized and convinced that they would be listened to, they started to realize that they would have to pay for these things. They started to demand that the people in the agency give them an accounting of what they were spending. They started to watch how the people in the agency were using the jeep, for example, and how much fuel they were putting into it, because part of that expense they were going to have to pay.

The government's accounting procedures, however, did not allow the farmers to look into this. So those in the agency found the need to change their own rules and procedures, also a need for more training for the people within the agency. The government helped them in these matters.

Other aspects of the new approach affected their engineers. They brought the engineers into a workshop and said to them: "You have to work with the people." Now working with the people takes time for efforts to coalesce. It takes much longer than just sending in a technical man to survey the place, lay out the canals, and start construction. While they kept telling the engineers to work with the people, the engineers found out that they still were being judged by their superiors on the basis of the deadlines set up under the previous system.

Having found this out, we began to work with them. How do you coordinate the community-organizing work with the technical work? How do you set up a work chart that shows when each stage will be complete, given the need for all this community input? The control elements themselves had to be revised. To measure the performance of the engineer under this grass roots approach, they changed the definition from "a completed irrigation system" to "a working irrigation system accepted by the farmers and managed by the farmers." But most of all, through workshops, we helped them develop a problem-solving style of management.

We are now working closely with them. They began with one project, and now they are running something close to 240 projects on this farmer participation basis. We are also using what we are learning from this experience and working with the Ministry of Agriculture to assess their experiments with farmer participation in some of their projects. In the process, we have had to help others develop community organizers. We have had also to learn about the technology of irrigation and the language of agricultural people. We find that you can learn very fast if you know what you are looking for.

In the course of our work, we have discovered that there are several other management institutes in the developing world which are concerned about the same things. With support from the Rockefeller Foundation, we have been meeting over the past few years with a group of them around the world to exchange experiences and to teach one another what we have learned. These include the Indian Institute of Management at Ahmedabad, INCAE in Managua, Nicaragua, and IESA in Caracas, Venezuela. In August 1982, we had a meeting at Bellagio where we exchanged ideas on how to mobilize communities.

The second issue that we are focusing on is how to reorient bureaucracy so that bureaucrats can work with communities that are now alive and demanding things. Also, we have been looking at how to help government agencies develop a congruence between what they're trying to do and their organizational structure, their processes and procedures. These should all work together toward the common end of moving their programs forward. We have published two books on some of our findings. Also, one of the professors at the Indian Institute of Management, Samuel Paul, has written an excellent book on strategic management for government agencies.[1]

Finally, I'd like to say something about the topic of this workshop, this new discipline of food policy analysis. Is it primarily an economist's exercise or are there other elements to make it an effective tool for government decision-making? It seems to me that it cannot be just an economic type of analysis. You cannot just tell people in government, "This is what you should do." "What" to do is not enough. The who and how and when also have to be answered. This need not be done in great detail, for that is the task of program analysis. But, in analyzing policy, one has to have some feel for who and when and how it is going to be done. One has to incorporate that into the design of what constitutes policy analysis. One needs to look not only at the economic dimension, not only at the technological dimension, but also at the organizational and political dimensions.

In private business, staff work is not complete unless it gives the decision-maker all that he needs to make a decision. Otherwise staff work is inadequate. This is one of the doctrines that business schools teach. One must give executives "completed staff work." It seems to me that we're talking here about staff work for the government. It has got to be complete or people are not going to be able to make a decision. We will have a lovely analysis which nobody is going to do anything about.

Finally, I believe that because part of that analysis is going to be political analysis, it will be very difficult for non-indigenous people to make that analysis. There are some things that can be said only if the speaker is a member of the family. If a foreigner says certain things about the country, he may raise a lot of hackles. Therefore, it is important quickly to build a capability into the staffs of government agencies to do this kind of analysis. The work of foreign analysts will have to be much more at an international level which can feed ideas to the people within the country, which they then have to digest and use in their analysis of their own circumstances. Nonetheless, there are other instances when the foreign analyst usefully can come in and say something shocking and then run away. This too is an important function.

To support this need for analysis by indigenous personnel, more training opportunities are needed at all levels. One of the principles is that wherever possible, it is preferable to have the training in the developing countries themselves. In the 1960s and the early 1970s, there was a big surge among the donor agencies to help in institution building. After a while that became "old hat"; now there is no more donor money for institution building.

Many of the institutions set up then all over the world have shown that they are viable, that they can do important work. Most of them have virtually stopped growing, excelling, achieving their potential. The amounts of money needed to push these institutions, to make them really centers of excellence, is small. Yet the administrators and faculty are spending half their time just trying to survive. They're going from hand to mouth; all that potential is being wasted for lack of small amounts of money.

In the developing world, there is no tradition of giving endowments to help support schools. Even government schools are having a hard time. They need to build up their capacity so that they can do a better job. They find it difficult to get this assistance because the fad for institution-building is past.

With assets already in place, capacity could be pushed up very quickly with only modest outside help. This could benefit not only the institution's own country but other developing countries as well. Taking an example from our own Institute, we have developed a one-week seminar on management of people-centered development for senior government officials. We're hoping from this to design a much longer program for lower-level government officials to help develop the kinds of managers really needed in the developing world. We are at the brink of being able to reach the neediest in our societies, of helping them pull themselves out of the morass of poverty in which they are bogged down. A little more help could give us the extra push needed, but it must be help for our own programs and priorities. For, while we can learn from Western models, people-centered development means we must develop our own approaches to managing our own problems.

NOTES

1. David C. Korten and Felipe B. Alfonso, eds., *Bureaucracy and the Poor: Closing the Gap* (West Hartford, Connecticut: Kumarian Press, 1983), 258 pp., David C. Korten, ed., *Population and Social Development Management: A Challenge for Management Schools* (Caracas: Instituto de Estudios Superiores de Administration, 1979), 179 pp.

2. Samuel Paul, *Strategic Management of Development Programmes: Guidelines for Action* (Geneva: UNDP Inter-regional Programs, ILO Office, 1983) 137 pp.

TRAINING NEEDS OF MID-LEVEL FOOD POLICY MANAGERS IN SUB-SAHARAN AFRICA

Barbara Huddleston

Introduction

The vital importance of improving the performance of African food production and distribution systems is widely acknowledged. At the same time, various observers have pointed out the difficulty of achieving this goal with the limited number of trained Africans available to carry out essential tasks at all levels of the system.

The need for training affects all aspects of African development. Further, the problem of developing cadres of trained personnel to plan and administer the modernization process in Africa may involve efforts which go beyond the traditional training techniques of the industrialized West. As Jon Morris has pointed out, the cultural and institutional environment of most African countries does not utilize Western-trained talent effectively for development purposes.[1] David Korten lays an important share of the responsibility for this situation on the inappropriateness of management training offered by the West since the mid-50s.[2]

With respect to the food sector, Uma Lele has clarified an important difference between the preparation and utilization of persons with higher-level training in South Asia and in Africa.[3] Whereas in Asia Western-trained persons working in the agriculture sector developed a professional network which fostered public debate about the importance of the sector

Based on a report to The Rockefeller Foundation submitted in December 1982.

to general economic development and the policies necessary to encourage agricultural growth, this has not yet occurred in Africa. Thus the perceived need is not just for more scholarships and training courses. It is for an approach to higher-level training which will foster a bureaucratic mentality favorable to food policy planning and agriculture development programs as central elements of a country's economic growth strategy. The purpose of this chapter is to define the nature of this approach more clearly and to identify various institutional mechanisms by which it might be tested and ultimately carried out.

Food Policy Management in the African Context

At the present time, food policy management in Africa displays the following characteristics. In most countries, public institutions were created after independence to supply credit, seed, fertilizer, and extension services to small farmers, and to procure and market grain. Previously, such institutions had become well-established for export crops but not for food staples. In general, these new institutions are still weak. Links with producers are imperfect, and private traders often operate side by side with government agents. Subsidized input programs reach a relatively small number of intended beneficiaries. Food distribution systems often reach no farther than the capital city and a few other major urban centers, with private traders again filling the gap. Official prices are fixed for the operation of the public grain procurement and distribution system, often with a view to keeping the cost of grain low for the increasing numbers of wage earners migrating to urban centers. In some cases, imports are used instead of locally produced grain to meet urban demand because they are cheaper and more easily accessible to the government officials who must manage the food supply system in the cities. Timothy Josling has observed that because of these policies, the price received by farmers in developing countries is substantially lower in relation to input costs than the price received by farmers in developed countries for locally-produced grain.[4] Thus, throughout much of Africa, agriculture is in effect taxed in order to support urban development.

Good information about farming practices and local market conditions is hard to obtain, and many policy decisions must still be made largely on the basis of guesswork 'about their likely effect. Policy priorities are influenced by the leverage donors exercise through tied aid. In the agricultural sector, this has meant emphasis on certain types of agricultural development projects and production practices according to the current fashion in development theory. More recently, price and storage policies have come under the scrutiny of donors, and food aid is being linked to changes in the policy environment, which it is hoped will improve incentives for local farmers and facilitate development of internal marketing and distribution systems.

Such conditions, coupled with the continuing shortage of trained and experienced administrative personnel, have forced most African governments to focus their own managerial efforts on a relatively small number of food-related programs and projects. Selection of priorities for utilization of their own manpower resources is usually based on short-term political requirements. Considerations affecting the longer-run evolution of the entire food system often play a secondary role in the decision-making process, with programs and projects having a long gestation period and a slow payoff being left to donor agencies to design and administer. As the World Bank Report, *Accelerated Development in Sub-Saharan Africa,* notes, outside personnel in Africa have played a much larger role in formulating development strategies, projects, and policy advice than elsewhere in the world.[5] Thus, responsibility for current conditions rests as much with donor agencies as with recipient governments.

During the early years after independence, a number of attempts were made to introduce improved administrative practices into Africa. The standard management model then in use distinguished sharply between the process of implementing specific policies and projects. Academic training provided students with the analytical tools needed to undertake planning and policy formulation tasks. At the same time, specific management skills, such as financial planning, accounting, personnel management, recordkeeping, and so forth were taught to individuals who obtained degrees or certificates from newly-created institutes of management and public administration. In practice, an individual with either type of training might rise to supervisory positions within the bureaucracy, but each lacked the skills and techniques the other had acquired in early training.

In general, it is easier to teach management skills to a person already trained in academic discipline than vice versa. One suggestion to improve managerial capacity in line agencies of African governments has therefore been to develop short courses and on-the-job training for individuals with an academic degree and a need for supervisory skills.

This approach may not succeed unless accompanied by a change in attitude about the relationship between planning and implementation. A newer theoretical model for administering development emphasizes the links between the process of policy formulation and the implementation process. This model requires an institutional structure in which individuals with one type of responsibility or the other are required to interact on a regular basis, and career rewards are given to those who identify problems and adapt policies and procedures so that development goals can be achieved and costs minimized. This model has been refined for use by private corporations, and it would probably require considerable adaptation before it could be taught in useful ways to officers of government. But it is interesting to note that in Africa, the preferred sources of training for management skills are not the public administration institutes modeled after the earlier pattern, but rather the schools of business administration and the economic development institutes where process as well as economic linkages are emphasized.

Within an organization, a critical mass of people must adopt a new attitude before it can take root. To bring about changes in attitude about administrative relationships and reward systems in African bureaucracies will require training programs which are country-specific and which reach sufficient numbers within each relevant agency to make change possible. If junior officers are released for four-to-six week courses, for example, their superiors can be brought to the training site for a long weekend of intensive introduction to the new perceptions and skills their staff members have acquired. If benefit to their operation can be demonstrated, they are more likely to allow the staff member to use lessons learned through in-service training.

In order to teach both attitudes and skills, it will be necessary to design training programs which offer more than tool courses for old-line managers. Some interaction among trainees with different kinds of responsibilities in the sector in which they work is essential to foster understanding of the interaction process which they are being trained to implement.

Recognition of the importance of such a process is increasingly acknowledged by top government officials of many African countries, but the means to bring it about is not clearly seen. The relevance for food policy is uppermost in the minds of many because of the crisis nature of the food supply problem for many of them. A number of countries have asked the World Food Council for assistance in preparing food sector strategies to help them to rationalize the policy framework and establish priorities for externally-financed programs and projects (Williams, p. 152). Like previous planning efforts, these food sector strategies will set general goals and policy directions. But through them it is hoped that the planning process will shift toward the entire food system and away from the earlier focus on agricultural production systems. It is also hoped that the process of developing such a strategy and institutionalizing procedures for following up on its implementation will bring food-related issues into sharper focus as a central feature of the development process in the eighties.

Even if food sector strategies or other similar planning efforts produce useful results, the broad objectives for food policy which they delineate still will have to be transformed into operational directives and action programs. It is at this operational level that the need for trained manpower to carry out policy initiatives is so critical.

With respect to food policy implementation, the distinction between the two managerial styles referred to earlier is related to the difference between the food systems approach and the agricultural development approach to conceptualizing policy issues. Under the latter, which has prevailed until quite recently and still dominates some donor assistance strategies, 90 percent of total resources expended for food-related activities went to production projects. Further, projects were utilized almost exclusively as the vehicle for channeling additional resources into sectors designated for assistance, such as agriculture, health, education, infrastructure, and so forth. This has meant that government agencies have faced constant pressure to improve their capacity for project analysis and evaluation, and numerous short-course training programs have been created to teach African agriculturalists the skills needed to prepare projects acceptable to donor agencies.

As Ralph Campbell also observes (pp. 183ff.), because of the distinction between planning and management, project analysts do not necessarily bear the responsibility for carrying out the projects in the field. If charged with monitoring and evaluation, these analysts frequently have no formal links with field managers and cannot be assured good feedback. Evaluations based on data analysis with such numbers as can be obtained to quantify the progress of the work satisfy the academic standards to which the analysts have been trained, and the system offers no reward for investigating actual field conditions more deeply.

At the same time, project managers in the field often struggle against conditions which virtually preclude success—late arrival of essential supplies, late payment of promised funds, lack of funds or spare parts for maintenance, lack of storage facilities for perishable items, lack of project acceptability to intended beneficiaries for local cultural reasons or because of inappropriate or inadequate incentive structure. Since field supervisors were not part of the planning process, no channel had been created for their problems to be identified and corrections introduced into the project plan as work proceeded. This situation often prevails even when the field managers are expatriate technical assistance experts, though presumably the fact that they represented external resources can sometimes generate a quicker response from the central government.

In the African context it will not be possible for governments to concern themselves simultaneously with the entire range of issues which a fully-developed food policy would address for some time to come. Yet a change in managerial style and a training effort concentrated on bringing about this change could improve the current fragmentation of effort and enable governments to define clear priorities for the use of domestic and external financial resources and technical skills.

Training Requirements of Mid-Level Food Policy Managers in Africa

Examples of tasks which mid-level managers might be asked to perform in an African country attempting to transform its approach to food and agricultural policy include the following:

1. Create and maintain an early warning system to monitor weather conditions, planted area, yields, private stocks, and local grain prices;

2. Supervise the delivery of food aid relief to drought-prone areas through targeted feeding programs;

3. Rationalize official grain procurement and release prices in relation to anticipated offtake from government stocks, planned imports, and producer response to price incentives;

4. Supervise grain procurement operations and management of government held stocks;

5. Direct research programs for processing and marketing locally produced foods;

6. Administer farm credit and fertilizer subsidy programs through a network of local agricultural officers;

7. Direct agronomic research programs to develop drought-resistant varieties of corn and millet.

This list is indicative, not comprehensive. However, most countries would need to develop some short list of food policy priorities if implementation efforts are to be effective. Selection of activities for priority attention would be made by senior ministerial level decision makers in the country, in consultation with aid donors where external assistance is involved. Project preparation and cost/benefit analysis of various alternatives ideally would be part of the selection process. In any case, this work usually will be done before tasks are assigned to managers designated to implement policy objectives. This means that at the stage when the manager takes over, some kind of plan will have been prepared stating the goals of the activity he or she is to oversee and indicating the tools and resources which will be made available to him to accomplish the task.

Most of the tasks mentioned above require knowledge of one or more academic disciplines. Agronomy, statistics, nutrition, anthropology, agricultural economics, stocks management, and marketing all would be useful tools for carrying out various of the tasks mentioned above. There seems to be little dispute that those aspiring to occupy managerial positions will continue to need solid grounding in some academic discipline or skill related to the career path they intend to follow. Further, there is general agreement that these basic skills and disciplines can be taught best in traditional Western-style university degree programs, although within these degree programs there is need for adaptation of teaching materials and techniques to local conditions and policy programs which students are likely to face upon graduation.

In addition to academic training, however, the tasks listed earlier also require organizational and supervisory skills which academic training does not usually supply. In an established bureaucracy, these often are learned through observation and apprenticeship under the tutelage of those with more seniority and experience. Similarly, in Africa new entrants into government service learn the practical applications of their academic training and the unwritten rules of bureaucratic behavior and career advancement through on-the-job experience. However, in the existing institutional environment, the cadre of senior officials under whom new entrants can apprentice is very thin; and for the reasons discussed in the previous section, the nature of their bureaucratic experience has not prepared them to guide today's mid-level managers in carrying out tasks requiring complex organizational interactions.

Thus there are two points at which training interventions are needed to improve the managerial capacity of individuals occupying positions of high responsibility with respect to implementation of food policy objectives. First, those who are immediately responsible for carrying out innovative programs need help in broadening their vision to encompass the contributions of academic disciplines in which they are not trained and to see more clearly what managerial options are available to improve communications with subordinates and field workers and provide feedback to senior level policy makers. Second, those who are completing their academic training need supplementary exposure to specially designed courses or field experiences which will introduce them to an integrated approach to food policy planning and implementation and help them conceptualize their assigned tasks within a continuously evolving goal-orientated framework.

Innovations and Experiments in Food Policy Management Training for Africans

One of the most active U.S. training agencies with a food policy management orientation is the office of International Cooperation and Development (OICD) in the U.S. Department of Agriculture. Since 1976, OICD has put more emphasis on management training in the agricultural sector, and many projects use training teams comprised of an agricultural economist and a management trainer who work together to develop curricula and lead class sessions. These trainers offer short in-country courses for a number of trainees from within a single agency or small group of interacting agencies. OICD is now attempting to tie courses to a country's development strategies, plans, and programs, and is tying into local training institutions and initiatives wherever possible.

The U.S. Agency for International Development (AID) does not carry out any training activities itself, but it has a training office to oversee contracting operations. In addition to short-course training, AID also funds students who come for degree programs at American universities. Fellowship students are nominated by their governments and are usually individuals with some previous government experience. Training funds may be given to countries for specific purposes, such as livestock development, small farmer credit, rural roads maintenance, grain marketing, agricultural extension development, and so forth. Or they may be in support of institutions which offer training of various kinds. A recent review of training support in Africa showed that about one-quarter of the total number of projects receiving support had a development management component. Brinkerhoff notes, however, that training offered under specific project loans or grants tends to be managed by persons with technical rather than managerial expertise, even when the focus is on developing management skills.[6]

The United States appears to be the most active bilateral donor in the management training field. However, the program of the Agricultural Administration Unit of the Overseas Development Institute in London, England, is also noteworthy for its attempt to grapple with problems raised in earlier sections. The Unit was established in 1975 and is funded by the British Overseas Development Administration, plus a number of commercial enterprises. It has three functions: research, dissemination, and advice. Although it does not offer training as such, research on administrative problems is conducted by ODI staff members in collaboration with networks of 400 to 600 individuals, each in the United Kingdom and overseas. Through these networks, the Unit hopes to provide a bridge between "thinkers" and "doers." Topics on which research is currently underway include design and management of pastoral development programs in arid and semi-arid areas, design and management of irrigation schemes, forms of cooperation in agricultural activities and farmers' participation in development, organization of the provision and utilization of government agricultural services, and organization of crop marketing in low rainfall areas. Because of its wide contacts the ODI unit is a good resource for persons with ideas and skills related to food policy management training.

The Economic Development Institute of the World Bank (EDI) is a long-established multilateral training program covering all aspects of development planning and project implementation. In the agricultural sector, training in agricultural project analysis has been predominantly featured; but within the last year or two, more attention has been given to the training requirements of agricultural project and rural infrastructure managers. More recently courses have been added specifically addressing food policy. The EDI cooperated with the African Development Bank (ADB) and the Pan-African Institute for Development (PAID) to offer a short course on Project Management for Rural Development in May–June 1981.

This course was the brainchild of the Training Department of the African Development Bank. The Department previously offered courses in project analysis and loan administration for national development bank personnel and other officials charged with these responsibilities. The ADB uses regional training facilities and supplements its own staff with lectures from PAID. Recognition of the need for management training grew out of the observation that in many Bank-funded projects, expatriates come in as technical experts with the goal of training counterparts to take over when they leave. But often this did not happen.

The objectives of the new course were to furnish financial, technical, and sociological tools for directing rural development projects and to give participants a chance to exchange views on their practical experience. The subject was approached from five angles: agro-techniques, finance, human aspects, organization, and environment; and it was taught in three phases: theory and conceptualization, project site visits, concepts and tools of analysis and synthesis. The general reactions of the 22 participants from 15 French-speaking countries were the following: (1) material on human aspects, while interesting, was given too much emphasis in relation to other topics; (2) more background on financial aspects and on-going and ex-post evaluation techniques would have been helpful; (3) evaluation as a concept should be taught before project site visits; (4) logistical support for project site visits should be improved, and visits should be more closely linked to individual experiences and responsibilities of participants; (5) the overall cohesion and appropriateness of the training was excellent; and (6) the exchange experiences and development of new contacts among participants was extremely useful. With these generally favorable comments and helpful suggestions, the ADB intends to improve on this course and will offer it for English as well as French speakers.

PAID is another African institution with leadership capacity for continent-wide training. In addition to a Headquarters staff in Douala, Cameroon, it operates four regional training centers, one in English and one in French in Cameroon, one in French in Burkina Faso and one in English in Zambia. It has a professional staff of about 60, almost all of them African. Staff are involved in both curriculum development and teaching. In addition to courses offered at the centers, training teams also offer in-country courses upon request.

PAID has concentrated its training efforts on technicians and lower-level field workers and has little experience with training the mid-level manager whose needs are addressed in this chapter. Also, food and agricultural issues have not figured prominently in the training program, except for a course in Nutrition and Food Policy which is offered primarily for women working in nutrition projects. Two issues on which PAID is concentrating are institutional constraints to participation of women in rural development and application of business management techniques to the private sector in Africa. The Institute has open membership for individuals, corporations, and organizations. Governments cannot be members, though most of the support comes from the aid agencies of various governments, particularly France, but also including Canada, Netherlands, Switzerland, and the United States. A needs assessment is currently underway, and PAID is open to suggestions for training at higher levels of education and responsibility, if countries indicate this would be useful. The needs assessment will also weigh heavily in their decision whether to put more emphasis on the food and agriculture sector in developing new course material. Regardless of the outcome, PAID will continue to support the collaborative effort with ADB and EDI for the one course on Agricultural Project Management Training.

Other African institutions with programs which could be adapted for training mid-level food policy managers include: East African Management Institute (Arusha), Institut Africain de Developement Economique et de Planification (IDEP), Mananga Agricultural Management Centre in Swaziland (MAMC), and the Centre Africaine de Recherche et d'Administration in Morocco (CAFRAD).

The total amount of funding required to support innovative approaches to training mid-level food policy managers in Africa is substantial. Nevertheless, there are a number of specific activities which would benefit from small start-up grants, in particular (a) support for research on training, (b) support for research and training network activities, and (c) direct support for food policy management training for Africans. In these ways a start can be made at laying the groundwork for a better understanding of the training needs of mid-level food policy managers in Sub-Saharan Africa, fostering communication among them, and developing materials and courses directly relevant to their needs.

NOTES

1. Jon R. Morris, "The Transferability of Western Management Concepts and Programs, and East African Perspective," pp. 73–83, in Stifel, et al., eds.,

Education and Training for Public Sector Management in Developing Countries,
RF Working Papers, 2d Printing, April 1978.

2. David C. Korten, "Toward a Technology for Managing Social Development," pp. 45–55, in *Development Digest,* Washington, D.C. NPA, January
1981.

3. Uma Lele, "Rural Africa: Modernization, Equity, and Long-term Development," *Science* 211 (1981):547-553.

4. Timothy Josling, "Developed Country Agricultural Policies and Developing Country Supplies: The Case of Wheat," Research Report No. 14, International Food Policy Research Institute, Washington, D.C., March 1980, p. 45.

5. World Bank, African Strategy Review Group, *Accelerated Development in
Sub-Saharan Africa: An Agenda for Action,* Washington, D.C., 1981.

6. Derick W. Brinkerhoff, *Review of Recent and Planned Field Projects With a
Development Management Focus or Component in the AID Bureau for Africa,*
National Association of Schools of Public Affairs and Administration, Wash-
ington, D.C., May 1981.

USING THE CASE METHOD TO IMPROVE FOOD POLICY

Charles K. Mann
and
Malcolm F. McPherson

> *Nothing ever becomes real till it is*
> *experienced—Even a proverb is no proverb*
> *to you till your life has illustrated it.*
> *—John Keats*

Keats' insight is the key to understanding why the case method approach to policy analysis is proving to be a valuable tool for enhancing the analytical and managerial skills of those making food and agricultural policy. Long used by the Harvard Business School and others in improving business management skills, the method more recently was adapted by the International Center for the Improvement of Maize and Wheat (CIMMYT) for use with government officials of food deficit countries. With the development of fifteen cases and five successful policy seminars, CIMMYT has demonstrated the usefulness of the method to promote more effective policy making. Since they do not have the mandate to continue such programs as part of their core activities, they have encouraged other agencies to use these materials in programs to enhance the skills of senior policy officials. There appears to be interest at such management training centers as the Indian Institute of Management, the Asian Institute of Management, and the Southeast Asian Regional Center for Graduate Study and Research in Agriculture (SEARCA), as well as the International Service to National Agricultural Research (ISNAR).

227

The authors participated in the early CIMMYT food policy seminars and have explored the case method with many of its leading advocates and at least some of its critics. We, too, are convinced that it has substantial potential as a useful tool in promoting more effective food policy making. We have tried to identify some of the reasons why it works so well; why it may be particularly well-suited to the task of improving skills of busy, nationalistic, over-seminared senior policy makers.

Why does the Case Method Work?

To paraphrase Keats, one's experience serves to define what information one regards as "relevant." Information perceived as relevant is readily internalized and acted upon. That perceived as irrelevant is disregarded. The cases used in the CIMMYT seminars present situations with which policy makers can identify. They can recognize themselves or those of their associates throughout the case materials. As life illustrates the proverb, so the policy maker's experience must illustrate for him the case. Engagement with the policy issues under discussion occurs because of identification with the situation presented. The case method captures attention in a way that a journal article with a comparable message cannot.

Although identification with the situation captures attention, it is not sufficient to assure learning. There are other key conditions for successful learning which the case method also satisfies to a greater degree than more traditional approaches.

First, new knowledge must be integrated with existing knowledge. This demands an active thinking process. While a good lecture, book, or article can stimulate such an active thought process, the nature of the case method demands it. By intent, there is no explicit message. This is precisely the opposite of a traditional written approach. Indeed, one test of a good writer is how explicitly and clearly the message is presented. In the case approach, part of the exercise is for participants to draw some message or lessons from the welter of facts presented. Moreover, in shaping that message, one is encouraged to draw upon one's own experience. In the educator's language, one is asked to integrate the new knowledge with the old.

Through repeated confrontations with a variety of realistic situations, one develops an ability to separate trivia from essentials, to isolate the central issues, to seek the alternatives open to the policy makers, and to develop an overall approach to problem-solving across a broad spectrum of real problems. To reinforce these skills, the skilled case leader works to integrate the individual contributions into some sort of overall framework which helps people perceive the problem in a structured way. While the leader contributes to this structure, all elements have come from the group. Hence, they recognize it as their diagnosis, not the case leader's. In contrast, the objective of traditional teaching is often considered to be receiving the teacher's analysis of the issues.

The creation within the group of the framework for analysis appears central to the success of the case method. Often through grouping elements of the dialogue on a large blackboard, the leader provides a means of helping the group to make sense of their many disparate contributions. Typically, the lesson starts with a question such as: What is the problem here? It goes on to such other dimensions as: What is the real objective, what are the constraints, and who are the primary and secondary decision-makers?

Unlike standard economic analysis, the case method places great stress on developing awareness of the context within which a decision must be taken. Typically, the economist presents his work in terms of maximizing benefits subject to purely economic costs. The social and political context is outside his professional boundaries. In contrast, policy makers are at least as sensitive to this larger context as to the economic issues strictly defined. Because the case method recognizes explicitly the importance of the context of the analysis, it appears more realistic to participants. While cases often illustrate the usefulness of a particular analytical technique, it is seen as only one element of the total picture. This emphasis on context both represents good learning strategy and helps engage the policy makers. When they say that traditional economic analysis is irrelevant, what they usually mean is that it ignores this contextual dimension of the world in which they operate.

In addition to relevant materials, another prerequisite to effective learning is active participation. This is essential to the process of integrating new with existing knowledge. Simply listening to a case discussion will not produce the same learning as participating in discussion. This fact is reflected in the careful sequence of activities in which the case method involves the participant. First is individual reading of the case, then small group discussions, then the full session, and finally individual reflection. Everyone in a four to five person group meeting for an hour or more must make some contribution. In turn, this contribution demands a careful reading of the case. Talking out one's own ideas and listening to other group members prepares one to be an active participant in the full group discussion which follows. One has already articulated some contributions and developed enough understanding to provide the basis for further contributions to the plenary session. The small group discussions seem to convert a relatively passive reader of the case into an active participant—active not only as contributor but also as a listener who attends carefully to the perceptions of others and to the leader's development of the collective understanding of the case and possible solutions. The active mode of learning which the case approach engenders is a major reason for its effectiveness as an educational method.

What Are the Advantages of the Case Method?

The case method promotes strategic thinking; it forces awareness of the inter-relatedness of various facets of problems. Accordingly, it highlights the need for coordinated efforts to solve food problems. Moreover, if enough key individuals from a given country are participating, it provides a non-threatening situation in which these individuals work together, perhaps for the first time, to solve a realistic and relevant problem.

Yet another advantage of the case method is the role which falls to the expatriate, if one is involved. If the case leader is a foreigner, he or she acts the role of moderator or facilitator, not that of the expert with the answers. Humility is built into the role itelf. Contrast this to the role played by the usual foreign expert who is brought in to provide the answers. On technical issues, it may be true that the national group does not have answers. In the policy area, they must feel the answers to be their own if they are to act upon them. The role of facilitator is more apt than advisor.

In cases where the foreigner is a technical expert, participation as a peer in the case process may provide a more effective context for absorption of technical information by policy makers. They go through a process whereby they discover their need for such information. They then draw it in from their technical colleague as the need arises. In other circumstances, his information may go unheeded because the need for it is unrecognized.

Lastly, the case method draws upon the oral traditions characteristic of many non-industrial societies. In contrast, Western development experts are steeped in a highly literary tradition. Think of the books that begin, "This book is addressed to policy makers in the less-developed countries." Yet the target policy maker is more likely to be found talking than reading. More than in Western countries, people acquire and internalize knowledge by asking, listening, and talking rather than by reading. Hence the case method with its successive levels of learning through discussion seems to be a good cultural fit.[1]

In summary, the case method uses conceptual frameworks and communication to improve strategic, technical, and administrative capacity. It is effective because it requires active participation and it allows participants to see how to apply their new knowledge in their own work. Case method seminars, such as those organized by CIMMYT, can bring together, for a particular food issue, both the policy makers and those whose support is necessary for the policy to be implemented. A skilled case leader can help the participants to develop a framework for discussing the issue and to realize that together they often possess, or can identify, the knowledge needed to resolve the issue. The process tends to improve communication among individuals working on similar problems, whatever their institutional affiliation. It also helps to develop a sense of group cohesiveness and an awareness of local sources of expertise.

NOTES

1. Language structure can give clues to the importance of oral communication. For example, Turkish has a separate form for every verb to denote whether the speaker knows something from his personal knowledge, whether he has learned it from hearsay, or whether he simply believes something to be so. When a primary source of information is oral, such shadings are important enough to shape the structure of language itself.

Part III:
The Future Agenda

THE FUTURE AGENDA

Charles K. Mann and Barbara Huddleston

An important element in coalescing the ideas presented in this book was three days of discussion among most of the authors at The Rockefeller Foundation Study Center at Bellagio. Professor Schuh chaired a concluding summary session there in which he addressed to the group the following questions:

With respect to the *state of knowledge*
1. How adequate is it? How complete?
2. How much confidence do we have in what we know?
3. How transferable is our knowledge?
4. What is the state of country-specific knowledge?
5. What do we know about the international system?
6. How complacent are we? Are we keeping up with constantly changing systems?

With respect to the *state of policy analysis capability*
1. How transferable are the skills people have?
2. What mix of skills are needed?

With respect to the *state of training capacity*
1. What kind of training is needed?
2. How can informal training be provided to complement formal training?
3. What is our capacity to train? Is it adequate?
4. What kind of training should be provided and where?

Answers to these qustions can be grouped under several categories. Two in particular have important implications for the future. The first relates to the kinds of skills needed in building food policy analytical capability. The second concerns particular activities or actions which various agencies can take to improve this capability.

There was general agreement that policy analysis is part science, part art. On the science side, analysts need training both in micro and macro level analysis. Moreover, much of policy analysis is rooted in welfare economics, in that market failure provides the rationale for most interventions. Despite this fact, the theoretical basis for these interventions is little understood. In addition to training in theory and quantitative methods, preparation should include institutional and political economics as well.

For agronomists or other agricultural scientists involved in policy analysis, an understanding of marketing may be the most important new subject to be learned. For economists, perhaps the best general training is a background in trade theory. The microeconomics orientation of agricultural economics needs to be supplemented more effectively with macroeconomics, analysis, welfare economics, and trade theory. In the World Bank, the weakness of agricultural economics as the basis for policy analysis is suggested by the fact that less than one-third of 90 slots for operational agricultural policy analysis in the World Bank are filled by agricultural economists.

A much broader understanding of various institutional options (ways of organizing national economies) should be covered in policy training programs: centrally planned economies, barter systems, contract systems, as well as market systems. Efficiency as the principal criteria in analysis is inadequate and should be supplemented with a broader perspective which includes attention to equity issues.

In identifying specific actions to develop capacity, both the science and the art dimensions of policy analysis were addressed. Central to the discussion was the question of the transferability of knowledge. If all knowledge has to be country-specific, we don't know very much. But if much of social science theory is applicable to all countries, then transferability is a function of local capacity to adapt knowledge to a particular situation.

As noted above, there was wide agreement that various branches of economic theory provide the foundation for policy analysis—the science side. This knowledge is relatively transferable. On the other hand, the "art" in policy analysis lies in how this body of theory is applied and adapted to particular country and institutional situations. It is in developing this "art" dimension that there is the greatest scope for creating new programs.

Building national food policy capability will require a combination of opportunities to learn the basic theory involved and the art of its application. This suggests both fairly traditional graduate training supplemented by innovative special programs. People with experience in the art but lacking the theory could be sent to existing graduate programs.

Most of the discussion, however, focused on how existing theoretical training could be supplemented to develop the art of policy analysis. Drastic cutbacks in dissertation funding present an attractive opportunity. Making funds available for applied policy dissertation research would stimulate the growth and development of the field. It would both increase the numbers of people entering the field and advance the knowledge base. In effect, this would expand both the demand for analysts and the supply. FAO and World Bank in particular were cited as potential sources for dissertation funding.

Other suggestions were support for developing appropriate curricular material and short courses—post-doctoral training in the application of theory to policy problems. There was particular stress on the usefulness of apprentice/mentor relationships.

There is an important continuing role for workshops and seminars to stimulate communication, to disseminate knowledge, and to identify specific research and training gaps. The capability of individuals can be multiplied by linking them with other individuals with complementary skills. Modern telecommunications should facilitate easier access to research materials, library and bibliographic resources, and professional colleagues. The Rockefeller Foundation and other organizations can help to innovate and move forward activities in this networking function.

There may be substantially more demand internationally for policy analysis skills than there is within national institutions. This emphasizes the importance of a demand-focused approach toward strengthening national capability. The current recognition of past policy weakness in such documents as the Lagos Declaration may presage growing national demand for food policy analysis.

To advance knowledge, to offer broader training and research opportunities, to provide mentors for junior colleagues in the developing countries, there is a strong case for building up three or four centers of excellence which offer a concentration in food policy training. Working to improve several such centers would be one important way in which interested donors could help support the growth of this field.

In closing, no hard and fast prescription emerges for improving national food policy capability. Policy analysis requires a variety of analytical skills and a broad perception of interrelationships—technical, economic, political, institutional, and international. While the problem is difficult to define precisely, there is broad agreement that a major problem exists. Increasingly, inappropriate policies are cited as principal causes to lagging agricultural productivity and widespread malnutrition. Improved policy must be based upon an improved understanding of the effects of various alternative policies. While international advice and expertise can be useful, ultimately nations must have their own sources of advice and guidance to their own policy-making processes. The progress reported in this book suggests some of the approaches which can be used in developing this capacity. It also suggests that better analysis alone is not the answer; management capacity as well will have to be improved if the potential of improved policies is to be realized.

CONTRIBUTORS

Robert H. Bates is Professor of Political Science at the California Institute of Technology.

Alan Berg is Senior Nutrition Adviser, Population, Health, and Nutrition Department, at the World Bank, Washington, D.C.

Donald Ralph Campbell, former Field Staff Member, The Rockefeller Foundation, Nairobi, Kenya, is Director of the International Development Office, Ottawa.

Lincoln C. Chen, former Representative of the Ford Foundation in New Delhi, India, is Takemi Professor in International Health at Harvard University.

David O. Dapice is Associate Professor of Economics, Tufts University.

George E. Delehanty, former Field Staff Member of The Rockefeller Foundation in Nairobi, Kenya, is Visiting Research Scholar in Agricultural and Applied Economics, University of Minnesota.

Graham Donaldson is Chief of the Economics and Policy Division in the Agricultural and Rural Development Department, The World Bank, Washington, D.C.

Hasan Gençağa is Secretary-General of the Turkish Development Research Foundation in Ankara, Turkey.

Arturo A. Gomez is a Professor in the Department of Agronomy, College of Agriculture at the University of Philippines at Los Banos.

Barbara Huddleston, former Research Fellow in the International Food Trade and Food Security Program of the International Food Policy Research Institute, Washington, D.C., is Chief, Food Security and Information Service, Commodities and Trade Division, in the Economic and Social Policy Department of the Food and Agriculture Organization of the United Nations, Rome, Italy.

Charles K. Mann, former Associate Director of Agricultural and Social Sciences of The Rockefeller Foundation, New York, is Visiting Scholar at the Harvard Institute for International Development.

Malcolm F. McPherson, former Visiting Research Fellow in Agricultural Sciences, The Rockefeller Foundation, is a Research Associate at the Harvard Institute for International Development.

Joan Mencher is Professor of Anthropology at The Graduate School and University Center of the City University of New York.

Gabino A. Mendoza is President of the Asian Institute of Management in the Philippines.

David N. Ngugi is the Dean of the Faculty of Agriculture at the University of Nairobi, Kenya.

Theodore Panayotou, former Associate of The Agricultural Development Council, is Research Associate, Harvard Institute for International Development.

Kosit Panpiemras is the Assistant Secretary-General of the National Economic and Social Development Board in Bangkok, Thailand.

John A. Pino, former Director of Agricultural Sciences at The Rockefeller Foundation, is Adviser in Agricultural Sciences at the Inter-American Development Bank, Washington, D.C.

Per Pinstrup-Andersen is the Director of the Food Consumption and Nutrition Policy Program at the International Food Policy Research Institute, Washington, D.C.

G. Edward Schuh is Director, Agriculture and Rural Development at the World Bank. At the time of writing, he was Head of the Department of Agricultural and Applied Economics, University of Minnesota.

Marcelo Selowsky is Research Adviser in the Operations Policy Department at The World Bank, Washington, D.C.

Laurence D. Stifel, former Vice President for Program at The Rockefeller Foundation, is Director General, The International Institute for Tropical Agriculture, Ibadan, Nigeria.

C. Peter Timmer is John D. Black Professor of Agriculture and Business at the Graduate School of Business Administration, Harvard University.

Snoh Unakul, former Governor of the Bank of Thailand, is Secretary-General of the National Economic and Social Development Board, Bangkok, Thailand.

Alberto Valdés is Director of the International Food Trade and Food Security Program at the International Food Policy Research Institute, Washington, D.C.

Maurice Williams is the Executive Director of the World Food Council, Rome, Italy.

INDEX